FIBER

FIBER

The Coming Tech Revolution—and
Why America Might Miss It

SUSAN CRAWFORD

Yale

UNIVERSITY PRESS

New Haven and London

Yale University Press books may be purchased in quantity for
educational, business, or promotional use. For information, please
e-mail sales.press@yale.edu (U.S. office) or sales@yaleup.co.uk
(U.K. office).

Set in Janson type by IDS Infotech, Ltd.
Printed in the United States of America.

ISBN 978-0-300-22850-2 (hardcover : alk. paper)
Library of Congress Control Number: 2018944752

A catalogue record for this book is available from the British
Library.

This paper meets the requirements of ANSI/NISO Z39.48–1992
(Permanence of Paper).

10 9 8 7 6 5 4 3 2 1

To scrappy cities

Contents

Acknowledgments

In the course of working on this book over the past five years, I have been fortunate to have had the help of hundreds of people and dozens of institutions. If I leave anyone out, forgive me; my heart, I hope, is in the right place, even if my powers of recall are limited. The Rockefeller Foundation hosted me for a crucial month of work during the summer of 2014. The Ford Foundation has supported me generously for many years. I cannot thank them enough for their encouragement of me. The Roosevelt Institute gave me a desk for a time. My employer, Harvard Law School, has given me summer research support as well as access to an extraordinary group of kind, thoughtful, and talented students. The school's former dean Martha Minow, in particular, really understood the idea that telecommunications policy is central to social justice in America and gave me every encouragement. She came by that understanding around the dinner table, because her father, a former chairman of the FCC, Newt Minow, is one of the great heroes in the communications arena.

In DC policy-land, I am forever grateful to Jim Kohlenberger, Gerry Salemme, Tom Wheeler, Joanne Hovis, Jim Baller, Chris Mitchell, Catharine Rice, Colin Crowell, Paul de Sa, Sam Gill, Ben Scott, Lev Gonick, Elin Katz, Jory Wolf, and Deb Socia.

John Horrigan and Waide Warner have been consistently wise and helpful.

Students at Harvard Law School and Harvard generally have been of enormous help to me, often in ways they could not have known at the time. I am in their debt: Andrew Crocker, Mary-Catherine Lader,

Laura Kremen Adler, Danielle Kehl, Lizzy Schick, Tim Koay, Benjamin Goh, Zoe Wolford, Maxwell Gottschall, Emily Kline, Rauvin Johl, Kayla Haran, and I'm sure there are others.

Other students or student-age people, not at Harvard, involved in this project have been highly important to this journey, and I thank them from the bottom of my heart: Caitlin Howarth, Alyssa Taylor, John Randall, Maria Smith, Robyn Mohr, Melissa Nally, Andrew Glantz, Dana Walters, Jess Goldfin, and Madeline Lemberg.

I have been inspired by Ron Suskind innumerable times. Clay Risen has been by my side for many projects and I cannot thank him enough. Katie Hafner gave me advice at several crucial junctures; Steven Levy, my longtime column editor, has had a major influence on me.

I traveled to Seoul, Stockholm, Tokyo, Amsterdam, Berlin, Copenhagen, Havana, and Oslo (some several times) along the way.

In Seoul, former presiding judge, Seoul Northern District Court, Jongsoo (Jay) Yoon, who always has a bass guitar in the trunk of his car, made dozens of introductions for me. I treasure his energetic, curious way of moving through life. I was accompanied in Seoul and Pyeongyang by several Harvard College, Harvard Law School, and Harvard Business School students: heartfelt thanks to Kylie Chiseul Kim, Seongmin Lee, Dianne Lee, and Sun Woo Lee, in particular. Soohyun Pae and Ye-seul Kim provided expert translation services. Korea Telecom executives agreed to be interviewed (but did not pay expenses of my trips, at my request). Other interviewees included Jinhee Park, Professor Jae Chon Park, Ram Lee, Joo Yeon Kim, Hyunseok Shim, Hyun Woo Nam, Jisoo Seo, SuhYoung Yun, Prof. Seokho Bang, JiHo Yoon, Yeon Sung Choi, Mayor Wonsoon Park, and many others.

In Stockholm, Anders Broberg made introductions that changed my life: Staffan Ingvarsson, Jonas Birgersson, Nicol Villa, Ulla Hamilton, and many others. Herman Wagter taught me about fiber in the Netherlands and northern Europe generally. In Tokyo, Seo-in Kwon took great care of me. In Havana, former ambassador John Petter Opdahl was extraordinarily helpful to me. William Ruiz was my guide in Cuba.

In Kansas City, Cate Zollicker was my guide and adviser. In Chattanooga, mayor Andy Berke opened the gates of the city to me, pointing me in all the right directions. I'm a big fan of Mayor Berke's. In Greensboro, Jane Nickles was an extraordinary colleague to me. In Nevada City, John Paul was my introducer and guide. I will be forever grateful to Mark Erickson, the indefatigable beating heart behind fiber to the farm. Wilson's Will Aycock and Rebecca Agner were patient and wonderful.

I am grateful to everyone who has spent time with me. It has been quite a journey. I hope this book does your stories justice.

CHAPTER ONE

The Fiber Future

ERE IS THE TECH revolution America may miss:
On a gray, cloudy weekday morning in August, I
drove across the wide Han River that divides the
northern and southern parts of Seoul. I turned east
onto a furiously busy highway that runs alongside the river. I
was noticing everything at once: the enormous pale forests of
concrete apartment blocks, each forest pointed in a seemingly ran‐
dom direction, each building labeled with a number; the traffic;
and the Lotte Group tower ahead of me, the tallest building in
South Korea, narrowing to bat-like ears at its top—it had been the
CEO's dream to build the tallest tower in the country, but the
structure is roundly disliked, and sinkholes have started opening
at its base. The traffic in Seoul is crushing and constant, an oppres‐
sive fact of life for the ten million impatient citizens of that
booming metropolis.

After a few minutes, a huge concrete stadium with fading Olym‐
pic rings decorating its side came into view. This was the Seoul
Olympic Stadium, built for the 1988 Summer Olympics but not
used for a major world sporting event since then.[1] I drove on, and
the forests of apartment towers and the crushing traffic continued
for another twenty minutes but then fell away; I was in the suburbs
and heading toward the mountains.

I had been on many journeys over the previous five years, in-
terviewing hundreds of people in Stockholm, Seoul, Tokyo, Singapore, Berlin, Amsterdam, Copenhagen, and Havana, as well as in a
long list of U.S. cities, about the possible effects on human lives of
virtually unlimited, cheap, ubiquitous communications capacity.
This was my third trip to Seoul. I had come to see what South
Korea, the most wired nation on the planet, would show the world
when it hosted the 2018 Winter Olympics, six months away.

My destination that morning was a rural, hilly area three hours
east of Seoul—about ninety-five miles away—a small town of some
thirty thousand people called Pyeongchang. There was no way to
get there other than by driving. Although a high-speed rail link between Seoul and Pyeongchang was being built that would make a
one-hour trip possible, the line hadn't been completed. No one
knew how expensive the rail tickets would be, and these calculations mattered: there weren't enough hotel rooms in Pyeongchang
for the anticipated seventy-five thousand fans, even though buildings to house visitors were hastily being thrown up near the event
venues and older structures were being pressed into new roles as
hotels. Many Olympics enthusiasts would have to make a daily
round trip by train from Seoul, a gigantic place with thirty thousand hotel rooms.[2] There is no housing to speak of between Seoul
and Pyeongchang and the Pyeongchang Olympic hockey center
and ice arena can hold up to twenty-two thousand spectators.

And so I found myself driving east of Seoul on a brand-new
four-lane freeway, specially built for the upcoming Olympics.[3]
I checked my phone: my 4G coverage throughout the three-hour
trip was spectacular.

The ice track ahead of you slopes steeply down and curves sharply
to the right and out of view. And then you're off, at unimaginably
high speed, slamming into the banks of the track and zipping forci-
bly around every curve, while you keep an eye on the stopwatch
and the heart-rate indicator projected on the top-right corner of
your view. You are seeing and hearing a bobsled run—your stomach is convinced you yourself are hunkered down in the body of
the streamlined bobsled—from the perspective of your favorite
athlete, a young man from Seoul who is a luge prodigy and hopes

with his team to snag the gold medal for his country. Seconds later, you're in the virtual company of your friends, chatting away; they're all around you. The bobsled, meanwhile, is taking an alarming turn, high up on the side of the track, to gain crucial momentum for the end of the run, and you and your buddies, sitting in your living rooms or standing on street corners, have been granted your favorite athlete's point of view and insight into his climbing heart rate. You collectively hold your breath: will he win?

Later that day, you visit the ice arena to see the high-pressure couples ice-dancing competition. You are still in your living room in Seoul, but it doesn't feel like it. You can see every corner of the arena from any one of a hundred cameras, your view moving easily around the enormous building with its sky-blue seats and bright digital displays. As your attention wanders to the VIP boxes, you miss a crucial dance moment; the roar of the crowd brings you back, and you quickly speak, asking for a replay.

The replay you are instantly shown allows you to see the ice dancers' perfectly choreographed jump and to freeze the image, leaving both dancers above the ice, graceful and eternal. You move the skaters backward and forward a few times to see how they got to that height, before smoothly, slowly allowing them to continue their flawless joint routine. You marvel at their skill. And the image you see is so detailed, and seems so real, that you feel you could touch the woman's silk sleeve and feel the thinness of the fabric.

That evening, the visitors to the events who have made the physical trek out to the Olympic venues—not you, because you are still at home in your living room in Seoul—ride around the city in an aquamarine bus; on the side of the bus, bold white letters read "World's First 5G Connected Car." The Olympic visitors touch the windows of the bus and write there with their fingers, interacting with displays showing them live coverage of the Olympic events around them. A man with a long white cane suddenly walks right in front of the bus. The bus has no driver. The riders realize the pedestrian is blind and feel powerless to do anything about the collision that is about to happen—but the bus, guided by tsunamis of data running over 5G networks, smoothly rolls around him, avoiding an accident. The riders turn back to bantering with their personalized window displays sometimes the face of a guide, sometimes a map, sometimes text, whatever they're interested in. And when they go inside the physical arenas, their smartphones speak softly to them about where they are in relation to their ticketed seats and where snacks are being sold.

Late at night, stirred by the bravery and heart of the athletes you've seen and whose perspectives you've shared, you walk around Seoul. You're interested in knowing more about your favorite athlete; you want to hear from him about his childhood dreams, and Seoul is having a special digital event in his honor. Wearing glasses that allow you to see digital overlays on physical objects, you are fascinated by the stories told by the buildings that were part of the athlete's past. You're touched by the connections to your own life and delighted by the digital scenarios and jokes your favorite athlete has left for you to enjoy.

Welcome to the future, the first hints of which were visible at the Winter Olympics of February 2018 in Pyeongchang. Korea Telecom (KT) unveiled its very-high-capacity but very-short-range 5G wireless communications network (at least ten times faster than 4G) to the world during those games, so South Koreans really could be part of speed skating or ski jumping events from the perspectives of the athletes involved, and ride autonomous buses on an eighty-eight-acre test site—the world's biggest.[4] It was a major collaboration: the enormous South Korean companies Samsung and Hyundai, together with Intel and Ericsson, committed to the enterprise and built hardware to handle the flood of data moving around the Olympic venues before a global standard for 5G communications—not expected until 2020—even existed.[5] South Korea simply wanted to be first. And South Koreans with 5G-enabled devices were the most engaged sports fans on the planet during those Olympics. They could see and hear anything they chose, in real time, from any angle, including the athlete's view, while surrounded by their friends and other South Koreans as fellow commentators.[6] Interactive holographic projections, along with augmented reality (the digital overlay made possible with glasses or smartphones or interactive bus windows) allowed for new forms of engagement. KT's "360 Virtual Reality" technology made viewers feel as if they were right there in the stadium, no matter where they actually were, and its "time slice" technology allowed watchers to roll these visuals back and forth at will.[7]

The Seoul traffic, the distance, and the lack of hotel rooms were less of an issue, as was the incomplete state of the Seoul–Pyeongchang high-speed rail link. Except for the self-driving bus, which has to be physically experienced, anyone in Seoul with a 5G-enabled handset could have a real-time experience of the Olympic Games that was much the same as what those "actually" present had. Minus the crowds.

What makes these astonishing feats of communications transport possible—floods of data flowing back and forth, from an athlete to millions of fans and back, without an instant of hesitation—is South Korea's extensive fiber optic network. The country is wired with 375,000 miles of fiber optic cables, formed of hair-thin filaments of unbelievably pure synthetic glass, which channel light across the many miles between rural Pyeongchang and homes and businesses in the rest of the country. Sang-jin Oh, the cheerful, bespectacled director general of the technology bureau for the Pyeongchang Organizing Committee for the 2018 Olympic Games, told me that "fiber serves as a basic infrastructure for telecommunications services in Korea." To beef up the fiber capacity in rural Pyeongchang and the nearby coastal town of Gangneung, Korea Telecom added thousands of additional fiber strands in the area. All the TV cameras broadcasting the Olympics had direct fiber connections that allowed them to integrate and upload data simultaneously. KT did the same at thousands of other physical locations, providing sensors to which data was sent across very short distances over the air using KT's 5G wireless network: think tiny, tiny cell towers receiving and sending a ton of data for short distances—without fiber optic lines connected to those tiny cell towers, 5G doesn't work.

South Korea has this amazing fiber optic connectivity because years ago its government, still rising from the rubble of the Korean War and urged on by the giant electronics conglomerate Samsung, decided that world-class data networks would be key to the future success of the country.[8] KT and other telecom companies were urged, through a combination of subsidies, tax breaks, and low cost loans, to upgrade to fiber optic connections. In his Next Generation

Connectivity report from 2010, my colleague Yochai Benkler wrote that South Korea had invested "$24 billion in its first transition on connecting schools and government centers in the 1990s, over $70 billion in low-cost loans to providers, and over $12 billion per year from 2004–2007 on [its] transition to the next generation ubiquitous [fiber] network." He noted that it was unclear who exactly spent the money—public authorities or private companies.[9] But the results have been dazzling: South Koreans take virtually unlimited, cheap connectivity, both uploads (performing) and downloads (consuming), for granted, and the country is now poised to have advanced wireless services that are possible only because fiber optic cables run to just about every home and business in the country.

As Mr. Oh solemnly told me the day I visited, in August 2017, "Through the . . . Olympics, we are preparing thoroughly to show to the world what cutting-edge telecommunications services we have in Korea."

In the United States, we have fiber optic cables between cities, called "long-haul" or "backbone" lines. And within any metro area of significant size, there are "middle-mile" or "business data services" fiber optic lines. These cables often connect to telephone poles or other network elements, but don't go all the way to retail customers' premises. What Korea, Japan, Hong Kong, China, Singapore, and the Nordic countries have that the rest of the world does not are fiber optic cables running physically, directly, into neighborhoods, homes, and businesses in both rural and urban areas—the so-called "last-mile" network. Inventors have found ways to encode stunning amounts of information on pulses of light vibrating billions of times a second, and then send that light on its journey through a channel made of the purest glass on earth.

If the information-carrying capacity of copper wire is like a two-inch-wide pipe, fiber optic is like a river fifteen miles wide; you wouldn't even try to download a 4K movie using a copper connection, but using fiber you could download ten movies in a second—or run your own business remotely, or see your doctor or members of your family, when needed, as needed.

Most of the phone calls going on throughout the world at any moment could be carried simultaneously across a single hair-thin strand of fiber. But because people send and receive information from where they physically are, fiber optic cables need to be physically distributed to reach individual buildings in order for fiber's capacity across all the parts of the network—middle-mile, long-haul, and undersea cables linking continents—to be fully harnessed.

In many developed countries, that last mile is the weakest link in the network, its materials (copper or coaxial cable) serving to throttle communications just as they are starting on their journeys from individuals to the rest of the world, and slowing incoming data just as it is about to arrive in those individuals' lives. Once the fiber cable reaches an individual living unit—that is, a home—data can be sent over the air to devices we wear or hold in our hands. The plan is for 5G wireless to allow for the sending of enormous amounts of data over the air across very short distances, to reach humans, handsets, sensors, or anything else capable of receiving or transmitting data.

Because the last mile has to connect to individual buildings, it is also the most expensive part of any communications network to install.[10] Most of that expense—perhaps 80 percent of it—is the high fixed costs of the labor needed to dig up streets or attach fiber optic wire to poles and buildings, and revenue will not flow in to cover those costs until the last mile is actually in use. Just like electricity or water service, last-mile communications networks are often called a "natural monopoly." Those high fixed installation costs mean that it simply does not make economic sense for two separate fiber cables to be attached to any given location. To avoid allowing the resulting natural monopoly position to be used to extract unreasonably high fees from subscribers, telecommunications regulators often require that the basic communications line be made available on a wholesale, price-controlled basis to competing retail providers.

Back to the 2018 Olympics. The fiber optic lines very close to the locations where Olympic athletes in Pyeongchang wore cameras and microphones allowed them to beam information about their experiences across the airwaves by way of 5G connections to the installed fiber. Fiber can carry a virtually unlimited amount of data at the speed of light, so all those cameras and tiny cell towers

surrounding the athletes and self-driving buses, picking up on their
movements and perceptions, were able to spew data to their hearts'
content. All of that local, "last-mile" fiber in Pyeongchang and
Gangneung is connected to the existing intercity fiber optic lines
running to Seoul and elsewhere in South Korea. Think highway
system, with interstate freeways acting as long-haul networks, local
highways acting as middle-mile connections, and residential roads
and driveways playing the role of the "last mile." That final seg-
ment, made up of those last-mile fiber connections, is what allowed
everyone in any South Korean living room with a 5G handset to
be present at the Olympics, with virtually zero delay between an
athlete's gesture in Pyeongchang and the perception of that gesture
ninety-five miles away in Seoul. "Latency," the word used for delay,
has been reduced to about one millisecond across this connection.
Humans love zero latency; we are genuinely bugged by delay between our touch of a key and the reaction of a remote computer,
hundreds of miles away, to that touch—just as we are put off by
delay in human interactions.

In the United States, we cannot even imagine cheap, unlimited
communications capacity in our homes. Because of decades of political maneuvering by the enormous private companies that sell
internet access to American consumers, a lack of leadership at the
federal level, and the invisibility of this entire policy area, we have
failed to make the upgrade to cheap last-mile fiber connectivity.

  We suffer from a whole series of digital divides as a country. On
the global stage, there is a deep and widening divide between the
United States on the one hand and Japan, South Korea, Singapore,
Hong Kong, and China on the other. Those places, where fiber
now reaches or soon will reach all residents, are where new industries and new ways of making a living are likely to emerge first.

  We also suffer from huge digital divides between richer and
poorer Americans that will make inequality worse and weaken the
fabric of democracy. These infrastructure divides are driving
wedges between rural and urban Americans and between white and
nonwhite Americans. All the policies important to us as a country—becoming the most advanced health care nation in the world,
the most energy efficient, the most innovative, the most resilient—

depend on having last-mile fiber and advanced wireless services available cheaply to everyone. We must do better.

Fiber optic, as a category, is both old and new. The cables running under the oceans and among the major cities of the world began to be upgraded to fiber thirty years ago. And once a fiber optic cable is in the ground, it lasts for forty or fifty years; it is essentially future proof, because its information-carrying capacity can be almost infinitely upgraded without digging up the cable, merely by swapping out the electronics that encode and power the pulses of light that travel within its walls.[11] Most people in non-fiber countries (including the United States) can't even buy what in fibered countries counts as a standard, modern internet connection. About 11 million American households, out of 126 million total, are connected to last-mile fiber, and that service is usually available only at very high prices from a single unregulated provider. Meanwhile, South Korea, Japan, Hong Kong, and Singapore have virtually 100 percent fiber adoption at low prices, and often scores of competitors.[12]

This is a big problem.

Here's why: Those hair-thin fiber strands, capable of carrying billions of phone calls simultaneously, plus advanced wireless communications that depend on that fiber extending into the last mile, will make possible virtually unlimited, cheap communications capacity wherever you are—which in turn will give rise to new businesses, new transport capabilities, new ways of managing our use of energy, new forms of education and health care, new ways of earning a living, and new forms of human connectedness. For these things to happen, both fiber and advanced wireless technologies need to be widely and competitively available. Without these basic pieces of open infrastructure in place, your country will be missing out on the future being lived and built elsewhere.

Much of the world gets this. China is installing twenty thousand last-mile fiber optic connections every single day. In June 2017, the *South China Morning Post* reported "China set to build the planet's largest 5G mobile network for US $180b."[13] Listen to that: the "planet's largest."

Fiber plus advanced wireless capability is as central to the next phase of human existence as electricity was a hundred years ago.

Just as countries that quickly ensured cheap access to electricity revolutionized their economies and provided dramatically improved quality of life for their citizens, countries that figure out how to get fiber to everyone will have ever-increasing advantages over those that do it slowly.

Take the 2018 Olympics in South Korea: Korea Telecom was smart to focus on sports—and the Olympics in particular—in demonstrating its prowess. Sports grab humans in real-time emotional ways, and the Olympics mark the global pinnacle of inspiring athletic achievement. KT got the world's attention in 2018.

But KT's display of its 5G fireworks is far more significant than any Olympic event could possibly be. Korea is going through a phase change in digital communications that has implications for almost every occupation and source of economic power of which we're aware today.

In the crowded city of Seoul, for example, I met many twenty-somethings who did not distinguish between online life and "real" life; for them, these are simply layers of life as a whole. This generation is so accustomed to cheap, unlimited connectivity everywhere that they have forgotten its existence—just as people in other countries forget the existence of electricity until it is suddenly not there. South Koreans are impatient. For them, going to almost any city in the United States is a little like going off the grid.

In Seoul, I met Yeon Sung Choi, a professional e-sports player who is as famous in his sport as Lionel Messi, the best goal-scorer in the world, is in soccer. Yeon Sung, who now works as a coach for the SK Telecom T1 Starcraft II team (telecommunications companies are major investors in the e-sports industry in Korea), told me he'd lived through the transformation of Korea that took place following the installation of high-capacity networks that permitted any number of people to play games simultaneously.[14] At age twenty, he realized he could beat just about anyone. The essential factor in connectivity, he says, is latency, or response time; any delay makes it very difficult to play. Some players say latency starts to become obvious when there is a gap of 150 milliseconds or even less between pressing a button and a visual response. Fiber connections generally have lower latency than cable or copper wires. "In Korea the response time is really short," he said, laughing. He sees a bright future for the gaming industry in Korea, but there is much more than gaming. The same technology will revolutionize business, medicine, education, manufacturing, energy use, and real-time translation functions between spoken languages.

Fiber is also revolutionizing cities themselves. Because the city of Seoul years ago installed fiber optic last-mile connections throughout the city and its subway system, it can provide free Wi-Fi, which means the private sector can experiment with Internet of Things (IoT) services that will improve its citizens' lives. On the same trip that had me clambering around the empty ice arena in Pyeongchang, I visited the city's IoT testbed office. Taejin Kim, director of the testbed, told me that the city is testing its ability to provide personalized services to elders, to provide data from road surfaces and public transit so that navigation systems function well, and in general to "solve urban problems, wherever they are." The conference room next to the mayor's office houses an enormous dashboard that, fed by public data, allows the mayor to see the site of an accident or fire, talk in real time to public officials at the site, visually understand traffic congestion, and manage the city's budget. Because fiber is everywhere, this enormous amount of data can be shipped whenever and wherever it is needed.

The next wave of applications making use of fiber and advanced wireless services is likely to be in health care, education, or other fundamental areas than has been seen so far in Korea and Japan. I am confident that innovative American businesses will come up with services that use much more significant amounts of bandwidth when there is a critical mass of users with capacity. If and when the United States becomes a last-mile fiber sandbox for this inventiveness, the huge market here will drive those developments. We will also support our commitment to genuine liberal democracy: the rising tide of cheap, ubiquitous, unlimited connectivity needs to reach everyone in order for the country as a whole to thrive.

This same virtuous cycle of innovation happened with electricity more than a hundred years ago. In 1907, when just a small part of life in the United States had been electrified—mostly street lamps

and streetcars—appliance makers had little incentive to manufacture mass-market devices that used electricity, because the adoption of domestic electricity was minimal. During the 1920s,
America's private utilities were focused on the enormous profits to
be made in industrial electrical modernization. Not until the Great
Depression weakened that industrial sector did they pivot toward
domestic electricity.

It was hard at the time to imagine why vast amounts of electricity would be needed in daily life. Some houses were wired for
lighting but not for general electricity use, and appliances initially
were plugged into lightbulb sockets. Wall switches at an entrance
were considered a luxury. Nonetheless, according to David Nye in
his 1990 book *Electrifying America*, the introduction of electric
lights in the homes of the very wealthy was "an entering wedge"
into home use of electricity, prompting appliance makers to think
of other devices that could be plugged into the network—which
eventually, in turn, motivated mass electrification.[15] Manufacturers
introduced electric irons, toasters, vacuum cleaners, electric wash-
ers, hot plates, and many other labor-saving devices. The electric
fan was a big success. Electricity use soared, creating a need for additional capacity and the business case for building it.

Electrical "apps" proved not only that usage would justify
further buildout but that a model based on affordability and
mass consumption was feasible. This app-based wisdom prompted
federal investment in projects like a traveling exhibition of farm
equipment in rural areas—a sort of agricultural circus that reached
about a million farmers in twenty-six states between 1939 and
1941—and the provision of financing options for appliances.

The federal effort was not limited to rural areas: the Roosevelt
administration expanded consumer credit to low-income houses to
advance electrical modernization. With no down payment, home-
owners could buy a refrigerator using low-interest loans for as little as three dollars a month—thus bringing refrigeration, the
essential ingredient of a modern kitchen, into the lives of millions.
The private utilities had thought of their market as consisting only
of the one-fifth of American households that were already modern-
ized, but the use of electricity ballooned. Where the average early
1920s household had been using 30 kilowatt-hours or less each

month, by 1950 most households had modern electrical services and were using more than 150 kilowatt-hours monthly. The secret to mass electrification was twofold: lower the price of electricity and get more "appliances" out to more people by whatever means possible. Electricity became normal and invisible.

Today, when we do not yet have effective distribution of last-mile fiber capacity at competitive prices to a giant marketplace of users, the next killer apps are just emerging. One thing we know, however, is that humans have never preferred less connectivity at higher prices.

Imagine being able to make eye contact with your doctor, even though there's a thousand miles between you—to be seen and understood as clearly and as fully as if you were in the room with her. Imagine being in touch with distant relatives and feeling part of their lives, even if you're in a different country. Imagine being present in a classroom, not just downloading files or watching a lecture but participating fully, speaking up from wherever you are. Imagine the implications for advanced research of being able to upload, download, visualize, and stream huge data files without thinking twice about the capacity of the networks you're using. Imagine a city that can pull together, analyze, and understand all the data being collected by its transportation, water, and energy networks. Imagine technical directions being conveyed by way of augmented reality, so that you can be an apprentice in a remote factory rather than traveling to a physical central training location. Imagine being over eighty and able to live a dignified, socially connected life while staying in your home, connected to far-flung relatives and able easily to summon people who care about you to your side. Imagine having eye contact with anyone, anywhere, and communicating the empathy and concern that humans need to thrive.

Somewhere in our evolution, socializing and connecting with each other became a species characteristic, and fiber will allow us to be present in others' lives in ways we cannot now imagine. By permitting genuine eye contact at a distance, and the empathy and connection that contact can bring, high-bandwidth, no-delay fiber connections could make the experience of online connection much more like physical presence. Real eye contact, so far, has been impossible over existing copper wire and cable lines; too little information is flowing symmetrically to make this kind of presence possible.

Over the past five years, I have been learning from people around the world what they have found useful about last-mile fiber networks. I've traveled to American cities to meet the pioneers who are struggling to install them here in the United States. I met many twenty-somethings in Seoul and Tokyo who talked to me candidly about the transformation of their friendships and way of life in their busy cities. "Things just work here," I was told, over and over again; transit tickets and schedules are entirely electronic, cash is never used in Seoul, and robots guide you through the airport. In Stockholm, the mayor volunteered to help me persuade American government leaders that fiber last-mile networks are essential to modern life. In Nashville, Tennessee, a leader of fiber installations in Asia told me, quite seriously, that America's lack of decent connectivity amounted to child abuse; in his view, we were systematically relegating our children to lives of insufficient opportunity to find meaning and dignity.

Outside a noisy restaurant in Lund, Sweden, I met the man who has been labeled the Swedish Broadband Jesus: Jonas Birgersson. He was wearing a tall black motorcycle helmet with the visor tilted up, making him look a bit like a welder in a science-fiction movie. After we sat down, he told me that he and fellow students in Lund had showed his country the way in last-mile fiber, installing their own 100 megabits per second (Mbps) network in the early 1990s that connected to the basements of apartment buildings. Birgersson, who was then a twenty-year-old busy starting online companies, became an agitator for fiber. Along the way, he gathered several home truths: fiber, he told me, "is like a window. Whatever you send, there will be no barrier." For him, its importance was not about speed per se but about not having to wait for your computer to do something. "If you want to get things done and then move on to the next thing, you need fiber," he said. "Don't think about gigabit access, think about time. If you enjoy sitting watching the colorful wheel turn, then cable is for you." Today, more than 70 percent of Swedish residences have last-mile, "fiber-to-the-home" connections.[16]

I met a young Cuban woman on the porch of the Norwegian Embassy in Havana who first experienced internet access when she left the island on a scholarship and was heartbroken, when she returned, by the realization that nothing of the kind is likely to come to her country for a long time. I will never forget Yaima Pardo crying in front of me. She felt that Cuba was missing something crucial that the rest of the world took for granted. For her, internet access was not a matter of technology. It had become elemental, like water or fire, and Cuba had been left out; a child alone in a trackless forest, without a helping hand. She had made a documentary about the issue, called *Offline*, and had shown it around the country; at each screening, local state security officials monitored the crowds. At one of the showings, an older man came up to her afterward and thanked her. And then he said, "The internet, to me, is like death. I've heard about it, but I've never experienced it." When it comes to high-capacity access, Cuba is to the United States as the United States is to Korea.

When journalist Robert Caro moved to a house on the edge of Hill Country fifty miles outside Austin, Texas, to interview people for his biography of Lyndon Baines Johnson, he heard one phrase repeated over and over again: "'He brought the lights. No matter what Lyndon was like, we loved him because he brought the lights.'" They meant that when Johnson, from the Hill Country, became a congressman in 1937, at the age of twenty-eight, there was no electricity, but by 1948, when he was elected to the Senate, most of the district had electricity. The people of the Hill Country were so grateful they named their children after him. Before electricity, the women there had rounded shoulders from lifting heavy buckets of water, moving innumerable loads of wet clothes by broomstick between a washboard and a vat of boiling water, and working with hot irons in oven-hot summer kitchens. Caro called all of this "brutal drudgery," and called LBJ's ingenuity in bringing electricity to his district "one of the most dramatic and noble examples of the use of government that I have ever heard." For Caro, this story is "the seeds of the Great Society in the young Lyndon Johnson."[17]

We are walking the same path today with last-mile fiber optic networks. Almost every American is like the people of the Hill

Country: we suffer from totally inadequate, horribly expensive connectivity that cuts whole populations off from opportunity, adequate health care, and a decent education, and thwarts the development of new businesses. A handful of private companies dominate last-mile data delivery in American cities. They choose the richest, densest areas to serve with expensive second-class services—not with malign intention, but with a detrimental effect on the country. Hundreds of American cities, fed up or ignored, have decided to call for the construction of their own last-mile fiber networks. But it's not easy: the incumbents go after them systematically, hiring academics and "experts" to attack these city planners as socialistic and mounting epic campaigns in state legislatures to block cities with legislation. Meanwhile, rural areas are unconnected and out of touch. The only thing we are missing is widespread public recognition of the depth and significance of the last-mile fiber problem—and either a young LBJ or a more seasoned FDR to address it.

At the same time, we routinely underestimate the long-term impact of any new fundamental technology, and I suspect any guesses of mine about the effects of fiber will similarly fall short. We are already seeing dramatic improvements in agricultural productivity that have been driven by fiber-to-the-farm: detailed automated treatment of land that is possible only with the aggregation of enormous amounts of data. Fiber and advanced wireless capability will allow us to manage our use of energy and incorporate renewable sources into local and national power grids. The fiber story in Chattanooga, Tennessee, began with its "smart grid," and the cost savings of monitoring and moderating the city's use of power at very fine-grained levels paid for its last-mile fiber installation. With a large enough consumer market, we could see vastly expanded retail opportunities that allow sellers and buyers to touch and feel goods from a distance—something we can't now do online. With fiber, you can work where you live, rather than the other way around; you can be "in the office" in every way short of smelling the new paint on the wall. Effective, real-time business meetings drawing on expertise from widely dispersed geographic locations can actually happen on an end-to-end fiber network. New forms of collaboration among musicians and other artists will emerge over fiber. We cannot be the most advanced health care nation in the world without fiber everywhere, permitting Americans to avoid costly, unnecessary visits to hospitals and clinics. Advanced forms of transportation—driverless buses, personalized, demand-driven subways—that are better for the environment, require less human intervention, and are better suited to their context will be created. New forms of virtual reality entertainment will become part of our lives (you have to experience this to understand why it is so important). Augmented reality applications—mixing digital and "real" events and objects—that allow us to see and understand everything around us far more deeply will become standard.

Everything I have suggested here, and much more that we cannot imagine, will become possible in countries where last-mile open-access fiber can be easily connected to competitive 5G wireless communications. These developments will also cause enormous disruption to existing occupations. And only the countries that are thinking ahead about the new industries made possible by these technologies will have the wherewithal to manage the dislocation of their labor forces—to smooth the runway to new sources of economic growth and human thriving.

It's going to be amazing. But it won't happen without substantial public energy and intervention.

CHAPTER TWO

Transmitting Light

O NE HOT JULY MORNING in Corning, New York, I opened the door of my car and gazed across the parking lot at the huge steel and glass building. I had driven alone across the entire width of the state of Massachusetts and most of New York over two days. In this building, I hoped, someone would be able to explain to me the magic of how fiber optic cables are made.

For me, the name Corning had meant hefty, chipped white cookware, seemingly hand-painted with a primitive looping swirl on the rims of the lids. But in the building I was looking at now, Corning had been researching high-tech glass for decades, often without a clear commercial application in view—the kind of pure science that many companies can't afford these days. The super-thin, scratch-resistant glass on the iPhone was developed by Corning scientists. And the company is not just about smartphone glass: the nine-story glass building in front of me was the home of Corning's long-term research in fiber optics.

Walking around the town's historic downtown district the afternoon before, I'd found restaurants, shops, and art galleries; it's a welcoming few blocks that seems to be thriving. Corning is a small place—once a village, then a hamlet, now a town, population about 11,000, that grew up around the glass-making industry during the nineteenth century. Abundant coal supplies, railroad connections, and canal links lured Brooklyn Flint Glass to Corning right after the Civil War, and the company soon changed its name to Corning Glass Works. The town attracted competitors and knock-on businesses; glass arts flourished. But it was industrial production of glass for railroad lanterns that drove the company into profitability, and when World War I blocked the import of German glass, labware from Corning Glass became a major business. The company sponsored its own band and sports teams, and the tall glass furnaces of its main plant spewed smoke just north of downtown's Market Street until it moved its operations outside of town. Even in June 1972, when three days of flooding caused by Hurricane Agnes caused disastrous, extensive damage to Corning Glass Works and to the town, the company didn't leave; instead, it actively helped rebuild the region, and Corning was transformed from a factory town to a tourist destination—named by Rand McNally in 2013 as the "most fun" among the best small towns in America. The company, which changed its name to Corning Inc. in 1989, is still the largest employer in the county. The fortunes of the town of Corning have been tightly tied to those of Corning Inc.: the city of Elmira, twenty miles east along the Chemung River, where Mark Twain coined the term "Gilded Age," hasn't rebounded from the 1972 storm.[1] It didn't have a stabilizing corporate citizen like Corning Inc.

Corning is an old town, with houses meant for Corning executives perched on the top of the hill above the village. The night I arrived, one of the Corning executives had a group of his colleagues over to meet me; they were all men, and most of them were commuters. They had found it hard to convince their wives to come to the town of Corning or stay for any length of time.

But first, coffee.

Claudio Mazzali, a bright-eyed, energetic Brazilian physicist who has been with the company since 1999 and now leads technology efforts for two of its divisions, met me in the lobby of the research building and showed me to a large room lined by screens and gadgets.

I spent many hours with Dr. Mazzali that day, and I was delighted by his wry sense of humor and somewhat goofy smile; he had first worked in Corning's Brazilian regional office as an optical communications specialist and had transferred to upstate New York about fifteen years earlier. I could see that he loved his job. He's helping to run the enormous centralized research lab—the Bell Labs of our era—for a company that keeps reinventing itself as a manufacturer and annually invests about 10 percent of its revenue, no matter what, in research and development.[2] Turnover at Corning is very low; employees come for life, by and large. But Mazzali had a sense of humor about his location: "We're in the middle of everything. Five hours from New York, six hours from Boston, five hours from Toronto." Because the rest of the country doesn't have fiber connections into homes and businesses—yet— he feels intensely the remoteness of Corning.

Mazzali brought me a cup of steaming coffee; as I drank, he said emphatically: "When you think about glass, some people say, 'Oh, I get sand, and I melt that, and then I make glass.' Of course it's much more sophisticated than that for optical fiber. It's totally different."

Fiber optic cable is made completely synthetically. It has to be so pure, so clear, that it can transmit light over many dozens of miles without any boosting or encouragement, and without losing any of the information that has been encoded onto that light. To get that clarity, its manufacturers control every micron and every second of the manufacturing process.

The history of fiber optics goes back to the 1960s, with the invention of the laser. Lasers apply energy to billions of atoms, exciting their electrons and making them emit photons that then turn around and make already-excited atoms give off even more photons. When some of the photons are allowed to escape, the result is an amplified, concentrated beam of light—Light Amplification by Stimulated Emission of Radiation, or LASER.[3] That light has a frequency; it is wobbling at a rate of millions of millions of times a second, and each of those wobbles can be modulated to carry data. That data then travels at the speed of light.

The trouble was how to transmit that focused data reliably from point A to point B. Light can be carried by water—just imagine a nighttime fountain lit by purple light from below—but light can't carry information through water very far. You need the waves to maintain their strength and definition in order for the information they carry, encoded in the height or frequency of these waves, to be understood. Back in the late nineteenth century, a Viennese medical team identified only as "Dr. Roth and Prof. Reuss" experimented with guiding light through bent glass rods to illuminate body parts during surgery.[4] With the arrival of the laser, scientists saw the possibility of guiding information across many miles with very little loss of accuracy.

Enter "optical fiber." Researcher Charles Kao (now Sir Kao), while a PhD student in Harlow, England, in 1964, posited that glass—a later generation of the glass tubes that had been used to illuminate surgery—could be used to guide many "colors," or frequencies, of laser beams. But Kao pointed out that for this guidance to occur without significant loss, the glass had to be much purer than anything then available; his work was purely theoretical.[5]

His work got Corning interested in the idea of optical fiber.[6] In 1965, Corning was in the glass business but not the telecommunications business. Telecommunications companies were using copper lines to transmit the electrical pulses that carry voice calls and data between cities and into homes.[7] To make it worthwhile for those companies—a potentially huge new group of customers—to replace their copper lines with fiber, Corning would have to show that fiber was so much better at conveying data than copper that it would be worthwhile for those customers to replace their existing copper lines. But at the time, there was no glass strand that could transmit light more than about fifteen centimeters before the signal fell off (or was "lost" or "attenuated").[8] Corning needed to figure out how to create glass that could transmit a signal not for centimeters but for many miles.

The head of Corning Glass Works research at the time, William Armistead, was skeptical. Nevertheless, he approved funding for Robert Maurer, a physicist, as well as colleagues Pete Schultz, a senior chemist, and Donald Keck, an engineer and physicist, to work on the problem. And they did, without a customer in sight.

Maurer and his team knew that the glass would have to have a clear core surrounded by a skin—called cladding, and also made of glass—so that the cladding could reflect laser light back into the core and keep it traveling along its path. For four years, he and his team at Corning kept experimenting with different chemical compositions of the core to create the greatest possible clarity. Failure followed failure.

One Friday evening in August 1970, Donald Keck was alone in the Corning R&D lab, testing one last piece of fiber before the weekend. Ira Magaziner and Mark Patinkin, in their book *The Silent War*, tell the story of Keck bending over his microscope and lining up the laser, watching as the narrow beam of light got closer and closer to the core. Suddenly, Keck was hit right in the eye by a bright beam of light. The fiber had transmitted light without losing more than a tiny amount of the beam's strength. "Eureka," Keck wrote in the lab notebook that day. It would be ten more years before Corning found a customer for its optical fiber.[9]

The remarkable thing about the hair-thin strands of optical fiber that Corning and other companies sell today is that any single strand of glass can carry many different beams of light at the same time, each beam wobbling at its own frequency and using its own method of encoding information. This is the enormous advantage of fiber: its overall bandwidth potential (how many different signals it can transmit and how fast you can encode or modulate them) is much higher than any other transmission medium. Unless the transmission medium itself somehow gets in the way, as a deep pothole or a truck might block the road when a car wants to go by, a single fiber optic cable can carry the entire weight of data on the internet.[10]

It's an amazing idea. Now, copper wires—sometimes called "twisted pair" because they are made of pairs of strands of copper twisted around one another—also carry data and telephone signals to homes and farms in much of rural America. But because of the characteristics of copper as a transmission medium, signals that travel over copper don't have the extraordinary frequency range that light signals do, are subject to interference from other signals, and in general degrade very quickly over more than a short distance.[11] That's why if you have a copper-wire DSL (digital subscriber line) subscription you have to be very close to the phone company's "central office" in order to get a download signal into your house. A "DSL" house is connected to a copper wire, not a fiber optic cable.[12] Not only can light travel over fiber for hundreds of kilometers with little attenuation (impossible with copper), but signals zipping around via fiber don't get interfered with by other electrical transmissions nearby (which happens all the time with copper). Fiber is also, once it's installed, far cheaper to maintain than a copper line.[13]

As Mazzali explained, the traditional ways of making glass—blowing and pressing melted silica, for example—create a bubble-filled, flawed product that can't do what Maurer's team required. "Because you need purity and transparency," he said, "you cannot start from sand or anything like that and melt it and make glass." Instead, you use gas traveling through flames to create particles of soot—glass soot particles—that are deposited on a rod in a controlled pattern. And then he showed me a line of small blue flames that were slowly, mechanically being moved sideways up and down a white rod. This was the beginning of the creation of a strand of fiber: printing soot in carefully orchestrated layers on a solid rod.

The composition of every layer of each hair-thin strand of glass—and each strand consists of thousands of layers—is controlled by tweaking the composition of gases traveling through the flames. Once you have laid each one of those thousands of layers meticulously on top of the previous one, and you have heated the whole thing at a precisely controlled rate to a precise temperature, when it cools you will have glass with very specific properties. "That's how you control the light," Mazzali said. "That's how you can trap the light inside, by playing with different attributes of the fiber." He was smiling, excited. I asked for the recipe—the identity of the gases being blown through the flames to create the soot particles—but he wasn't telling. "A little bit of germanium, a little bit of this, a little bit of that."

Mazzali was showing me a demonstration version of the printing-on-a-rod process that Maurer and Keck had created at Corning; the real process, he says, takes several hours. He led me to a tubby, short white tube and had me touch it. This was what all the printing of soot I had seen ends up creating. A white chalky substance came off on my fingers. "Sorry about that," said Mazzali. "Those are actually particles of glass. It's not just silica. We are doping each one of those layers with different materials and different amounts of materials, to change how they reflect light." That white tube, called a blank, already has most of the attributes of the end product; all the ways that glass will treat light are already built in. "When you make that," Mazzali said, "you know exactly that that fiber will have that dispersion, that attenuation, that geometry, all that." When companies transform the blank by pulling or "drawing" it into a single skinny glass strand thousands of kilometers long (think of pulling a very long single strand from a thick skein of wool), all they're doing is making the chunky blank thinner.

Mazzali was warming to his task. "Now," he said, "you have to transform this coarse white thing into glass." The fat tube certainly did not look like glass to me. "So now we go to the next step, consolidation."

Consolidation involves placing the chalky thick blank into a giant furnace. The heat gets all the water out of the blank, and then the material starts to consolidate, or "sinter." This sintering step transforms it into a transparent and smaller thing that is labeled a "preform." Mazzali handed me a sample transformed preform, sleek and transparent, about the same size as a very large salami from a local supermarket. The ceramic rod on which the soot had been printed was gone.

"If you look very carefully in the middle, can you see a different sort of color?" Mazzali asked me. I looked, and saw a very narrow, thin band of something-ness in nothing-ness. "That's the core," Mazzali said. "That's where the light will be." Maurer's team had decided that the way to make glass transmit light most effectively was, somewhat paradoxically, to make the core less pure than the cladding so that the latter would act as a mirror, trapping light inside the core. So chemicals were mixed into the core—through the tweaking of the soot layering—that did that. "You put a light in that core," said Mazzali, "it keeps reflecting back and forth."

It all seemed magical, and it was about to get even better. That sleek preform goes into a draw tower—imagine a grain silo on stilts up near the ceiling of a giant warehouse—to be melted. Then from the gob of stuff that initially protrudes from the bottom of the tower following the melting process, a single strand is pulled or drawn straight down toward the ground. That is the hair-thin strand that is a single fiber optic cable.

The melting and drawing process, like the other steps, is tightly controlled. First, the tip of the preform is heated, causing a gob of hot glass to descend. Once the gob drops, it's taken away, and the thin thread behind it is threaded through a device that minutely controls the speed of the draw (the speed at which the strand is drawn toward the ground) and the diameter of the resulting fiber. Every micron is documented.

The glass cools rapidly, within seconds, but according to precise timing. Meanwhile, inside the draw tower, a coating made of several layers of different plastics is applied to protect the glass and cured using ultraviolet light. The secret sauce of all of this is the precise controlling of the timing and temperature of the draw; that's what gets the pristine transparency and low signal loss that communicators want. "If you do something very abrupt with glass, the material is not homogeneous anymore," Mazzali said, because the chemicals will clump up and you'll lose the architecture that has been carefully engineered into the glass. Any variations in density—however minor—will cause the light to scatter. And scatter means loss.

Mazzali led me into the wide white hall outside the prototype demo room to take the elevator to a higher floor of the R&D lab. As we went up, he told me what was about to happen. "We're going to need safety glasses." We came out of the elevator, put on the glasses, and looked up at a big steel box with one side missing. "What comes after the blank?" Mazzali quizzed me. I tried hard to remember what he had told me minutes before: "You've got the big thick thing and then you take out all the moisture and all the impurities and slenderize it," I gamely responded. Mazzali pointed out a clear post-processing glass tube, with the core visible. "After you have that piece of glass, what's the next step?" He was enjoying being the teacher. "You draw, the globule comes first and then the very skinny stuff comes next," I said, gabbling a bit.

He pointed up again: "Can you see there, the gob going down?" A big blob, glowing white, was hanging off the end of an enormous clear glass tube. That one tube, he said, would produce a few thousand kilometers of glass strand. He smiled; he wasn't going to be any more specific. "This is the top of the draw," he said. "We're going to go down a few floors."

We ran down the stairs, with me clattering after Mazzali. He opened the door on the floor just below where we had been and pointed ahead of us: "Can you see the fiber?" he asked. "No," I said. "Look carefully," he said. And there it was, an impossibly thin strand, descending from a big hole in the ceiling to the floor.

"Now you're going to see the last stage, which is putting it on a spool," he said.

We clattered down more stairs into the basement. There a calm, tall man named Matt was watching gauges as the strand of fiber wound onto a spool. He was looking for imperfections. "Remember that the fiber is 125 microns in diameter, plus or minus less than a micron," Mazzali said. "We have to control the diameter of this glass, every single meter over more than a thousand of kilometers, by all of this equipment that we have on the draw, the tension, the temperature, the speed, and all that," so that whenever a splice has to be made—a connection between one strand of fiber optic cable and another—the fiber will transmit perfectly.

"At this point it's cold already," Mazzali said. "The coating is there, you can touch the fiber, it goes on the spool. After this, you put it in a box and you can ship it to the customer. There is nothing else to be done other than putting it in a cable." The strands of fiber would be bundled inside a cable—a cable with 576 strands will have 24 colored "buffer" tubes, each with 24 individual fiber strands inside.

The coating, the layers of plastic cured around the fiber, doesn't stop the fiber from bending. By serving as a kind of very thin cushion, the coating keeps the individual fibers inside any given cable from interfering with one another. (Corning fiber, these days, is made to bend easily, even around tight corners inside buildings or when wrapped around rods, without losing signal strength.) Months later, many hundreds of miles south of Corning, I would see that coating being carefully removed in order for one strand of bare glass to be precisely spliced to another strand of fiber.

Low-loss fiber was invented forty-five years ago, and fiber that was installed just a few years later in places like Long Beach, California, and Dorset, United Kingdom, was already high quality and is still working today. Glass is very, very stable. If no one cuts into it, there is no degradation—for decades, as far as we can tell—of the extraordinarily high bandwidth of data it can carry. One single strand of glass can carry three billion phone calls or web sessions. The submarine cable connecting China and the United States contains just eight strands.[14]

And to improve that capacity, as the science of photonics improves, you can merely swap out the electronics producing the photons—the glass stays in the ground or on the poles. Once the photons shoot out into the glass, no power is needed to boost the transmission of data, for many, many miles. The photons just keep going for tens of kilometers, traveling inside their perfectly mirrored channel, and can't be interfered with by electricity, water, or anything else.

The problem with fiber is not capacity or longevity. It's distribution. You need to distribute those fibers to everyone who might want to carry out those phone calls or web sessions, so the fibers have to go to different locations. The submarine cables between continents are all fiber, the lines between American cities are almost all fiber, and the data centers run by companies like Google and Akamai are all fed by fiber. But there's an enormous distribution bottleneck close to you and me: less than 10 percent of Americans have "fiber to the home," or FTTH.[15]

The FTTH distribution issue isn't easy to fix. Although several countries have made installation of FTTH an industrial policy priority and have steadily upgraded their "last-mile" networks, a series of federal- and state-level policy missteps over the past ten years has left America with awful fiber adoption. The completely deregulated private companies on which we depend for wired communications have systematically divided markets, avoided competition, and established monopolies in their geographic footprints. The results are terrible: very expensive yet second-rate data services, mostly from local cable monopolists, in richer neighborhoods; the vast majority of Americans unable to buy a fiber optic subscription at any price; and many Americans, particularly in rural and poorer areas, completely left behind. Several cities are showing the way, insisting on inexpensive, competitive fiber connections for their residents, and I visited some of those places to meet the people who carried this out. I also went to Seoul, Tokyo, and Stockholm to gather information about what's possible when the policy arrows are pointed in the right direction.

In June 2016, Verizon CEO Lowell McAdam told Wall Street analysts that his company was planning to deploy the next generation of wireless technology, called 5G, and described it as "wireless fiber"—intimating that it would substitute for fiber lines. But it's not quite that simple.[16]

Although over-the-airwaves wireless connections sprayed out by an antenna can carry a great deal of information over relatively short distances, those connections are shared, so the actual experience depends on how many users are connected to one antenna. And when higher frequencies are used to improve wireless bandwidth, you have to manage degradation by distance, weather, walls, and big walking bags of water—otherwise known as people.

That doesn't mean that McAdam's plan is wrong. In 2017, he made clear that fiber is essential to 5G. Mobile wireless connections are extraordinarily useful add-ons to fiber. But they depend on fiber being installed everywhere: in order to carry the tsunamis of data that 5G devices of every flavor will be producing, and given the very short distances those wireless communications can travel, we will need more than twenty times the number of existing cell towers or cell installations—every 15,000 feet or so, deep in neighborhoods and cities. "And they'll all need a fiber connection," Bob Whitman, Corning's vice president of market development, told me.[17] You can think of wireless as the end point of a fiber connection; the place where the pipe bringing water into your home is transformed into a showerhead—except that it is spraying not water but data.

This fiber-plus-wireless combination is alluring: with fiber to every cell site and every Wi-Fi access point, you could be constantly connected and never think about it. In the fall of 2015, Corning set a record for bandwidth use in conjunction with Texas A&M at its Kyle Field, getting fiber into antennas separated by just a few seats; fans were able to use their tablets and phones without constraint.[18] But wireless-everywhere is no less labor intensive than fiber-everywhere: tens of thousands of skilled workers will have to install and maintain hundreds of thousands of towers and connect them to readily-available, reasonably-priced fiber. It is a complement to fiber, not a substitute for it.

Another sunny morning found me in Austin, Texas, looking for wisdom from someone who knows all about the physical installation of fiber optic cable. I was in Austin because Google Fiber was installing last-mile fiber optic cable there, and I wanted to see it being done. Google had upended the policy discussion in the United States in 2010 by declaring it would wire a winning town or two with fiber; since then, it had moved into a handful of U.S. cities. Although Google's impact on America's actual fiber adoption has been minimal—it simply wasn't serving many houses, and didn't plan to—its activities have contributed to growing awareness of what's gone wrong with America's internet access. Austin, with its vibrant cultural scene and major research institutions, is an important part of the Google Fiber story.

My guide was Mike Leddy, a calm, soft-spoken man with tufty eyebrows. Leddy had moved to Austin about a year before I met him, shifting from being in charge of Verizon's New York City fiber installations—territory: the Upper East Side and Midtown, home to a lot of picky people—to working on squeezing all extraneous costs out of Google Fiber's FTTH network.

To deliver last-mile fiber optic lines directly to individual buildings, fiber has to be attached to poles ("aerials") or be put in trenches underneath streets or sidewalks. Google decided to design its FTTH network in Austin by stringing fiber from a backbone, or ring of metro fiber, to a series of squat brown buildings—Google calls them "huts," or "local active sites"—each of which serves about twenty thousand households.[19] Each air-conditioned hut has, inside, the electronics needed to split the signal received from the backbone onto multiple fibers that go underground or on poles to each neighborhood, where the signals are split again, until eventually, each Google customer gets his or her own fiber.

If this sounds easy, it isn't. It turns out that every street in every single neighborhood has its own set of issues. Fiber installation is a very local process.

Construction of last-mile fiber networks would be straightforward if there was conduit—plastic tubing of various kinds, easy to access and wide enough to enable individual fiber strands to be pulled through it—already installed under the streets, running from an underground "vault" or network access point. The vault in turn serves as a distribution center in each neighborhood for single fibers running to the side of each house. In many European cities, including Stockholm, that conduit exists, and can be used as a shared asset by many carriers. But it didn't exist in Austin. So, Google had to build its own path underground. Austin sits on very hard limestone.

I put on a hard hat—Mike had to adjust it to stay on my head—and a green fluorescent vest, and we set off on that sunny morning in an unremarkable section of suburban Austin. As we walked, Mike explained that Google had looked at two ways to do underground construction. First, you could use a big drill to carve out a path underneath all the other utilities (gas, electric, water) already under the ground. This is called "directional drilling" or "horizontal boring," but Google had decided before I arrived that it was too risky and disruptive. The drills are hard to direct, and you have to back a big, noisy machine (to grind through all that limestone) onto someone's front lawn to get enough of an angle to dig deep. The second way to do construction, he said, was "microtrenching," which is a popular method in Asia and Europe.[20] That's what was going on in Austin.

Microtrenching involves less digging and disruption than ordinary trenching, and it's also cheaper.[21] It could be used successfully in many parts of the United States. So I spent the morning watching an almost cartoonish parade of special-purpose machines that had lined up to do the microtrenching job. They proceeded, one after the other, each truck with its own character, color, and set of fantastic attachments, moving at about a mile an hour down the quiet suburban street. Men wielding big STOP signs stood nearby to direct traffic.

First came the vacuum cleaner truck, with a giant hose flowing back behind it. Why a vacuum cleaner? Because the hose was attached to a digging truck carrying a giant circular steel saw festooned with drill bits. That saw-wheel digs into the street; its job is to cut out a narrow, two-foot-deep trench alongside the curb, flush with the street. The vacuum truck's job is to remove all the material from the microtrench so that the cables can be installed at a uniform depth. It also keeps the neighborhood clean. The men running the digging truck stopped the action and pulled up the drill-bit-wheel from the trench so that I could see it. The vacuum cleaner truck sucked up all the mess created by the saw. Any six-year-old would have loved the show.

The resulting trench is small and shallow, but it's above the limestone and above all the other utilities, which are three feet deep. No one has to have a drilling machine with a mind of its own on his or her lawn; the trench is built on the street side and is protected by the giant concrete obstacle that is the unseen, underground part of the curb structure. Mike pointed to another machine coming up behind the digging truck: "There's the conduit!" he said proudly.

The next truck had a flat platform on which three giant wooden spools were mounted. Two spools had orange high-density polyethylene conduit pipe wound around them; the third one had green. A man in a hard hat was expertly drawing out a strand of orange pipe from one of the spools and laying it in the just-dug trench. Mike told me that the conduit would go underground accompanied by a copper tracer wire, so that later, the location of the conduit would be easy to detect from above the ground.

And then came the dramatic part: covering the conduit and filling the trench with concrete that was made on the spot. A first truck, grimy white and tall, with a bright blue nose, bristling with dials and chutes, was responsible for mixing the concrete. Another worker moved next to it, checking the consistency of the concrete slurry that was beginning to edge up a conveyor belt connected at about a forty-five-degree angle to the back of the mixing truck. Mike told me the resulting concrete would be less dense than sidewalk concrete, so that if necessary, it wouldn't be too difficult to dig up the microtrench. Another benefit of low density: like a fluffy baked good, it takes less time to set—thirty-five minutes rather than the hour that normal concrete would take.

Behind the mixing truck, receiving the slurry, was a narrow, mid-height orange machine with a kind of grate on top of it and a big screw inside it. A man was jabbing with a shovel at a dial next to a chute coming off the orange machine. "This machine," Mike explained, "actually agitates the cement mixture and releases it down the chute. It's designed to fit down into the trench. They'll just make their way along and fill the trench up." I asked Mike what the guy was doing with the shovel. "He probably got a little plug in there," said Mike, smiling.

It was time to say goodbye to the conduit for the next forty or fifty years. The narrow orange filling truck was rolling along, depositing the gunky concrete mixture in the trench, and a smoother-guy was walking along behind the truck smoothing the surface of the mixture. Mike had seen it a thousand times, "but I still like watching this," he said quietly. The crew we saw had done two thousand feet of microtrenching the day before, a tenfold improvement over what's possible with directional drilling.

The next step was restoration, which was not as dramatic; we went to a neighborhood to see a finished set of microtrenches. They'd been sealed with a black substance that left an innocuous narrow line against the white curb. The city of Austin believes this process improves the seal between the curb and the street, and that the street drains better after microtrenching. "One of the issues here," Mike said, "is that it rains really hard in Austin. I didn't know until I moved here. They have water that gets down between the asphalt and the concrete, so it undermines the base of the road. The idea is that this seal over our microtrench prevents this."

But the fiber hadn't gotten to the homes, not yet. At the same time the trenches are dug, filled, and covered by that fabulous lineup of special-purpose machines, the "outside plant" crew, the group we'd been watching all morning, cuts sideways across the curb near each pair of houses and digs a small square hole in the public right-of-way on the house side of the curb. Mike told me that single pipes of conduit are pulled into this hole from the microtrench in the street, the hole is covered up (later, a flat structure is built around the hole, and the whole thing is called a drop vault), and the next crew, the installers, come in when a homeowner makes an appointment to be connected.

We drove to another location to watch the installation. The day was becoming more and more pleasant, and the trees were even taller in that next neighborhood. The microtrench was all done and neatly sealed, and a big coil of PVC conduit was sitting on the ground next to a hole on the house side of the curb. I saw a man digging a shallow trench from that hole across the front of the property to the driveway. Another man named Zack, sporting a strong southern twang and a bright blue polo shirt stretched over a hefty belly, offered to be my tour guide. He pointed to the man digging the trench. "What you see him doing now," Zack said, "is basically what we call whomping." The PVC conduit would be brought from the drop vault to the side of the driveway through the trench, and then under the driveway using a nondirectional small boring device called a PortaMole. The PortaMole, which looks like a rotary tiller, was described to me as the "Chitty Chitty Bang Bang" of equipment: "It kinda comes out where it comes out." Once the hole under the driveway was done, the fiber would be brought up to the left side of the house in another shallow trench. Why there? Because it was a two-family house, and only the left side wanted fiber service.

On that side of the house, about three feet up from the ground, Zack was planning to install a small gray plastic box called a network interface unit (NIU). Inside the NIU, fiber that had been pulled through the conduit all the way from the trenches under the street would be spliced to the very last link in the network: the fiber that would go inside the house to provide connectivity. A hole would be poked in the house wall to allow that fiber in, and then, inside the house, a fiber jack would be installed to which the homeowner could attach a laptop or Wi-Fi router by an ethernet cable. Then the homeowner would be online.

Many installers are true characters; they've come to the job of installing fiber after decades of working for local cable monopolies, and they have lots of stories to tell. While Zack was explaining how the house would be wired, an older man named Bill with sleepy blue eyes, who had clearly spent a lot of time sidling up to bars, sidled up to us. Upon being told I was writing a book, Bill said, "Well, just make sure whoever plays me in the movie, you check with me. Channing Tatum would be nice, you know what I mean?" I promised to get that done. He told me he moves around a lot, was originally from Delaware, but didn't want to go back there. I got the sense that Bill isn't connected to much. "Yeah, it's nice for about three days. And then I'm ready to leave." Zack's voice softened in bantering with Bill; he was used to Bill's stories.

Although the drop vault was on publicly owned land because it was less than ten feet from the curb, all the whomping and PortaMole activity I saw was taking place on private property. The homeowner, who had already given permission for the installation, wasn't around for me to talk to, although I heard that he had been coming and going all day. People often come out of their homes and thank the installers.

There was just one more step in the deployment process: the splice inside the NIU between the outside plant fiber and the fiber destined to run inside the house. Zack told me how this was going to happen: "Wes is gonna start to get his machine out, get a scrap piece of fiber and a pigtail, and in about two, three minutes he'll be ready. We can go down there and he'll actually show us how—strippin' it, cleanin' it, and putting it all together." The whole gang, including Mike, Zack, Bill, and the whomper (whose name I never heard), repaired to the side of a pickup truck in the shade. The guys leaned on the side of the truck and watched, making only a few cracks: splicing is serious business.

Although the NIU splice is usually done on the side of the house, the team wasn't ready for that at the moment I showed up, so Wes demonstrated his splicing technique on the truck's tailgate.

I had a question: "What's a pigtail?" Wes showed it to me. The pigtail in the NIU on the door of the pickup truck was about four inches long. It's basically a fiber cable with a green connector (Wes called it a "jumper"), a kind of premade splice holder made of ceramic on one end, and naked fiber on the other. Wes would take the fiber coming from the street and attach it to the connector end of the pigtail, and then splice the inside-house fiber (fiber ready to curve around walls) to the pigtail's naked end. The idea behind everything Wes was about to do was to ensure that all the excited photons coming from the fiber running from the hut miles away would actually get to the inside of the house. His target was no more than .03 decibels of loss.

Wes found a scrap piece of fiber that could stand in for the inside-house fiber. I told him that I'd been to Corning to see fiber being made. "I've always wanted to see how they manufactured that," he said wistfully. "Because I wondered how they've been so consistent with it, down to the micron." When I described the soot printing and the other marvels I'd seen, Wes listened attentively. "That's unbelievable," he said. Then he got down to the business of splicing.

He lifted up the green ceramic end of the pigtail, inserted a strand of fiber in it, and said, "There's a tiny, tiny little hole that the light comes through. You can actually take a laser up to it." He held up the other end of the pigtail, the naked fiber end, and showed me that the hair-thin strand was glowing. "I'm not going to point it at anybody's eye." Bill made the obligatory joke: "I used to have a cataract, thanks." Wes ignored Bill and went on to show me that the fiber at the working end of the pigtail could be bent or stapled without any light being lost. "There's a lot of things you can do to it now that would have been absolute no-nos" in the past, Wes told me.

Now it was time to mechanically splice the working end of the pigtail to the scrap of fiber. Mike showed me the splicing device, which was a footlong sort of console, with several horizontal sections. When the fiber was ready for splicing, Wes would put the pigtail end and the scrap end facing each other underneath two metal sections that would automatically align the two fibers together. Then: "Those two pins you see in the very center shoot a plasma arc that melts the glass together." At that point, you can measure the light lost between the incoming and the outgoing fiber strands. If the measurement is low enough, you take the resulting spliced fiber and put it in a different section of the splicing device, which obediently melts a plastic section over the splice to protect it.

Then followed a series of steps aimed at creating a seamless communication path from the neighborhood fiber distribution vault to the homeowner. First, Wes had to get to the naked fiber inside the PVC conduit. He cut away the orange conduit wall, revealing two white fiberglass rods within which a bright blue tube was set—the "buffer tube," within which the fiber itself was resting. He stripped away the buffer tube, and there it was: the fiber strand I'd seen manufactured at Corning, or one just like it, a hair floating in the Texas breeze. Very, very carefully, he stripped a half-inch or so of the polyurethane layers off the surface of the fiber.

Mike stepped in to explain what was going on while Wes kept carefully stripping and revealing the fiber strand. "The device that he'll use to cut it, cuts the fiber at a slight angle to prevent reflections from bouncing directly back down the center of the glass," Mike said. This process, called "cleaving," ensures that any reflected light does not create interference with the signal.

Wes stayed focused. He did the cleaving by scoring the glass with a special green circular blade—not actually cutting it; the glass falls away from itself once it is scored—and put both ends of the different lengths of fiber into the splicing machine. He bent low. "That's the zap melting," Wes said. He'd seen the plasma arc melt the two ends of glass. He checked the loss readout: .04 decibels. More than the required .03. "So I'll do it again," Wes said.

When a splice is done in the field, the splicers create a digital record that includes their location and the place the distribution fiber came from, and then they upload a picture of the splice they've made. None of Wes's splices have ever been rejected. Bill spoke up: "Some nights, Wes," he said, "we make popcorn, we'll sit back and look at it, you know what I mean?"

Wes tried the whole thing over again. ".07," he said glumly. Mike was sympathetic. "We have to press on," he told Wes. "I at least offered to redeem myself," Wes said.

CHAPTER THREE

Why U.S. Internet Access Is Awful

A LTHOUGH JUST ABOUT EVERYONE in America has contact with the internet, the high cost of that access and the low quality of service most people get is hidden in plain view. That's the odd thing about internet access in America: it's always in the news, with daily stories about the wonders of augmented reality, the Internet of Things, and driverless cars. No one seems to stop to ask whether those advanced uses of data will work reliably, where, and for whom.

Connectivity is not only an invisible problem but a hard one to explain. You have to know a bit about three kinds of wires and what wireless access is, and then reason through reams of industry talking points about "5G" wireless access. And you have to understand that the "last-mile" issue is a problem for different reasons in different places. And that the available data on all this is far scarcer than it should be.

Here's the bottom line: of the 119 million households in the United States, only about 10 million (give or take a million or two) subscribe to high-capacity fiber connections. About 75 percent of U.S. census blocks have no residential fiber provider at all. Something like 10 percent of Americans are connected to fiber optic lines, mostly in the very richest parts of the country, and they pay sky-high subscription rates; where fiber last-mile connections do exist, they are often extraordinarily expensive compared with international benchmarks. The problem is worst in rural areas, but it is awful in most cities as well.[1]

The cable and telephone monopolies that dominate access have no particular incentives to upgrade to fiber. These local monopolies are largely unconstrained by either competition or oversight. For services providing what the Federal Communications Commission (FCC) now labels high-speed access, defined as 25 Mbps download and 3 Mbps upload, almost 90 percent of Americans have *at most* one choice of high-capacity provider.[2] (Why the FCC chose to privilege downloads over uploads in setting this standard is a mystery to me; this standard fits the plans of the giant companies that control internet access in America, most of which themselves also sell packages of TV channels and thus have a business interest in ensuring that consumers think of the internet as a means for consumption of entertainment rather than for use in education, health care, or work, through video calls—all of which require symmetric connections, with equal upload and download speeds.) High-capacity connections in the United States are shockingly rare: 53 percent of the census blocks that have housing units in them have *no* provider selling download speeds at any price with a capacity higher than 50 Mbps—which itself is a tiny fraction of the standard capacity in Singapore and Seoul.[3] Think trickling garden hose versus a vast river. In most cases, given the scarcity of fiber connections in the United States, the provider of any existing high-capacity access is the local cable monopolist. Fiber accounts for just 14 percent of all high-capacity connections in the United States, and local cable companies account for 84 percent of such connections. When you consider subscriptions for at least 100 Mbps in the United States, about 94 percent are sold by cable companies.[4]

The ability to buy a modern connection is correlated with population density.[5] A quarter of Americans, or about 74 million people, live in areas where less than 40 percent of residents subscribe to even copper-line access; the rest have no access at all. People in rural areas are just one-tenth as likely to have access to modern-day high-capacity connections than those in urban areas.[6] They are even less likely than Americans in other areas to have a choice of providers: the fraction of census blocks with no service providers at all, even at the FCC's current "high-speed" level of 25 Mbps, is just 7 percent in urban areas but 58 percent in rural areas. Over 80 percent of rural census blocks have no provider of 100 Mbps download service.[7]

Where access is present, subscription numbers ("adoption" in industry lingo) are tightly correlated with socioeconomic status. About 60 percent of people making $20,000 a year or less don't have wired access—even copper-wire access—at home, but 80 percent of people making between $50,000 and $75,000 do. Price makes a big difference in adoption.[8]

We don't compare well internationally. The United States ranks twenty-sixth out of the forty countries in the Organisation for Economic Co-operation and Development (OECD) in average download speed; for plans that offer downloads at speeds greater than 50 Mbps (likely over fiber), Americans pay more than people in all but six other developed countries—including Mexico, Chile, and Brazil.[9] For plans offering speeds of between 25 and 50 Mbps over fiber, people in the United States pay less than residents in just *three* other developed countries, including Turkey and Chile.

Residents of South Korea, Japan, Singapore, and Hong Kong can subscribe to gigabit access (offering ten times more capacity than a 100 Mbps subscription) for between the equivalent of $30 and $50 a month; in Sweden, which has announced plans to have 98 percent of its residents connected to gigabit fiber by 2025, the 100 Mbps symmetrical fiber connections already available to more than 70 percent of residents cost between $35 and $40 a month.[10] Singapore's connectivity is simply astonishing: you can buy gigabit last-mile fiber access from any one of a large number of providers for prices ranging from $40 to $60 per month.[11] By contrast, Verizon New York charges almost three times as much per month as providers in Sweden do, $105 a month, for its very-limited-availability 100 Mbps access (a tenth of what's standard in Singapore). It also charges a ridiculous $305 a month for symmetric access speed of 500 Mbps for both uploads and downloads, and doesn't offer gigabit fiber access at all.[12]

Adoption of residential fiber is far higher in Asia and northern Europe than in the United States. Fully three-quarters of the world's adoption of fiber in residences (or in apartment buildings) has happened in Asia.[13] Of the six countries that have greater than 50 percent fiber residential adoption, four are in Asia: South Korea, Singapore, Hong Kong, and Japan, all of which are now considered 100 percent covered.[14] Adoption of residential fiber in Malaysia, China, and Taiwan exceeds that in the United States; China, making a massive push toward building a giant middle-class market, already has 120 million households connected to fiber and will have 300 million of its 455 million households connected by 2020.[15]

Almost two-thirds of Swedes and 31 percent of Norwegians already have fiber at home; adoption of residential fiber is also higher in Finland, the Netherlands, and Denmark than in the United States.[16] The rest of Europe is plodding along, but nearly all European countries—even those whose fiber residential adoption is lower than in the United States—consider fiber the endgame.

I've already noted the deep parallels between the stories of communities building fiber optic networks today and the history of electrification in America. Gary Evans, a Minnesota fiber visionary involved in many early fiber network efforts there, put it this way: "Those areas with people with the greatest vision prospered earliest in the days of electrification."

Right now, not enough people around the country understand the fundamental importance of fiber, just as in the 1920s they might not have understood the fundamental importance of electricity. Often we squabble over things that are not nearly as important to the success of the United States.

When electricity was young, it was a luxury, sold by private companies following a "demand-driven" model. Where investors saw the possibility of a reliable stream of revenue, they would borrow or put up the initial sum of money necessary to wire businesses and homes with electricity. But they didn't foresee that their product would be everywhere. For instance, even though San Francisco's streets were first lit with electric light in 1876, the first home to get electric lighting in San Francisco had to wait until 1899.[17] (The home, which was on the market in 2016 for $7.9 million, is at 7600 Jackson Street, in the heart of Pacific Heights.) The electrification of America, by and large, followed a set pattern: municipal buildings and businesses first, wealthy urban dwellers next, then poorer urban dwellers, and last of all, rural homes and farms. This was the demand-driven model in action.[18]

What explains this pattern? The answer is simple: the physical network for the delivery of electricity involved very high up-front costs, and the handful of large private companies that dominated the electricity market in the United States in the early part of the twentieth century were, reasonably, looking to make the greatest profit on their investments as quickly as possible. That's why the densest areas with the most reliable potential returns got service first. There was also little or no public oversight of these companies' activities, and what oversight existed was largely ineffective.

The rural situation, with 90 percent of farmers in the 1930s lacking electricity, was especially dire, but poorer areas of rich cities were getting second-rate service too: at a time when richer homes had refrigerators and electric heating and cooking appliances, low-income households were likely to have electric lighting but nothing more.[19] To address this problem, many cities and localities launched municipally-owned power systems. For example, despite stiff resistance from the competing private company, the city of Detroit in the 1890s established a municipally-owned power system that reduced prices by 50 percent within seven years and extended service to many stores and homes. Consumer-owned power soared in popularity between 1897 and 1907.[20]

Meanwhile, smaller local lighting companies were gradually absorbed by private systems that consolidated them into enormous utility holding companies that were vertically integrated to handle long-distance transmission as well as retail distribution. Following World War I, the major private electric holding companies mounted a massive propaganda campaign—paid for by their customers' fees—to trumpet the virtues of their services and discredit consumer-owned power systems. These efforts included flooding grade schools, high schools, colleges, libraries, and civic organizations with literature; investing heavily in newspaper and radio advertising; lavishing entertainment on media executives to ensure the dissemination of favorable news stories; subsidizing advantageous research at leading universities; paying poorly compensated adjuncts to give speeches and classes in colleges; and enlisting thousands of industry executives and employees as speakers.[21]

The information campaign often went beyond the benign. The private utilities described advocates of consumer-owned power as "un-American," "Bolshevik," and "an unholy alliance of radicals."[22] Franklin Delano Roosevelt later denounced these efforts as "a systematic, subtle, deliberate and unprincipled campaign of misinformation and propaganda, and if I may use the words, of lies and falsehoods."[23]

In Mississippi, the private power holding companies set up fake associations to defeat votes in Mississippi towns about whether to set up cooperatives rather than rely on the private utilities. (A cooperative is a not-for-profit business voluntarily owned and controlled by the people who use its services. Unlike investor-owned utilities, a cooperative utility is operated by and for people of the community. Its goal is to provide reliable power, not make a profit.) They took over a grocery newspaper and turned it into a vehicle for promoting the power company line. On election day they gave out free liquor at the polls. They still lost.

Nevertheless, by the late 1920s, a handful of unregulated private holding companies were supplying most of the country, and, unsurprisingly in light of the holding companies' public relations onslaught, the number of consumer-owned municipal power systems had declined from a peak of 3,066 systems in 1923 to 2,320 four years later.[24]

Farmers and rural areas in the United States were struggling without electrical services. At a time when most farms in Sweden, Denmark, France, Germany, New Zealand, and Canada already had electricity, America's reliance on unregulated private power left rural areas unserved: for-profit companies considered it unprofitable to build lines in sparsely populated areas. In the early 1920s, less than 1 percent of farms in North Carolina had electricity. As Clarence Poe, the editor of *Progressive Farmer*, put it in 1931, "Canadians are willing to take hold, go ahead, and work out experiments against which we Americans would be completely frightened away by cries of 'Socialism! Bolshevism! Paternalism!'"[25]

Meanwhile, electricity was becoming a major domestic policy issue. In 1928, as public concern rose about the size, prices, and practices of the private utilities, Federal Trade Commission general counsel Robert Healy "sweated blood" over a four-year investigation of the so-called Power Trust.[26] In a scathing report that ran to 486 pages and 84 volumes of evidence, Healy documented a range of abuses, including financial manipulation, stock watering, padding of operating expenses, overpayment of executives, questionable transactions with subsidiaries, milking of operating companies, and massive lobbying and propaganda campaigns. The Healy report singled out the industry's efforts to "mold the thoughts and belief of the present and future generations in conformity with utility interests."[27]

The pain of the rural situation, the growing centrality of electricity to modern life everywhere, the FTC investigation, and the evidence from the Great Depression that private companies were not the only agents in a position to promote the general well-being of society led to acceptance of the idea that effective government needed to be involved in America's electrification. And the right president was in office.

As governor of New York in 1928, FDR had led the charge against private utilities attempting to control the development of the St. Lawrence River that had steamrolled any state oversight of their operations. He had an aide collect bills from (private) New York and (public) Ontario, Canada, power systems. All the New York bills were at least three times more than what the Hydro Electric Power Commission in Ontario was charging.[28]

During the 1932 presidential campaign, FDR issued a statement signed by thirty-seven congressional leaders from both parties that stated that the "power question . . . is one of the most important issues before the American people in the campaign of 1932. . . . Its political significance cannot be overestimated. . . . The combined utility and banking interests . . . have the most powerful and widely organized political machine ever known in our history."[29] FDR also delivered a long attack on Samuel Insull, the owner of an enormous private utility holding company (the "Insull Monstrosity"), whose collapse in the Great Depression had eliminated the life savings of six hundred thousand shareholders. "The public has paid and paid dearly," Roosevelt said, "and is now beginning to understand the need for reform after having been fleeced out of millions of dollars. . . . Judge me by the enemies I have made. Judge me by the selfish principles of these utility leaders who have talked of radicalism while they were selling watered stock to the people, and using our schools to deceive the coming generation." He attacked state power and public service commissions—entirely captured by Insull and his colleagues—for betraying the public trust, and he endorsed government ownership and operation of power utility services, saying, "The very fact that a community can, by vote of the electorate, create a yardstick of its own, will, in most cases, guarantee good service and low rates to its population."[30]

Although power industry supporters temporarily derailed Roosevelt's nomination at the 1932 Democratic National Convention in Chicago, they were unsuccessful in blocking him from the popular vote. In 1935, Congress passed the Public Utility Holding Company Act, breaking up Insull-like holding companies, as well as the Federal Power Act, giving the federal government the power to regulate the sale and transportation of electricity.[31] President Roosevelt created the federal Rural Electrification Administration (REA) in 1935.[32]

The REA was enormously successful: it gave loans and assistance to hundreds of new municipal and rural power companies and cooperatives—as well as, starting in 1949, telephone cooperatives.[33] Conservative elements within FDR's administration urged that private companies also be eligible for loans and guarantees, but David Lilienthal, a level-headed lawyer who brought years of experience in the private utilities' tactics to his 1933 appointment as one of the original directors of the newly formed Tennessee Valley Authority, believed that municipal utilities and cooperatives alone should handle electrification. President Roosevelt backed him and replaced the Tennessee Valley Authority's chairman Arthur Morgan with Lilienthal.[34] By 1950, nearly half of U.S. farms had electricity.[35]

Today's urban and rural efforts to ensure publicly overseen, inexpensive fiber optic connectivity to everyone are the modern equivalent of the community-based electricity endeavors of a hundred years ago. The contexts are the same: essentially unregulated privately owned cartels are in charge of data transmission. Because they often have effective monopolies in their geographic footprint, it is not in their interest to sell inexpensive world-class services, to serve rural areas, to upgrade their lines to fiber (unless under pressure from a community system), or to open their transmission lines to distribution competitors (as the energy companies have been forced to do). But today there is no FDR to lead the fiber optic revolution. And so hundreds of cities and communities around the country are struggling to control their own destinies by calling for the construction of community-controlled fiber networks. Bernadine Joselyn of the Blandin Foundation quoted Jerry Garcia of the Grateful Dead: "Somebody has to do something, and it's just incredibly pathetic that it has to be us."

If you're looking for hard national-level data about all this, it turns out that we have it, and it's awful. The carriers (chiefly Comcast, Spectrum, AT&T, Verizon, and CenturyLink) self-report data every six months to the Federal Communications Commission about where they have deployed last-mile wires, be they fiber, cable, or copper.[36] There is little check as to whether the information is accurate. The data say nothing about pricing. Not only that, the FCC's standards allow the carrier to say that a particular census block is "served"—meaning that it has service of a particular capacity—as long as *one location in that block* has access to service. This is called the "one-served, all-served assumption."[37]

Census blocks are the smallest geographic areas that the U.S. Census Bureau uses to count things and people. They are anything but uniform: they are drawn based on natural topography, railroad lines, and many other invisible factors, and there are more than 11 million of them. Many census blocks are 6.4 acres or less, particularly in urban areas. My own census block in New York City—36061006300—spans the square block of West Ninth Street and West Tenth Street, between Fifth Avenue and Sixth Avenue; that's a dense area with many buildings in it. When any unit in one of those buildings has the capacity to be "served," meaning to receive fiber service at some price, however outrageous, the FCC considers the entire census block "served." But not all census blocks are necessarily small: one census block in Alaska measures 8,500 square miles.[38]

The FCC also has carriers report data about adoption of high-speed internet access in an extremely limited way. The threshold for considering a line "high speed" is 10 Mbps or more, which means that the category includes DSL copper lines, now hopelessly out of date. And the carriers report the data as a percentage band in a *census tract*, the next largest measurement area after a census block.[39] A census tract covers anywhere between 1,000 and 8,000 people.[40] Any given census tract could have a highly heterogeneous population; any tract could be incommensurable with any other when it comes to geography. Additionally, adoption figures at the census tract level are reported in quintiles: 0–20 percent, 20–40 percent, and so on.

Data at this level can be somewhat helpful when you are trying to understand who is generally providing service in a geographic area, but this won't represent your experience in your living room or give us any useful information about which populations are signing up for what technology. The FCC tells me that Verizon offers its FiOS (fiber-to-the-home) service where I live, but it isn't available in my apartment building.[41] (Perhaps someone else in my census block is able to subscribe to FiOS.) And when it comes to adoption numbers, the metric that would allow us to compare geographic areas and costs for particular wires, the threshold for what constitutes acceptable service is too low and the bands are too broad to give any sense of people's actual experience in, say, participating in an online class, visiting a doctor, or transmitting data. The absence of data about *what kind of service* (fiber, cable, copper) people have is particularly shocking. And sometimes, service providers even include small business locations in general counts that policymakers may assume include only residences.[42]

Also, crucially, none of this public data includes information about prices. (The FCC does do a survey of urban rates charged for high-speed internet access, picking a sample of census blocks from each state for this purpose; that survey shows generally what the range of prices might be in a given state, but locally it is useless.)[43] There is no way to gather that information just by looking up offerings online. We know that carriers routinely advertise special, limited-time offers for people who are switching services, launching subscriptions, or buying bundles (such as pay TV plus internet data), so the "real prices" Americans pay for data transmission are buried under mountains of indirection.

In short, even though two-thirds of Americans view internet access as a utility, we simply don't know, as a public matter, who is served at what address at what price with what service. We also have zero public information about the location of or cost to access poles, conduits, fiber routes, cell locations, and other key infrastructure that is essential to assessing gaps and efficiently targeting public funds.

The coarse and mysterious nature of these data, and particularly the absence of fine-grained data about price and adoption, helps shield policymakers from pressure to do anything about the problem—especially when they sit in federal offices far from local constituents.

There is a problem, and a large one. Although the copper-line phone system in the United States was the envy of the world when it was installed, and provided Americans with the same high-quality service at roughly the same price wherever they were sitting, we are falling far behind when it comes to upgrading that set of lines to fiber optic internet connections to homes and businesses—the modern-day standard if you live in most parts of Asia or northern Europe.

Today in America, local cable or telco monopolies, unconstrained by either competition or oversight, can charge whatever they want for whatever level of service their shareholders will accept. The central problems posed by inadequate last-mile connections are latency and scarcity. Those households and businesses that have wired connections are having to wait an unthinkably long time to accomplish simple tasks involving large amounts of data, if they can even do them at all. American households and businesses also don't do all they could with data because bandwidth is scarce. We have to think about whether we're online and how much that access costs. And we are leaving out tens of millions of Americans for whom connectivity is a luxury. This reality is causing problems for our future as an innovative and just country, as we fall further behind in the global race to create new jobs and new ways for citizens to make choices in their lives. We are amplifying and entrenching existing rural/urban divides and, even more starkly, inequality of opportunity.

This state of affairs didn't come about by accident. It happened because of lapses in policy and an uninformed, vague belief that the private market could be relied on to give Americans great communications infrastructure. That mindset hasn't brought us the economic growth or social justice the country needs.

I remember sitting at my desk at a Washington law firm reading about the initial public offering of stock in Netscape Communications Inc. on August 9, 1995. Netscape Navigator, largely forgotten today, was the first widely adopted browser software that made simple graphical web pages available to all of us, and that IPO marked the beginning of the commercial internet in America. Those pages had to be simple, because complicated graphics involve more data and thus more download time, and there wasn't much bandwidth available to American homes at the time: Americans were dialing in over their last-mile copper phone lines to banks of computers that were sending and receiving small numbers of packets of data. The constraint was the amount of data the copper phone line could carry: the standard connection was 28.8 kilobits per second (Kbps).[44] Screens were small and had low resolution for the simple reason that larger screens and sharper images require more data.

In 1995, the phone companies loved the idea of dial-up internet service. Households had to buy additional lines in order to be part of the new internet world while continuing to make phone calls. Left to their own devices, the phone companies would have moved very slowly into higher-bandwidth communications. By about 1997, competition from the cable TV industry began to push the telephone companies into providing digital subscriber line (DSL) services.[45] At the time, cable TV providers, whose networks were already designed to handle video rather than just narrow-bandwidth voice services, had moved into what they thought would be "interactive TV" services (two-way communications). Cable companies then invested in bonding some of those channels together over its hybrid-fiber coaxial ("cable," for simplicity) lines. Cable's substantial investment at this point made it possible to offer something much more interesting than interactive TV: high-bandwidth two-way data pathways (using what cable called its Data Over Cable Service Interface Specification, or DOCSIS, protocol) for internet communications, over channels that had been designed for two-way video. It called its product "cable modem" services.

The phone companies, nudged by this competition from cable modem services, finally began offering DSL services, which still exist in many parts of the country. DSL rides on existing last-mile copper phone lines, dividing those lines into high-frequency communications for data and lower frequency communications for voice. This allows for an always-on online connection that still keeps the line free for voice calls.

Cable wires have higher capacity than copper phone wires, meaning the physical properties of the wire itself make it capable of carrying more data. The cable industry's aggressive investment in improving its existing hybrid-fiber coaxial lines to make cable modem services possible followed a cheaper upgrade path than what the phone companies would have had to do to win and keep their internet access customers. Cable could work with its existing lines. To hold their own, the phone companies would have needed to dig up their last-mile copper lines and replace them with fiber optic wires. But the phone companies chose not to do this. The two major phone companies, AT&T and Verizon, had another existing line of business to go into that was more profitable and posed lower up-front expense than installing fiber: they could become primarily wireless companies. And so they did.

I've mentioned briefly our first two wires: copper and cable. And you've already heard about the third, which is fiber. This is our communications fairy tale, or standup comedy routine—the rule of threes operates in both contexts. The first two wires have fatal flaws; only the third will carry us into the future.

Copper's fatal flaw, its enormous shortcoming, is that a home or business has to be very close to a central switching office or other amplifying structure in order to be able to send or receive large amounts of data. Signals carried over copper are also subject to interference from other electronics nearby. There are lots of efforts to soup up copper DSL connections through fancy processing of data ("vectoring") so as to avoid interference ("crosstalk") from the multiple strands of copper lines that twist around one another to create DSL connections, and to avoid having to upgrade the last leg to fiber. But these don't defeat the distance limitation of DSL, which is sharp and real. You'd need to be within three-quarters of a mile of a central office to get the fastest speeds available from a copper DSL connection.

In contrast, cable's Achilles' heel is that its last-mile connections, between neighborhood shared points ("nodes") and houses, are sent over a coaxial cable that will never be as frictionless as glass. The pure glass of a fiber optic cable allows for virtually un-limited "headroom"—as far as we can tell, once the glass is installed, its signal-carrying capacity is limited only by the electronics attached to it. Signals can travel effortlessly and undiminished for many miles inside a fiber strand without needing to be amplified. Inside a cable wire, however, because the layers of material the signals are traveling through (which include copper and other media) are not as pure as glass, signals both move more slowly and bounce around much more, which makes them lose strength. Cable signals need to be amplified—by using additional equipment, which re-quires additional expense—in order to get where they need to go. As long as the cable industry relies on coaxial cable between resi-dences and shared neighborhood nodes, it will never be able to ex-ceed the information-carrying capacity and easy upgradability of a fiber-to-the-home connection.

Another issue: because cable's shared neighborhood nodes were built initially as entertainment-delivery vehicles, they vastly prefer-ence downloads over uploads. Every time they are redesigned to carry symmetric streams of data with equal uploading and down-loading capacity, lots of gear has to be swapped out—including the cable modems at consumers' residences. If this rebuilding were easy or inexpensive, the cable industry would have done it already. People who say "who needs symmetric access?" today are just like those who said "who needs electricity for anything but lightbulbs?" a hun-dred years ago. Because symmetric high-capacity networks don't yet exist in the giant U.S. market, the applications to use them, our twenty-first-century analogs to electric kitchen appliances, also don't yet exist. Building for the future requires inexpensive symmetric access, and that requires the headroom of fiber; cable has neither.

Fiber is a better technology than cable, both more flexible and easier to upgrade, which is why every other leg of the U.S. communications network is made of fiber. The "middle mile," or connections between cities, is all fiber; the "backbones" between areas of the country are all fiber.[46] Again, the only thing you have to do to make fiber carry more information is switch out the electronics, the lasers, at the ends of the last-mile segments. Once the glass is in the ground, it will last for decades.[47]

Even though cities were forbidden by law to make exclusive deals with cable operators, by the mid-1990s local cable companies had acquired monopoly presences in most urban U.S. areas and were selling pay-TV subscription services.[48] They saw the internet access opportunities and quickly made investments that allowed them to sell both data and video services. (I tell this story in greater detail in *Captive Audience*.) This nudged the telcos to go more enthusiastically into the DSL business in order to hold on to their subscribers. For a few years in the early 2000s, cable and telco internet access services in urban geographies competed neck-and-neck: roughly the same prices, roughly the same bandwidth.

Then things changed. The telcos' lines, including their DSL services, had been regulated as utilities, meaning that the owners of those lines had to share their facilities with competing retail services, at the same price. Cable companies had always been free of this requirement. The telcos had always found the arrangement unfair, and now that they and the cable operators were competing to provide the same service, they successfully argued that the regulatory difference seriously distorted the market. Beginning in 2004, the FCC deregulated high-speed internet access and ruled that basic lines no longer had to be shared by multiple competing providers.[49] To close the sale, the telcos added a sweetener: they promised to dig up their copper lines and install fiber—which really could have competed successfully with cable—if only the FCC would set them free from all that nasty regulation. Except that the sweetener was really more like an ultimatum.[50]

Ed Whitacre, the chairman of SBC, the predecessor of today's AT&T, told the *Los Angeles Times* in June 2004 that the company planned to invest $6 billion in fiber optic upgrades as soon as the regulatory environment for the company became "more rational." A Wall Street analyst, quoted in the same story, outlined the threat:

"SBC was 'sending a strong message' to the FCC, said independent telecom analyst Jeff Kagan in Atlanta: 'They have billions of pent-up investment dollars that they are planning to release into the market-place, assuming they consider the regulatory rules and environment to be fair.'" SBC and the other Baby Bells (now subsumed into to-day's CenturyLink, Verizon, and AT&T) would be "first replacing the copper wires in thousands of neighborhoods with fiber optic cable," the *Times* reported.[51] The message could not be clearer: the telcos would not invest in fiber networks unless the regulations were lifted.

There are many Lucy-with-the-football moments in telecom-munications history, and this was one of them. The telcos got the regulatory relief they sought, but they didn't invest in fiber.

Out of either naiveté or calculation, the FCC proclaimed that the competition it was seeing between cable modem and DSL ser-vices, and hoped to see from fiber, would protect consumers more than regulation possibly could. In 2004 and 2005 it steadily re-moved all oversight and all infrastructure-sharing requirements from all forms of last-mile high-speed internet access.[52] Nothing new was put in place to stop any of these companies from collabo-rating or choosing lines of business that they could dominate.

Through a series of mergers and combinations, the two largest remaining telcos (Verizon and AT&T) had already acquired sub-stantial wireless businesses at the time the internet access market-place was deregulated. Those wireless businesses—mobile cellular monthly subscriptions—were more profitable than wired DSL subscriptions, and AT&T and Verizon steadily transformed them-selves into mostly-wireless businesses. Fiber was too much up-front capital expense for their shareholders to swallow. Today, about 70 percent of Verizon's revenues comes from its wireless seg-ment, and AT&T is about 54 percent wireless. (CenturyLink, the third remaining large telco, doesn't have a wireless operation but is also backing away from residential last-mile wires in favor of a higher-margin line of business: more than 75 percent of its reve-nue comes from business customers.)[53]

Verizon, under the leadership of CEO Ivan Seidenberg, did briefly launch a fiber-to-the-home service, FiOS, beginning in 2005, but Wall Street hated the heavy up-front capital expendi-tures, and Verizon stopped expanding FiOS in 2010. Seidenberg left Verizon in mid-2011, and in early 2015 Verizon sold off its FiOS networks in California, Texas, and Florida.[54] So although Verizon is our only "nationwide" provider of fiber-to-the-home services, FiOS residential internet access actually reaches only about five million households, mostly in leafy suburbs on the east coast.

At the same time, the phone companies ceded the wired internet access marketplace to the cable companies in most urban areas of the country. The telcos' shareholders were happy with wireless, and it was cheaper for the cable industry to upgrade its cable modem services to provide higher capacity data flows than it was for the phone companies to dig up their copper lines and replace them with fiber. Cable modem services began to capture more and more new internet subscribers as well as people switching over from DSL. A huge percentage of net new residential internet access subscriptions went to cable: 89 percent in 2014, 106 percent in 2015, 122 percent in 2016.[55] (How could you have more than 100 percent of all net new subscriptions? When some of them are from people switching from DSL to cable.) Cable companies added about 855,000 subscribers in the fourth quarter of 2016, while telco companies lost 120,000.[56] This has been a steady trend. As Wall Street analyst Craig Moffett told investors in June 2017, "There are no signs of any moderation in Cable's win rate in broadband. . . . The first quarter of 2017 marked the eighth consecutive quarter when Cable captured more than 100 percent of market growth— that is, that the TelCos shrank in aggregate—and the seventeenth consecutive quarter that the Cable industry captured higher share than in the corresponding quarter a year earlier."[57] Cable companies have steadily merged and swapped systems so that they control entire markets and never enter each others' territories.

Today, if you are one of the 100 million Americans living in the most densely populated 37,000 square miles in the continental United States, it is very likely that your only choice for internet access over 25 Mbps is your local cable monopoly.[58] You've got one choice of a second-rate technology at a very high price. There may be a small competitor who is allowed to have 10 percent of your local market, but is careful not to radically underprice the big player so as not to be put out of business. There are two cable giants, Comcast and Charter Communications (now known as Spectrum, and including the former Time Warner Cable), both of which charge a lot for high-capacity internet access and charge even more if you try to sign up for internet access without also subscribing to their pay TV services.

Because of their explosive growth, their discipline in carving out exclusive territories for themselves, and the expense of their core high-speed internet access product (the prices charged for it are 95 percent profit), Comcast and Spectrum have few people left to sell to; their growth from now on is coming from simply raising prices on their existing customers.[59]

If you live in a suburban area, as one of the 100 million Americans in the less-dense areas that make up 158,000 square miles of the country, your local cable monopoly also likely has dominion over your internet access. If you're in a particularly wealthy suburb, one of the telcos or Google or an independent player may have shown up with fiber-to-the-home service, but it's unlikely.

And if you're in a rural area, all bets are off. About 123 million Americans live in the least-dense 3.2 million square miles of the country. If you're one of them, you're likely relegated to a local incumbent telco or cable company offering poor-quality wired service at best. You may have no wired service at all and be stuck with satellite—meaning that you have to send data packets 22,300 miles into space in order to communicate, which involves lots of delay and high expense.[60] Or your local telco incumbent may be trying mightily to persuade you to drop your copper line and be happy with mobile wireless service, which will limit your internet access to smartphone data plans.

I heard that wireless story several times during my travels. In the tiny town of Otis, in the foothills of the Berkshires in Western Massachusetts, selectman Bill Hiller complained to me about the town's DSL service from Verizon. "The service is not good," he said. "It's getting worse; it's degrading. And once you lose it, you don't get it back." Verizon was taking DSL lines out of service whenever it could and not adding new DSL customers. Aaron Bean at Westfield Gas & Electric, just outside Otis, told me that when a woman subdivided her property and sold off parcels, the parcels were no longer served by Verizon as DSL customers, even though the property as a whole had had DSL before it was divided. The same thing happened in rural Nevada City, California, where Michael Anderson told me that home buyers who thought their new houses came with DSL were being told by AT&T that the service wasn't available any more. "And so we've had people fall out of escrow, the realtors are out of their minds." Sellers are now keeping their names on the DSL bill even though they themselves have moved to Florida.

The crucial thing to understand is that the American wired data market has been very effectively segmented, both geographically and by service. Comcast and Spectrum overlap nowhere. Verizon and AT&T overlap nowhere for last-mile wired services. Although Verizon FiOS is a better service than cable, FiOS is present in very little of the territory of major cable companies: just 13 percent of Comcast's territory and just 5 percent of Spectrum's.[61]

CenturyLink isn't even trying to compete with cable. Instead it sells inexpensive DSL, unchallenged, in large portions of the rural United States: CenturyLink faces competition from Spectrum in just 16 percent of its territory, and in areas where CenturyLink overlaps with either Spectrum or Comcast, its offers are concentrated in far lower speeds and are seldom comparable on speed with either cable provider. CenturyLink has done small demonstrations of fiber-to-the-home in some neighborhoods, but mostly to gin up interest in the lower-capacity copper network options that it actually makes available to customers in those places—to take advantage, in other words, of the halo effect of fiber.[62] As CenturyLink's CFO, Stewart Ewing, told Wall Street analysts in 2016, "When customers called and weren't in the fiber footprint and realized they could get 20 Mbps or get 40 Mbps [over copper] and when they did they were willing to switch. ... The philosophy we have used when we have rolled out fiber to 16 markets is to be able to get the excitement in the markets, to have a gig available in certain parts of markets and generate the phone calls from customers, so we can sell them the speeds [over copper] that are available to them."[63] CenturyLink's fiber business, where it exists, is focused on businesses, not residences.

AT&T is pursuing the same strategy—selling residential DSL-based plans concentrated on lower speeds than cable offers. Interestingly, it prices those plans in line with, or even slightly higher than, comparable offers from the local cable monopoly. In exchange for getting its purchase of DirecTV approved in 2015, AT&T agreed to pass (note: not "connect," just go somewhere nearby) at least 12.5 million locations with a fiber network. Both business and home locations could be counted.[64] (This fuzzing between residences and businesses is often present in FCC data, making the entire area even more confusing.) But there was no regulatory oversight of where those locations were, and news reports make clear that AT&T has built its residential fiber-to-the-node services (in which copper wire runs from neighborhood fiber hubs into houses, creating a bottleneck for data before it reaches those hubs) disproportionately in higher-income communities.[65] It is impossible to know how many residents have actually subscribed. We do know that AT&T's pricing for fiber-to-the-node service is quite high— $90 a month for gigabit access, or $119 a month if you don't allow AT&T to track your web browsing preferences and target ads at you.[66] In Stockholm, the same level of service costs $25.

The giants in the wired market are the two enormous cable companies: Comcast, with about 25 million wired data subscribers, and Spectrum, with about 23 million. AT&T has about 15 million DSL subscribers, Verizon has about 7 million, and CenturyLink about 6 million. All three continue to shed DSL customers.[67]

Google Fiber made enormous waves and jarred the marketplace by announcing in February 2010 that it would bring fiber-to-the-home to localities that sent the best set of responses to a questionnaire.[68] The Google announcement—made the same year Verizon stepped back from FiOS—was accompanied by balloons, press conferences, and enormous excitement. I distinctly remember cheering when I watched the videos from my desk; finally, we would see in the United States what people in Stockholm and Seoul had had for years. Google's impact was mostly inspirational, because more than a thousand U.S. cities got excited by the offer and started getting their act together to attract Google. (Topeka, Kansas, temporarily renamed itself "Google" in order to get the company's attention.)[69] Although Google ended up building fiber in just a handful of places, serving fewer than a million customers, it made mayors jealous, triggered lower prices and better service from local cable monopolies, and launched many municipal efforts.[70] Google's investors found fiber too capital-intensive for their tastes, and Google announced in late 2016 that it would not expand to additional cities.[71]

As of spring 2018, the fiber-to-the-home picture in the United States was worse than spotty. Together, Verizon FiOS, AT&T GigaPower, and Google Fiber carried expensive services to about 10–11 million customers in about 119 million households, or less than 10 percent of the population, all in dense urban or suburban areas, mostly on the coasts, and all on a "demand" basis—not evenly across entire cities.[72] The connections are too expensive for many people. Cable modem monopolists powerfully dominate urban areas, and do this without constraint in locations that do not have fiber. Rural locations are often relegated to mobile wireless, poor cable modem service, or DSL over copper lines. Sometimes they have nothing other than expensive, jittery satellite access. AT&T and Verizon are aggressively backing out of the DSL marketplace across the country in an effort to shift subscribers to mobile-wireless-only services.[73]

The Obama FCC moved in February 2015 to relabel high-speed Internet access services as regulated services in connection with mul-tiyear "net neutrality" scuffles.[74] But under the Trump administration, the FCC has removed that label.[75] Under neither president has the FCC been willing to take on the fiber upgrade problem—the competition problem, the productivity problem—for the country. The Obama FCC launched a plan to give billions of dollars in subsidy funding (the money comes from a 17 percent fee added to the bills of long-distance landline customers, which is its own story) to existing carriers—AT&T, Verizon, CenturyLink—to ensure that they would maintain "high-speed" *10 Mbps* connections in rural areas. That's the standard the commission has set for rural locations at a time when the FCC itself defines "high speed" as 25 Mbps downloads.[76] This subsidy is a waste of federal funding: it supports a ridiculously low threshold of service and the wrong technology. Pre-dictably, AT&T is using the money to provide cellular service in those places, something it probably would be doing anyway.[77]

You may be thinking, "But isn't the world going wireless?" Of course it is. The important thing to understand is that 95 percent or more of a wireless connection is the wire that over-the-airwaves communications need to reach in order to get anywhere. Fiber and wireless are complementary technologies. Saying "the future is wireless, who cares about fiber" is like saying we can have airplanes without airports—those wireless signals need a wire in order to travel any real distance.

Exciting things are coming in wireless: vastly increased capacity, new ways of encoding information, better use of the airwaves. And we love our wireless devices. But if fiber is provided by a single private monopoly in each locality, and that private provider *also* sells wireless services, we'll be sunk.

All wireless connectivity works the same, simple way. Wires are connected to physical locations that host a transmitter of some kind. That transmitter, or antenna, transmits radio frequencies over the air. Your device receives those frequencies and understands what information has been encoded onto them. Decoded, that information can sound like a phone call or represent a database; it's all just information. Looked at from the other direction: you speak into a device, that device transmits the information over radio waves to some form of receiver, and that receiver sends your information over a wire to its ultimate destination.

You need both wires and radio frequencies for this system to work. But just as there are different flavors of wires, with different capacities to transmit data, there are different flavors of radio frequencies, all lying on a spectrum, with different levels of power.

The basic idea is that electromagnetic radio waves wobble up and down at regular intervals. We measure the frequency of those waves in hertz, where one hertz is one cycle per second. We're also interested in the related measurement of how much distance each wave cycle covers.

Imagine you're standing on a pier jutting out into the ocean, watching from the side while waves break on the beach. You're busy measuring the time between the crest of one wave and the crest of the next. If that time interval is one second, that means the wave frequency is one hertz (1 Hz). You then might want to measure the distance from one peak to the next: the wavelength. For light, there's an exact inverse correlation: the higher the frequency, the shorter the wavelength. (This correlation also holds for water waves, but it's not exact because bigger waves travel faster.)

The more waves per second—meaning the higher their frequency—the more information can be conveyed across a given distance. If you think about this, it makes sense. More wobbles per second means more opportunities per second to encode differences in information. As long as you've got something on the other end of the transmission that can decode what you've said, you can convey much more information at higher frequencies than at lower ones.

But at higher frequencies, in the gigahertz or billions-per-second range, the wavelengths get astonishingly short—close to a millimeter in the 28 gigahertz (GHz) range that is used for 5G communications.[78] Those very short waves have trouble carrying information over anything more than very short distances, particularly when they are sent out using low-power transmissions (as Wi-Fi currently is). In engineering jargon, very-high-frequency radio waves "attenuate" extremely rapidly, so to take advantage of their high communications capacity you have to be very close to the hotspot (the device connected to a wire that is sending and receiving wireless communications)—no more than a few hundred feet, for example, for transmissions in the 28 GHz range.[79]

At very high frequencies, transmissions can also be easily disrupted—the jargon for this is "interference." Walls, buildings, rain, leaves, and people can all get in the way of a millimeter-wave transmission.

To think a bit more about interference, imagine throwing a small stone into a smooth lake. The ripples going out in ever-widening circles from that stone, once it has hit the water, initially have a certain frequency—their peaks and valleys are regular and can be measured, just like the waves you watched from the pier. If it was just a small stone, the ripples won't spread very far, and the water will quickly be smooth again. If there is a rock jutting up above the surface of the lake, it will block and change the predictable propagation of those ripples.

You have just imagined a wireless transmission, in water form. The energy you used to throw that small stone is akin to the energy applied in sending a transmission. The ripples can be overlaid with data, and thus carry information in a circular area around where the stone fell. Leaves, trees, weather, other buildings, and humans are like the rocks sticking up above the water's surface—they disrupt the information-carrying ripples, interfering with them, often blocking them, and eventually make them unintelligible.

Beginning in the 1920s, the U.S. government took on the allocation of radio waves at particular frequencies, licensing their use to commercial and governmental transmitters.[80] Radio waves used for television and now internet access wobble at anywhere from 700 megahertz (MHz) to many gigahertz. That means 700 million waves a second, or several billion.[81] That's a lot of wobbling. The higher up the spectrum you go, the more information the waves can carry.

A few portions of radio spectrum, way up the dial (at 2.4 GHz, 3.5 GHz, 5 GHz) are already available for unlicensed low-power uses or will soon be available for low-power shared use (shared between the government and commercial operators).[82] If those airwaves were available for high-power, licensed use, they could carry a great deal of information. But that information might not penetrate walls at all, or as well as the carriers' existing 700 MHz spectrum does. The higher the frequency, the lower the penetration.

You can pick up AT&T or Verizon mobile cellular transmissions near windows inside your house because those companies are using relatively low frequencies for transmission—700 or 800 MHz—that can penetrate window glass and walls, particularly at the high power levels that their licenses permit.[83] But if you're in the basement, you're less likely to get a signal.

Higher frequencies require a transmitter in your house. Your device receives data transmitted through the air, and you quickly send data back. Here's the limiting factor: The transmitter has to have enormous capacity in order for your device to be able to send enormous amounts of data back to the outside world. The key mental leap you need to make is that wireless communication is two-way: you are uploading as well as downloading. (And in a creative, productive, working world, you are uploading a great deal. Everyone's download was once someone's upload.)

All modern mobile data transmissions need to be close to high-capacity wires. To get those transmissions anywhere, poles and other places where transmitters/receivers are placed have to be connected to thick, high-capacity pipes.

Here's the obvious payoff: now that we all want to be using devices chugging and sending reams of data—and every surface, gadget, and sensor in our homes, businesses, and civic operations may need to be communicating—we've got to raise the information-carrying capacity of our wireless communications as well as our wires. Carriers are seeing clearly that the untold amounts of data that residents and businesses are generating and demanding through their wireless devices will require using higher frequency spectrum, where broader swaths of frequencies might be available to use, *and* building many more towers and hotspots, *and* connecting all of those towers and hotspots to fiber—because only fiber will be able to cope with the flood. And that combination—more spectrum, more towers, more fiber—is necessary for all the 5G predictions you've heard to come true.

Now: What is 5G?

There are just three ways to increase the capacity of radio waves to carry internet-bound communications. The first way is to get more spectrum into the job of shipping data. So, for example, if you've had only 10 MHz of spectrum (in terms of width of the band on the dial—say between 700 and 710 MHz) to use for data, and you get 100 additional MHz, you'll be able to send a lot more data. But most of the relatively low-frequency (TV band-adjacent) radio-wave spectrum in the country has been administratively allocated, one way or another. It may be scandalously underused, but it's been handed out. We have allocational or regulatory scarcity of lower-frequency spectrum in the United States.[84]

Here's an example that mobile carriers would like to fix: A giant band of 150 MHz of spectrum, up around the 3.5 GHz area, has been allocated nationwide to air traffic control radars on aircraft carriers.[85] I don't know about you, but I hardly ever see an aircraft carrier in my neighborhood. The United States has about twelve of them lurking offshore. But they're sitting on that band, and they're probably not going to budge without a lot of political pressure. The Navy is hoping to get licensed access to broad bands of very-high-frequency spectrum (28 and 60 GHz get talked about) and use it for higher-capacity communications. The trade-off is that these millimeter-length waves will have trouble penetrating walls.

The second way to increase capacity of radio waves is to have cleverer ways of encoding them with information. You can think of this as dreaming up ways of forcing waves to carry more information across the same unit of time than they used to. We're making advances, but we're about to reach the limit that the laws of physics tell us is possible for information-carrying capacity. (This is called the Shannon limit, for Claude Shannon, a famous physicist who used to ride his bicycle in the hallways of Bell Labs.)[86]

This march toward the Shannon limit is represented by a blizzard of acronyms: CDMA, a transmission technology, allowed about 2.5 Mbps of information to be carried across 10 MHz of spectrum (2.5 million bits per second); HSDPA (or 3G) crammed about 8 Mbps of data into that same bandwidth; LTE (or 4G) gave us about 120 Mbps of information using, again, 10 MHz of spectrum.[87] That's about all we can do with coding efficiency with single radios working independently.

So carriers are moving to a third way to increase the information-carrying load of spectrum: reusing it by creating a multipath connection. If you (1) set up a whole cluster of cells, or base stations, that have tiny antennae on them, and (2) send out and receive simultaneous multipath transmissions over the same very high frequency (where more spectrum is available) but (3) coordinate the transmissions in a way that (4) can be understood by a very clever listener, you can in essence send the same communication across many different channels at once—busting through the Shannon limit.[88] The 5G part of this is the common protocol expected to emerge in 2020 as a worldwide standard that will set up the multipath encoding scheme.[89]

The hope is that 5G will deliver capacity up in the gigabit range to all of our devices. It's likely, at first, to operate on much higher frequencies than are currently used, way up in the 28 or 37 GHz range, because that's where more spectrum is available. And it will use more spectrum—perhaps an entire gigahertz.[90] In order to work using this very-high-frequency spectrum, the 5G protocol is going to require millions of additional base stations or cells in urban areas. These base stations will have to be much closer to one another than traditional cell towers because very-high-frequency transmissions cannot go very far before the signal fades. (And we still need to figure out how to send them through walls.)

How closely spaced will these base stations have to be? Well, when Verizon launched 4G in 2012, it needed to turn on just 30,000 base stations in order to cover 93 percent of the U.S. population. Verizon was using low-frequency spectrum, with its longer range. In order to get 5G into the marketplace, it will need ten million base stations. None of the private operators are talking about 5G outside urban areas; the distances you would have to fill with closely spaced towers or base stations are too great for private carriers to contemplate. Rural places will still require fiber, but it will be fiber to the home, which both South Korea and Sweden have already installed in rural areas.[91]

Here's the kicker: the 5G protocol will have us sending huge amounts of data from inside our homes and from our mobile devices, and in order to transmit it across any distance, we will need very-high-capacity wired connections—fiber—attached to every one of those small cells. Only fiber can do the job. It may sound paradoxical, but the future of advanced wireless services depends completely on how much fiber is in place.

Fiber will have to extend deep into neighborhoods and buildings to connect these tiny base stations. This will work fine in Japan, where companies can lease dark fiber (meaning fiber optic cable without electronics connected to it firing pulses of light) anywhere in any city for $50 a month.[92] But you can't do that right now in the United States: we don't have dark fiber to every corner, much less at prices of $50 a month. If 5G evolves as a worldwide standard, there's not going to be much 5G coverage in the United States because we don't have that much fiber.

We should not want Verizon or AT&T to be in charge of this new 5G world. If we want that world to be more competitive than the existing mobile wireless world—and we should!—we need to ensure that fiber is available for lease cheaply everywhere. Whoever controls the fiber controls the attachment to it—the 5G base stations. If a public actor controls the fiber, it can require that all 5G base stations be platforms, open to many competing players. But if a private actor, say Verizon or AT&T, controls the fiber under city streets, and in particular the fiber running all the way to these small cells, it can demand preferential treatment for its proprietary

5G base station installations (or allow only a few competitors to share them).

We do not want to replicate in the new zippy 5G world the grinding monopolies we now have for wired and wireless access. Wireless mobile data in the United States is only slightly more competitive than wireline access: AT&T and Verizon together have a comfortable "duopoly with a fringe" situation, with the two companies splitting the vast majority of wireless customers and almost all free cash flow. T-Mobile and Sprint are also-rans.

The yearning for control of the 5G world is already apparent. Verizon has said that its 5G plans require it to lay 1,700 strands of fiber for each cable it installs in Boston, with each fiber strand ending in a hotspot.[93] It's hardly conceivable that Verizon plans to share those hotspots or access to that fiber, except with a company whose services it needs in another city. The Internet of Things in Boston will consist of only Verizon's things.

Not only does wireless *not* solve our access problem, but both the need for more fiber everywhere and the need for that fiber to be publicly overseen (so as to avoid the risks of monopolization in the 5G world) are far greater in an advanced wireless ecosystem. In the United States, what we really need for the wireless revolution to occur is publicly overseen dark fiber available for lease at reasonable prices everywhere, with neutral, nondiscriminatory interconnection points for 5G platforms attached to that fiber at frequent intervals.

All we need to do is ensure that the dark fiber is leased at reasonable prices to anyone, runs to buildings and poles everywhere, and is accessible by way of a common interface controlled by local government, akin to a street grid. Here's the problem. AT&T has a lot of dark fiber, but it is not required to lease it to outside companies, and therefore won't. Verizon acts the same way.[94] (Remember that AT&T and Verizon don't overlap in their last-mile fiber builds that might reach small cells, ever.) It's well known that AT&T and Verizon, who need each other in their different last-mile territories, swap "backhaul" fiber (between base stations and aggregation points upstream) between themselves.

That reality, absent public intervention, will make life extraordinarily difficult for any new player wanting to get into the 5G or Internet of Things world: upstarts won't be able to get their data any distance at a reasonable expense without a public dark fiber option, because AT&T and Verizon, which can charge whatever they like for that transport, have a strong incentive to keep competitors out of the market.

But operators will need a zillion hotspot points to make 5G work, so cities will have a great deal of leverage. If cities made dark fiber available to a common infrastructure of interconnection points, they would make it possible for many different 5G operators to look for customers. One infrastructure, useful to everyone. If cities don't act affirmatively to set the stage for 5G, the single actors and duopolies that dominate wireline connections will extend that dominance into the wireless realm.

Confronted with a question about fiber optic last-mile connections, people who don't know better will often say, "Who needs fiber when we have Comcast?" These people are the modern-day equivalent of those who had just a lightbulb but no other electric appliances in the 1930s and could not imagine anything different. But even today, Comcast's last-mile wires are not good enough to provide the service that is cheaply available elsewhere, and millions of Americans are being left behind because they can't afford Comcast's services, or because the company has chosen not to expand its wires to where they live.

A private monopolist's incentives are not necessarily aligned with our public goals of social justice or even with economic growth. To be the place where new industries are born, health care advances become ubiquitous, and people get the education they need to thrive and move toward new opportunities, everyone needs high-capacity connectivity at a reasonable price, just as everyone needed electricity. Instead, after a sustained thirty-year attack on the idea that government should play any role in economic regulation, we're hanging on to a distorted idea of freedom that leaves everyone free to fail to thrive—to be without the basic connectivity, and the economic and social benefits it creates, that people elsewhere in the world take for granted. It simply *is not true that unrestrained private gain always leads to public good.*

The question "Who needs fiber when the future is wireless?" merits a similarly snappy response. Fiber is complementary to wireless. They do not substitute for one another. In order to work, very-high-capacity wireless connections—5G—require fiber to run deep into neighborhoods and buildings, and future wireless networks will look like present-day Wi-Fi in their architecture: relatively small areas, each attached to fiber. That fiber will need to be publicly overseen in order to avoid the monopolization we have already seen in wired internet access.

Jonas Birgersson of Sweden learned these same things, twenty years ago: privately owned telecommunications companies that are responsible to distant investors and operate existing copper networks will inevitably divide markets so as to avoid competition, and resist investing in any upgrade to fiber, claiming that it's impossibly expensive. "They only have one problem, the [incumbent] operators," Birgersson said. "They're wrong." Government officials believe these private incumbents' arguments "because there's a lot of money involved." You need proofs of concept, working networks, to persuade people. Open-access networks, allowing lots of competitive retail choices that run across fiber, are best for consumers and pricing—and require cities to rip up the streets just once. "Even in the [incumbent] cartels," Birgersson said, "the debate over fiber is over. The big guys inside the cartels understand that they need fiber to survive, and for wireless. The big bosses understand this. They want to figure out how they can get there without thinking like competitors."

The good news for the United States is that more than five hundred brave cities in this country are way ahead of the national trend.[95] They have realized that inexpensive fiber connections are critical to their survival, and the locations that have actually installed these facilities are thriving. Leverett, Massachusetts; Sandy, Oregon; Chattanooga, Tennessee; Wilson, North Carolina; Cedar Falls, Iowa; and Lafayette, Louisiana, all offer their citizens gigabit last-mile fiber access.[96] But as Bill Hiller of Otis, Massachusetts, diplomatically put it to me, "It's a lot to get up to speed. It's a long learning curve. It's a long move to get there." The city leaders I have met are determined to help others get up that learning curve.

CHAPTER FOUR

Community Stories

W HEN AMERICANS TALK ABOUT economic growth and social justice, we are often stuck at the national level and we are often complaining. You might think that the fiber story is a national one as well. But it turns out that America's awful, expensive data connectivity is a national problem for which the solution is intensely local: cities and localities are leading the way. Why? Because people live locally. Pain is felt locally. And local officials and entrepreneurs are responding with a thoroughly bipartisan, thoroughly practical movement.

I spent many days in Chattanooga, Greensboro, Wilson, Otis, Winthrop, Nevada City, and San Francisco. I also went back to my hometown of Santa Monica, California. Each of these places stands for a different part of the story.

Chattanooga's history of public electricity and public planning was a source of great strength as it built its gigabit fiber network. Greensboro, although similar in size to Chattanooga, has no such history and is struggling to solve its connectivity issue. Wilson, a very small town in eastern North Carolina, has a history like Chattanooga's and has gone even farther in making its fiber network affordable for poor residents.[1] Otis, in the foothills of the Berkshires in Western Massachusetts, used town meetings—the most direct form of democracy—to gather support and public funding

for its fiber network. Winthrop, a tiny Minnesota farming community, joined together with more than a dozen other nearby localities to create a cooperative for laying fiber—a very promising form
of collective action.[2] An entrepreneur named John Paul is trying to
bring fiber to Nevada City, California, just as Google brought it to
Austin, but is having difficulty without the strong support of public
officials.[3] San Francisco, the shining gem of the country's largest
cities, is the first major city in the country to take on its fiber problem.[4] Santa Monica, where I went to high school, is reaping the
benefits of extraordinarily long-term fiber planning by city hall.[5]

These community efforts show us that public involvement
in fiber networks—whatever specific business model is followed
locally—leads to lower prices and better communications services
for everyone in a given locality; clear and reliable prices rather than
"teaser offers"; better customer service, profits, and payments that
benefit a local community rather than distant shareholders; and an
ability to plan for a community's long-term future. Public control of
basic fiber infrastructure provides solid ground on which everything
else the private marketplace wants to do—sell particular data services, increase productivity, support new forms of industries—can
flourish. I found these developments in every corner of America. But
I started off in Stockholm.

In the early 1990s, Stockholm's businesses and its 900,000 citizens
were highly interested in fiber connectivity, but there was very little
fiber around. The incumbent phone company, Telia, had no great
incentive to upgrade its copper lines to fiber. The city's leaders decided that they wanted to have the streets dug up just once—Swedes
are orderly—and that the public sector should be responsible for
fiber as it had always been responsible for transport and other infrastructure. Any fiber line would have to be provided by a neutral
player and open to all service providers on equal, nondiscriminatory,
and easy-to-understand terms in order to create competition in
retail-level services. Stokab, a city-controlled corporation, was created in 1994 to build out dark (passive) fiber over city rights of way
and to lease that capacity to telecom operators, businesses, local authorities, and others.[6] Stokab recouped its original expenses in 2001
and now throws off about $27 million a year in profits that help

finance the city's other needs.[7] In Stockholm, leasing dark fiber costs less than a quarter of what it costs in New York City—where a purely private, unconstrained market operates.

Stockholm is one of Europe's fastest-growing cities, with talent arriving on its doorstep from southern Europe as well as the United States. New digital businesses are thriving, to the point that Stockholm has become the world's second largest startup hub after Silicon Valley.[8] The tech companies Skype and Spotify came from Stockholm, as well as financial technology companies Klarna (online payment company) and iZettle (card reader manufacturer) and many others; Amazon is building multiple data centers there.[9] "We've built for the last twenty years the best open fiber network in the world," Staffan Ingvarsson, Stokab's CEO, told me. "Did we know that one of the things coming out of that would be Skype or Spotify? Nope." Instead, Stockholm set general goals: to be the "smartest city in the world" and to be fossil-fuel-free by 2040.[10] It has a host of commitments in education, health care (a dedicated fiber strand to each house for health care services), city services, climate change, water use—all based on the assumption that moving data will be easy and inexpensive.

Not only that, but the horizontal strategy the region employed for fiber—neutral, reasonably priced infrastructure leased to private players on a nondiscriminatory basis—is being applied to every step the city takes in new services: cell towers open to all competitive carriers, traffic light data open to all, standard connections available to everyone, with the aim of improving opportunities for all residents. The same kind of planning also extends to "soft" social services, provided as basic assistance to anyone. As Ingvarsson put it, "The key here right now is to build in a platform way that really is open, that really makes it possible to go in various directions." The goal: to provide the highest quality of life to Stockholm residents and the best entrepreneurial climate.

The United States will never be Sweden. But Santa Monica led the way in America by providing a wholly municipal fiber network called Santa Monica City Net. It took more than a decade of work, led by Jory Wolf, the city's chief information officer, to get the network up and running. Wolf did the job incrementally, beginning in

1998 with a telecommunications master plan that put him in the room whenever a public works official was considering tearing up a street. Wolf's presence in those meetings ensured that every opportunity to install city fiber was taken advantage of, and he started by installing fiber infrastructure between municipal buildings and city schools.

The city initially invested just $530,000 to do this work, but then saved at least $700,000 a year by not having to lease lines from private companies. Through endless, relentless persuasion of city authorities, Wolf was allowed to reinvest those savings in a fiber network that now serves downtown Santa Monica businesses as well as the city; those businesses pay a third or less of what a private operator might charge. Today, City Net is extending its services to residents, operates free public Wi-Fi in tourist destinations, and makes possible (among many other things) real-time data for apps that help people figure out where to park.[11] Parking is an important issue in a beach town.

But media and medicine are also big businesses: the City Net 100-gigabyte network allows a business to transfer a 40-GB Blu-Ray movie in three seconds.[12] It would take nearly an hour to do the same thing over a standard cable connection. For "movie," substitute any large data file, including intense amounts of data associated with medical research. Santa Monica wants to be known as "Silicon Beach" these days, and the League of California Cities recently found that the city has seen new tech companies moving in while its existing health care and entertainment businesses stay in place.[13]

My favorite recent evening in Chattanooga, Tennessee, just four hundred miles west of Greensboro, was spent walking across the Tennessee River from downtown to the North Shore by way of the Walnut Street Bridge. It's a long pedestrian bridge with wide, soft wooden planks, and after dark you can stop and look back at the lights of the city's aquarium and many downtown hotels and businesses. On that particular summer night, the bridge was pleasantly full of diverse walkers and amblers, black and white, families and singles, strolling back and forth. The bridge wasn't always this pleasant a place; it fell into disrepair in the late 1970s after it was closed to cars, and decades of community and civic work were required to bring it to its current state.[14] That same narrative—desuetude to vibrancy with enormous collective effort—describes Chattanooga's story as a city. Today, that story is being pushed along by fiber: once a dying, dirty, old-industry city, Chattanooga now has one of the country's highest-capacity public utility fiber services, run by its electrical utility, EPB.[15]

Formerly known as the Electric Power Board, EPB was founded in 1935 as a public distributor of Tennessee Valley Authority (TVA) electricity to the residents of Chattanooga.[16] The idea for the board started with the downtown Kiwanis Club, which thought Chattanooga needed its own electrical system to take advantage of low-cost TVA power and bring new businesses to town. By the 1990s, EPB had become somewhat poky—many public electric utilities have forgotten their heroic past as key players in America's story of electrification—and "really had a very internal focus," in the words of its current CEO, David Eaves: "We would have businesses come into town [looking for electrical assistance] and we had hurdles and rules and stuff in place that were obstacles."

In 1996, EPB brought in a new CEO, Harold DePriest, who had already been with the utility for twenty-five years. DePriest, a heavyset, extremely intelligent man with an easy bearing, went to see mayoral candidate Jon Kinsey—a former real estate developer. DePriest remembered thinking, "Oh, here's another ol' mayor I have to train." Ken Hays, Kinsey's chief of staff then, was in that meeting. He remembered that EPB at the time seemed to think "they were God Almighty, and their job was just to run electricity" but not get involved in economic development. During the meeting, Kinsey and Hays challenged DePriest, asking, "What does EPB do for the city?" At first, DePriest was angered by the question. "Everybody knows what we do, we provide electricity," DePriest remembered muttering to himself. "If he's going to try to get into our money, or if he's going to try to push EPB around, I'll just resign."

But after he calmed down, DePriest took the question to heart and started to think about how EPB could actually advance the community's economic development. "If you think about it, back in the thirties, when we were created, that's what we did. . . . We really needed to go back to our roots," DePriest said. The talk with Kinsey and Hays was a "catalytic moment" for EPB.

Beginning in the late 1990s, DePriest led EPB through dramatic cultural changes, charging his employees to think of themselves as part of the city's economic development efforts rather than as bureaucrats at a difficult-to-work-with electrical company. EPB's electric grid clearly needed to get better and more reliable. Digital monitoring equipment able to sense and report electrical faults in the field was coming onto the market. But EPB's home office couldn't communicate remotely with that digital equipment. "In those days," DePriest remembered, "if you wanted to communicate with a digital relay, you sent a young engineer out with a microprocessor. You physically wired up to that one relay, and you sat there and punched buttons to change the coding." That was no longer workable: EPB's electrical system had a thousand relays, and the company was also starting to use personal computers. All of those digital devices out on the electric system needed to be connected by a communications system touching all of them as well as the desktop PCs. "We started out looking at getting into the communications business," DePriest said, and wondering, "how do you make a decision today that won't seem like a stupid decision in ten years?" As David Wade, DePriest's successor, put it, "What electric company around would build a substation that would meet today's needs? They would build it based on meeting a need that they're projecting to be out in the future."

DePriest and his team landed on fiber as an elegant solution to many problems. Some smaller electric utility systems in the Tennessee Valley had already put fiber in their last miles. By running a fiber optic network alongside EPB's electrical lines, the utility could reap enormous benefits in the form of reduced outages and quick responses to problems. Fiber was, as far as they could tell, future-proof. So in 2006, EPB went into the business of providing telephone service over fiber to its electric customers. There were many hoops to go through, including getting city council approval, EPB board approval, public comments, and approval by the TVA; getting a bond issued; and negotiating with Chattanooga and the eleven other municipalities and six counties served by EPB for phone franchises—all of this took more than a year.

With $229 million in bond proceeds, EPB was able to build fiber to Chattanooga's city limits.[17] The utility found many ways to reduce its installation costs: "This was one project that was built ahead of schedule, way below budget, and with sales that were eventually about twice what we had estimated in the business plan," DePriest remembered. The bond proceeds were used to pay for the headend (the brains of the communications network, located in a central office), the electronics, and the computers that ran the communications system. EPB started offering internet access and telephone services to its customers in September 2009.

Then, in 2010, an Obama administration smart grid matching grant of $111 million paid for more fiber, electric meters ("smart meters"), and 1,200 intelligent electrical switches, none of which necessarily had to do with communications.[18] But that grant did allow DePriest to keep building the communications network outside the city limits. "We'd already borrowed the money" to build the fiber network, DePriest remembered, "and we still had $100 million left to spend" when the smart grid money became available. "But because we got that smart grid grant, we were able to build our smart grid at the same time we were finishing the fiber."

Also in 2010, EPB started offering gigabit-per-second access, years before any other company in the United States did so. Chattanooga proudly adopted the nickname "Gig City." Today that gigabit connection costs about $70 per month—more than you'll pay in Singapore, but better pricing than almost anywhere else in America.[19] In the first three quarters of its 2016–17 fiscal year, EPB Fiber made more than $111 million in communications revenues and earned $14.5 million in profit.[20] The fiber is paying for the smart grid, helping to keep electric rates lower, and the smart grid is preventing and correcting power breaks. Chattanooga has decided that providing everyone with world-class technology at a reasonable price is the right thing to do, for both social justice and economic growth, and that decision has served the city well.

Chattanooga and Santa Monica are both urban places. I needed a new adventure, so I drove southwest from Minneapolis into the RS Fiber region on a blue-gray winter day. The "R" stands for "Renville" and the "S" for Sibley, two Minnesota counties into which a new fiber network is planned to run. I could not have felt farther from Santa Monica: on either side of the highway, the flow of bumpy brown fields edged with snow was moderated only by an occasional farmhouse or two. My destination was Winthrop, Minnesota, a struggling town of a few hundred buildings that is home to the extraordinary RS Fiber cooperative.

Stokab is a "dark fiber" wholesale leasing model controlled, essentially, by the City of Stockholm, in which retail services are provided by private companies rather than the city; Santa Monica City Net is a soup-to-nuts, city-owned and -operated model, a true municipal network in which the city itself sells services to businesses and residences. RS Fiber is yet a third flavor of community network. It's a fiber services cooperative, a nonprofit whose members are its customers: farmers, local businesses, and individuals. The network will serve, eventually, ten small towns and seventeen "townships," or large, sparsely populated areas that are smaller than counties. But the towns and townships in the RS Fiber region aren't members of the co-op themselves. They are not managing anything and have no formal power over what the cooperative does. Instead, they trust that the cooperative will do a good job, and on the strength of that trust have lent it money to string up fiber.

It's an amazing, many-years-long story. At the center of it is a former small-town journalist named Mark Erickson who used the GI Bill to go to the University of Idaho to study journalism and economics. In 2008, after serial careers as a journalist, a newspaper owner, and a leader of Hiawatha Broadband (the fiber company now stringing fiber for the RS Fiber cooperative), Erickson came to Winthrop as the city manager. He was disruptive—he had a lot of ideas and was willing to work hard. The only internet access service in town was provided by MediaCom, a local cable company, and its data service and customer service were both awful. "We'll come to Winthrop on Tuesday" was what people would hear from MediaCom—when they called the company on a Friday.

Within a year of his arrival in Winthrop, Erickson and Dave Trebelhorn, then the town's mayor, had met with local telecom companies asking them to upgrade the whole Renville-Sibley county region, both little towns and family farms, to fiber. They would figure out the financing later; they thought they could raise the money from issuing bonds. The telcos said no.

In the absence of company interest, Erickson and Trebelhorn planned a fully public network. The original projection—which took a couple of years to generate—was that wiring the area's farms and small towns with fiber would cost local government about $70 million, and the resulting network would be owned by the two counties and the towns in some sort of regional agreement.[21] About 40 percent of that funding would come from bonds issued by Sibley County. That plan didn't happen. Last-minute reluctance in 2010 on the part of two Sibley County commissioners blocked the county's participation. Shannon Sweeney, who did the financial work, said that happened because "you're entering a business that is traditionally a private business in Minnesota, and you're competing with other private businesses, and that's not something that units of government are always used to."

The Sibley County commissioners' 3–2 vote against participation in the fiber plan was a dramatic moment.[22] The whole plan seemed to be dead in the water. The county was representing the rural interest in having fiber, and I was told by several people that the "rural folks then went to the bar" right after the meeting was over and formed a cooperative, saying, in Sweeney's words, "'We're going to create this cooperative because we want to have a voice in this whole thing because it's important for the rural areas to be served.'" Erickson and his colleagues then spent months regrouping; the cooperative, they concluded, was a fine idea—in fact, a better idea, because having a private entity rather than local government own the network eliminated any discomfort over having government selling services that had traditionally been the province of private actors. But where was the money going to come from to build the network if the county wasn't involved?

Sweeney cracked the nut: interested townships and towns could issue "general obligation" bonds and lend the money they raised to the private cooperative.[23] This plan might have scared some people off: if future revenues from network services weren't enough to make debt service payments, the towns and townships could be sued by bondholders and forced to raise taxes to make those payments, meaning that money that might otherwise have gone to fire protection or road maintenance would go to paying back the investors in the RS Fiber network. On the other hand, general obligation bonds are low risk for lenders; there have never been any defaults, because unless all the taxpayers suddenly leave the area, the tax is going to be paid and the debt will be covered. And if the project was successful, the taxpayers would never make a payment.

The farmers and the towns were desperate for fiber. In the towns, they were sick of MediaCom, the local cable monopoly. The farms were struggling along on terrible and expensive mobile data plans. By 2014 it was time to figure out how to implement the plan—now slimmed from a budget of $70 million to $50 million in light of the county's exit.[24] The cooperative contacted Hiawatha Broadband, Erickson's former company, which had done fiber builds in more than a dozen rural areas.[25] Hiawatha's CEO, Dan Pecorino, recommended stringing fiber in the towns first, getting adoption and cash flow going, and then installing fiber to the farms in a second phase of activity. In the meantime, the farms could be served by a lower-capacity and less expensive "air" service—wireless high-speed internet access—handled by transmitter/receivers on water towers and cell towers that were themselves attached to fiber wire. By July 2015, the bonds were issued—after some elaborate joint planning between the ten towns—the loans for Phase One were in, and the towns started getting wired. The cooperative was determined to reach the fiber-to-the-farm phase as soon as possible.

One nearby town, Arlington, stayed clear of the RS Fiber planning and bonding. The city administrator was a dyed-in-the-wool Tea Party Republican, according to former Arlington economic development officer Denny Schultz, who thought government had no place in the utility business. Schultz thinks Arlington may end up as a ghost town, an island of non-connectivity in a sea of fiber. He's already worried about the town's inability to attract new business; these issues, he feels, go hand in hand. Bob Fox, of the city of Franklin in Renville County, was straightforward: "I'll feel sorry for any area, ten or fifteen years from now, if you don't have fiber. I'm guessing there's not going to be a lot of people."

The RS Fiber deployment was ongoing as of spring 2018. One of the key lessons the cooperative has already learned is the importance to people of both great customer service and just plain better telecommunications service. RS Fiber is always the "service provider of choice," meaning, said Sweeney, that "the majority of the market takes their service because they provide better service." And unlike cable, the fiber service can be infinitely upgraded. By contrast, people in the RS Fiber area felt they'd been begging the incumbents, both cable company MediaCom and telco New Ulm and others, for fiber for years and being ignored. Local phone companies said, basically, "We don't need that service here." These companies also spread rumors that RS Fiber was a startup that wasn't going to be able to give good service and would fail.

Fiber is just better than what the incumbent is selling. As the Hiawatha Broadband employee charged with wiring up the RS Fiber towns, Toby Brummer, put it, "The fiber's going to be there forever. Unless we invent something faster than the speed of light, you're not going to get anything faster." Upgrades to the electronics on either end of the fiber are available every six months or so. Meanwhile, the fiber will last: in the early 1980s, Brummer's father installed fiber that is still being used. There are no teaser rates, where people get a package for $29.95 for the first year and then the rate jumps to $300. The price is the price, and rural farmers will pay the same rate as the people in town.

People love the fact that when they call RS Fiber for help, they are talking to someone in either Winthrop or next-door Gaylord. Toby Brummer said, "If there's a problem, local people, from here, come out and we get it fixed. Right away. There's no waiting." People also love that the money stays local. "We want to be profitable," Denny Schultz, a member of the co-op board, told me. "but we don't have any shareholders in New York to answer to." Money going to Mediacom, by contrast, flows far away from the community.

The grassroots, stubborn character of the local farmers and townspeople is amply reflected in the RS Fiber project. People in the area are descended from homesteaders, as well as from Scandinavians who very early on brought the cooperative model to Minnesota; they are comfortable trusting one another, and with the idea that you can do much more working together than you can as individuals. The cooperative isn't in this business to make huge profits or dividends. It exists to bring a service to the area. And the people who stubbornly worked for years to get RS Fiber off the ground don't like being bossed around.

When I visited, the cooperative was feeling a bit undercapitalized. It had been planning to take advantage of a federal tax credit structure—New Market Tax Credits—that had gotten delayed.[26] Sweeney was optimistic that things would work out in the end, but he cautioned that, so far, private banks had not bought in to the idea of fiber startups sufficiently to be willing to lend money to them. It is crucial, he thinks, to get units of local government to finance the project costs and subordinated loans: "There are no banks that we're aware of," he told me, "that are willing to fund a startup cooperative that wants to build fiber without some other large cash infusion that's subordinate to their interest." At the moment, federal funding is almost inaccessible for regular projects. "Cities have to see this as their role," Sweeney said. Cities have to put up the necessary collateral to secure the private funding needed by any fiber cooperative. If they do, fiber becomes an ordinary city commodity, "the type of enterprise that you fund, build, and operate every day," like a street grid, public transportation, or a bridge.

Life in the RS Fiber region can be a struggle: the towns have to work every angle to get a new business to move in. San Francisco doesn't have that problem, for the moment, but it is suffering in its own way in terms of its connectivity. It has been embarrassing for the country's leading tech city not to have inexpensive gigabit access for everyone; right now, AT&T and Comcast are the leading internet service providers (ISPs) in the area, but although both companies have said they plan to deploy gigabit service, neither has given the city a timeline. Meanwhile, tens of thousands of San Francisco residents—12 percent of the city's population—lack high-speed home internet access, and 50,000 others have only dial-up service. Many of San Francisco's public school students—14 percent—lack internet access to do their homework, mostly because their parents can't afford to pay what AT&T and Comcast charge.[27] And because of the city's inadequate current wiring, its mobile access is often awful: RootMetrics ranks San Francisco as 58th out of 125 metropolitan areas in quality of mobile network service.[28]

And so San Francisco has become the first major American city considering a city-owned community fiber network that will reach every and business. Mark Farrell, the moderate and relatively young former member of the city's Board of Supervisors, is leading the effort. Farrell, like Chattanooga mayor Andy Berke, has political ambitions that are likely well served by working on a citywide fiber network. He said he's genuinely interested in having high-speed internet access viewed as "an economic right, not just a nice-to-have, in today's society." But, in 2017, his remaining time as supervisor was short—his term would be over at the end of 2018. He told me if he wanted to run for another office, he would need to show progress. Like many San Franciscans, he was sick of paying $250 a month to Comcast for inadequate services and upset that the city's "download speeds are on par with Mexico City right now."

A native San Franciscan with a private-sector background in venture capital, Farrell recently had the Budget and Legislative Analyst's office of the Board of Supervisors—a kind of internal consulting arm for the supervisors—work through different business models for providing fiber in San Francisco.[29] Spurred on by Farrell's efforts, the late mayor of San Francisco, Ed Lee, said he too was interested in taking the substantial political risk of a large, ambitious fiber project. This story has been bumping along for years; in the early 2000s, Board of Supervisors member Tom Ammiano proposed studying municipal fiber, but the effort was stalled by a failed multiyear effort to deploy Wi-Fi in the city in partnership with Earthlink.[30] A fiber study was done, but nothing happened. In the ensuing years, the city dug up all its streets to put in new sewer lines, but missed an enormous opportunity to address its fiber connectivity deficits.[31] Only now, pushed forward by Farrell's urgency and helped by his current role as interim mayor, is a plan beginning to take shape.

The city has multiple goals. It would like to help close the digital divide, ensure that world-class internet access over fiber is ubiquitous within its footprint, deliver the best value it can to taxpayers, have any agreements with private actors about internet access over fiber be flexible enough for changing circumstances, and generate competition in services. It is focused on a Stokab-like dark fiber model that will separate availability of a wholesale network from retail services. The city is considering charging a low monthly property-related fee for fiber and issuing general obligation bonds to support construction costs.[32]

The battle with the incumbents will be a kind of holy war. We've seen similar conflicts in other areas: the soda industry vehemently opposed the city's efforts to impose soda taxes and health warning labels, spending nearly $10 million on ads claiming that any soda tax would lead to higher prices for milk and bread.[33] That lobbying effort was likely a ripple compared with the tidal wave of opposition incumbent communications companies can mount to a big-city assault on private telecommunications services. We are likely to see every tactic that has ever been used in the past, including proposed new state laws, announcements of planned fiber networks from AT&T and Comcast that are short on timeline but long on special pricing promises, advocacy by telco-funded minority nonprofits and craven academics, announcements that fiber is passé and has been superseded by advances in wireless communications, a drumbeat of claims that any municipal network is destined to fail miserably and cost taxpayers unnecessary millions, and a variety of attempts to limit the scale (and thus the economic strength) of any San Francisco–led fiber plan.

It's important that San Francisco prevail, because cities are the counterweight to the state- and national-level swing toward increasingly individualistic policies. Farrell believes San Francisco's move to community fiber is of a piece with other city-led efforts aimed at improving citizens' lives. As he and former supervisor Eric Mar wrote in a February 2017 op-ed in the *San Francisco Chronicle*, "San Francisco has led the way for California and the rest of the country on advancing equal rights and universal health care, and improving the environment. Cities of similar size that have tried to deliver on this vision and goal have been met with stiff opposition. We can lead the way on delivering the 21st century utility—Internet access at home—to every San Franciscan."[34] If San Francisco succeeds, America's fiber story may begin finally to change. At the same time, city-level dedication to liberal democracy may ultimately strengthen the country as a whole. Laissez-faire is not serving us well.

CHAPTER FIVE

Sustaining Economic Growth

T HE CITIES THAT HAVE the leadership to establish utility-style fiber networks reaching all residents and businesses will have a leg up when it comes to economic growth. Fiber isn't just a story of technology. It is also a key ingredient in working toward communities of opportunity.

Chattanooga has clearly been able to harness its fiber for economic development, but it has much more work to do. Wilson, North Carolina, while it has a terrific fiber network, is still working to revive its downtown and attract new employers. Greensboro, North Carolina, by contrast, has business leaders who talk a lot about fiber but has neither a long-range fiber plan nor a convincing economic development plan; its future as a thriving locality is uncertain. Follow the money: the story of reaching for light is importantly about economic growth.

Chattanooga's efforts to reinvent itself didn't start with EPB fiber and will not end there. The fiber story in Chattanooga is just one chapter in a history of long-term collaborative planning. "The Chattanooga Way," people call it: working together for the greater good. From the many stories I heard there, the "Way" involves local philanthropy, local businesses, and local government putting aside their egos—a bit—in service of progress for everyone.

Chattanooga in the 1970s was an alienating, hollowed-out place. Walter Cronkite famously called it "the dirtiest city in America" in October 1969.[1] Massive layoffs and plant closings in the steel and textile industries had eliminated tens of thousands of jobs, created a discouraging atmosphere, and left empty lots downtown. The city was deeply divided politically and geographically by race, class, and religion, and its leadership was fractured and opaque. The place felt like a backwater. Ann Coulter, who shares her name with a famous conservative firebrand but has been working on Chattanooga's redevelopment efforts for decades, graduated from high school in Chattanooga in 1975 and is now a strategic planning consultant for Chattanooga's downtown Enterprise Center. "It was awful," she told me. "Everybody that could get out when I graduated from high school, went."

In 1980, Jack Lupton, a local philanthropist whose grandfather had had the foresight to own the world's largest Coca-Cola bottling company, commissioned a study examining Chattanoogans' perceptions of their city.[2] The report's author, Gianni Longo, wrote, "There is a noticeable lack of communication between the city's leadership and the citizens at large, particularly members of the poorer strata of society and blacks, who are conscious of an unstable relationship between people of different social and economic status as well as different races. There is a sense of powerlessness, a lack of receptivity to their needs and problems, and a feeling that the powers that be reflect entrenched local interests rather than taking into account the broad needs of the community."[3] Both wealthy and poor residents of Chattanooga, it turned out, were frustrated by the city's lack of progress and closedness. Something had to be done to improve its quality of life. The place was a mess.

Spurred by Longo's report, over the next several years Lupton's Lyndhurst Foundation invited many people from inside and outside the city to think through how Chattanooga could change. There wasn't a plan; they muddled through, sponsoring and co-sponsoring a huge range of events and activities, including publications, musical performances, art exhibits, and conferences, all aimed at increasing citizen engagement and stimulating downtown development. A sense of hope began to emerge. Over three years, dozens of open meetings focused on what should happen to Chattanooga's riverfront—to which access was blocked by big buildings and a four-lane highway. In 1983, about fifty Chattanoogans from all parts of the city traveled to Indianapolis to learn about how that city had created regional public transport, expanded its arts facilities, and renewed its downtown. They took home a wide range of ideas, including that a city could change its personality if it involved all stakeholders in its transformation, and that foundation funding could be a critical catalyst. An informal study group was convened to learn about how other cities had tackled similar situations.

All of this activity led to the creation, in August 1984, of a broadly representative public participation effort called Vision 2000, linked to a public-private partnership coordination entity, RiverCity Company, that was charged with answering the question, "What kind of city do we want Chattanooga to be?"[4] It had a young, diverse staff, funding from the Lyndhurst Foundation, and a sense of mission. Eight years later, encouraged by Vision 2000's work, RiverCity's implementation efforts, and a $20 million gift from Jack Lupton, the city opened the spectacular Tennessee Aquarium on its waterfront in 1992.[5] That was just the beginning.

RiverCity, in partnership with mayor Jon Kinsey (1997–2001) and his chief of staff, Ken Hays, subsequently carried out another major public-engagement process, Revision 2000, for several years.[6] By the time Bob Corker became mayor in 2001, the project recommended through that process—the 21st Century Waterfront—was ready to go: the city narrowed the riverfront highway to two lanes, eased pedestrian access to the river, and spurred more waterfront development, including a second phase for the aquarium, a children's museum, and an addition to the art museum.[7] Chattanooga's downtown, now connected to the river, experienced a substantial revival beginning in 2000, with many restaurants, several hotels, new retail outlets, and a slew of residential buildings springing up.

Another broad-based visioning/participation project, Create-Here, also funded in part by Lyndhurst, worked for five years beginning in 2007 to survey more than 25,000 local residents, host all-night parties, incubate small businesses and artists, and draw attention to the potential of Southside Chattanooga (Main Street in particular) for creatives and investment. At the end of the process, more than two hundred small businesses had been launched, artists had moved in, and real estate was beginning to change hands in a formerly blighted area.[8] A 2013 City Center Plan aimed at linking the revived riverfront to the revived Southside has resulted in nearly a billion dollars of investment in Chattanooga buildings.[9] More recently, in 2015, the city designated a 140-acre area of downtown as its Innovation District. It has consciously worked at creating an anchor for the area, open to the public and housing many new companies and community meetings, in the ten-story Edney Building at the corner of Market and 11th Streets.[10]

These processes of thinking together about the city's future have had a transformative impact on citizens' attitudes, willingness to connect, and readiness for change. The big idea is, again, the "Chattanooga Way": a long-term, collaborative public-private partnership with leaders from many walks of life "having those really challenging forward-looking conversations and thinking ahead," as Kristina Montague put it. It is a norm of behavior that is universally supported. One civic leader, who wanted to remain nameless, told me that "Just to protect the Chattanooga Way, there have been multiple coffees where I'd sit down with somebody and say, 'Man, I appreciate what you're doing but you need to shut up because you're distracting, you're causing disunity. That is not where we are right now, and we need to move this ball forward not backwards.' Because I've always believed that cities either grow or decline, but they don't stay the same."

Today, with the arrival of fiber, economic growth is a big story in Chattanooga. New jobs are flooding the area: in 2016, Hamilton County, where the city is located, was expecting ten thousand new jobs to arrive in the next few years, mostly in advanced industries.[11] Most will require some kind of post-high-school certification but not necessarily a college degree. Volkswagen and Amazon are the name-brand players, but a host of smaller businesses—automotive supply, logistics, aircraft maintenance—are also adding thousands of jobs. Tech startup guys and gals are buying each other coffee at The Camp House, a large, welcoming first-floor space anchored by a wide altar at one end and a DJ booth at the other; it's used for religious services and parties as well as pitches. Terrific restaurants are opening all around the downtown area, particularly on South

Main, the first area of the city to gentrify. The hype about Chatta-nooga's growth is powerful: today it is, for many city planners, a poster child for midsized success.

The connection between the EPB fiber network and Chatta-nooga's resurgence is obvious to Andy Berke, the city's ambitious, hardworking mayor. "We're supplying important economic develop-ment," Berke told me. A recent economic study by Bento Lobo, pro-fessor of finance at the University of Tennessee at Chattanooga, said EPB's fiber optics network, in its first three years, saved $130.5 mil-lion in power outages, boosted business energy efficiency by $234.5 million, and spurred $461 million in new business investment.[12]

Like Chattanooga, Wilson, North Carolina, had the advantage of having run its own electric utility for a long time before it launched its fiber network in 2010. Dathan Shows, who started the fiber project and now serves as the city's chief operating officer, was trained as a city manager after having worked in city operations. In the 1990s the Wilson city council proposed addressing citizen complaints about poor service from the local cable monopoly. "It was the typical cable industry, 'We can schedule between noon and five, and we'll let you know when.' And pricing seemed to just esca-late, arbitrarily, from year to year. Service interruptions, too," Wil-son lawyer Jim Cauley told me. The city council wanted to build a cable system to be run by the city, and it asked Shows to research the idea. He talked to people in Morganton, the only city in North Carolina at the time that had a cable system. "They're the ones who said, 'Don't do [cable wires]. It's dead. Copper's dead, it's dying." Morganton was moving to fiber, and Shows "looked at the throughputs of fiber versus copper and what was on the horizon for each, and it was a crazy difference. There was just no way." Shows kept learning, talking to the operators of an early municipal fiber system in Bristol, Virginia, and the people at EPB in Chatta-nooga. "Chattanooga had not done anything yet, but they had done a chunk of research. We talked with them."

Shows decided Wilson needed fiber. "I learned everything I could about fiber and how to build a fiber network." He brought in engineer Gene Scott to design the network. That was a good call: Scott arrived at Greenlight, Wilson's municipal fiber company, from a twenty-eight-year career with a telco in the eastern North Carolina area, "Embarq, which was Sprint, which was Carolina Telephone," Shows joked. "He knew how to build it, so we didn't have to figure that part out." And for operating the network, "we stole several people from Suddenlink [a cable company that is now a subsidiary of Altice USA]."

Shows had the good sense to give Scott freedom to oversee the design of the network. "I was just told, 'We're going to build this. We're going to do it for the community, and we want it correct. I had a clean sheet of paper," Scott told me. He wanted the network to be reliable, robust, flexible, and upgradable. He planned to have a dedicated fiber for each address in the city, which meant that there would be no active devices to maintain out in neighborhoods. There would be electronics in the central office and electronics in homes. "There are no active devices in between to go wrong or be damaged by lightning. If I can keep the squirrels off of it, it's going to work," Scott told me. He put all his fiber neighborhood access points below ground. "Unless you hit it with a backhoe, you're not going to get it."

Now, when upgrades are needed, Wilson can simply change out the electronics in the central office. "You don't have to go out and do a massive rebuild in the field," Scott said proudly. The fiber will last, he said. "Some of what we put in from my early career is already thirty-five-plus years old and still operating." Scott is also proud that he carefully documented the entire network; his records are immaculate and detailed. "I think many entities and maybe other cities that get into this don't realize the importance of documenting their networks," he told me. "Because you can build it, and you turn it on, and it works, and you go, 'Great.' But then the guy who had it all in his head retires.'"

Scott deliberately designed the Wilson network as a public utility rather than a demand-driven business. The entire network was built out at once. "Whether you want the service today or you want it a year from now, or you sell your house and somebody else wants the service, it's already there." The whole point was to have the network available to everyone in Wilson. "It wasn't all driven by, 'Are we going to make money in this neighborhood or not?' because we built every neighborhood regardless of their socioeconomic conditions, because it's supposed to be something to help," Scott told me. "Obviously we need to make enough money not to go out of business, but it's not all about funding Wall Street."

Shows and Scott, a good team on the operational side, were joined by an experienced city manager, Grant Goings, and Jim Cauley, a calm, resourceful lawyer who had survived a ten-year fight with the U.S. Army Corps of Engineers and the Fish and Wildlife Service over the city's water supply ("baptized by fire," Cauley joked) and worked for years counseling the city through its fights over fiber with incumbent cable providers both locally and at the North Carolina statehouse. Wilson had a city council that, according to Cauley, kept together and was consistently brave. "You don't see the infighting that you see on some boards," Cauley told me. "They are together, and I think that makes a big difference in what they're able to accomplish." Shows, Scott, Goings, and Cauley were a band of brothers, full of gallows humor, and all with different skill sets.

Wilson's employees also had needed skills: they knew all about poles from their electrical experience, and so were ready to cope with using poles and conduit for fiber. "Due to our extensive experience operating utilities, particularly an electric utility that owned most of the poles in town, we were not intimidated by the infrastructure build," city manager Goings told me. And, importantly, Wilson had Will Aycock, who Dathan Shows brought out of the city's information technology department to be general manager of Greenlight. Aycock, said Shows, was "the one who really took it to the next level and got the national attention for Wilson."

Shows said that high-quality local customer service, also ready to go because of the utility's electrical business, has been essential to Wilson's success: "The people we have here is why people switch to us and why people stay," Shows said. "Local customer service representatives of Greenlight pick up the phone and someone from eastern North Carolina answers it. And we will send a truck to you for anything that goes wrong. Even if your TV's not working right, we'll roll a truck to you. It has just amazed the citizens." And the citizens love that all the money stays local. "Customers love the fact that the people they talk to are local people," Scott told me. "You wouldn't have thought that would have made that big a deal. . . . I think it's a kickback to, right or wrong, a feeling that large companies don't care about the customer anymore." Working on a fiber system, according to Cauley, is not for every local government. "It takes a lot of skill; takes a good bit of assets; takes a staff that's capable. You've got to have all the pieces to make it work, and not every local government does," he said.

As Will Aycock put it: "The network undergirds and connects most everything going on in the community, but it's in really subtle ways." He was standing in front of a fifty-foot-tall kinetic sculpture of a man on a bicycle, a sculpture made of brightly painted metal shards, red, blue, yellow, its rider blunt-nosed and eternally capable of whirring along, high above the ground, as he circles in place: this is one of Wilson's Whirligigs, undergoing painstaking restoration before taking a starring role in a new downtown park.

Wilson's tobacco warehouses and auction barns, a dozen low-slung enormous buildings, were once a center of life in eastern North Carolina. Decades ago, everyone came to town for the auctions and the dances that followed them. Wilson's mayor told me, "It was the biggest thing in the world, right here." Every street would be lined with cars waiting to get to the tobacco sales. The local radio station's call letters reflect Wilson's identity in those years: WLTM, for World's Largest Tobacco Market. But the auctions have been gone for twenty years or more. All the small farms are gone, and restaurants and hotels have vanished from downtown. Wilson, in company with developers, is creating a new plan for its downtown. They've chosen whimsy as part of the attraction, and that's where Vollis Simpson's Whirligigs fit in.

Simpson, when he was alive, met the description of "curmudgeon," sometimes abrupt and sometimes a loner. He transformed old army surplus vehicles, rigging them up into wreckers, and dug stuck cars out of ditches; then, for his own amusement, he constructed a huge number of tall, playful Whirligigs made up of machine parts from Wilson's manufacturing past, and put them on his land out in the middle of nowhere. Where they rusted. After Simpson died, Wilson, in company with a family foundation, bought the Whirligigs from his family and began painstakingly restoring them.

The plan is to erect thirty of the Whirligigs on land downtown, three blocks from City Hall, where several tobacco barns have been removed; there will be walkways, gardens, and a grassy amphitheater around the ungainly, unlikely structures Simpson left behind. On the blocks of Goldsboro Street, looking at the Whirligigs, there's the beeping, bustling activity of construction: one of the last two auction barns in town is being converted into ninety loft-style apartments, with ten thousand square feet of commercial space below to be filled by shops and restaurants. There's a new brewery on South Street, the street that borders the new Whirligig Park, created by a husband-and-wife team where an old mule stable once stood. Wilson's planning and community revitalization director, Kimberly Van Dyck, told me the city can support hundreds of residential units downtown; their other projects have drawn young professionals and empty-nesters, and she's confident the new units will do well. "Give us ten years, come back here, and this entire place is going to be booming," she said.

Wilson's fiber invisibly connects and supports every element of this story. To get the Whirligigs moving and shining, restoration specialists are working with other experts around the world. They can do this easily because Wilson's fiber network allows them to share high-resolution digital imagery quickly and easily. A special-effects company, Exodus FX, moved to Wilson a while ago just for this reason. It does work for top-flight movies and television shows, and advertises that its location in Wilson allows it "to offer very competitive rates for high-end work, while providing access to gigabit fiber broadband to deliver our work faster." More people are commuting *to* Wilson to work these days than are commuting *out*, which is a dramatic development in a poverty-stricken region. Wilson County's population isn't declining even as nearby counties that don't have fiber are losing people. The city has the strongest manufacturing sector, with the most jobs, of any locality in eastern North Carolina.[13] "Our efforts to position Wilson for long-term success have been very intentional," Grant Goings said. "Our city council has repeatedly shown the political courage to make bold investments in our future, often before the projects were pushed for by the general population. Their leadership has made a difference for Wilson."

Kimberly Van Dyck says that she moved to Wilson because she heard about the fiber network. "I saw a small town that was doing big things and I thought, 'Oh, my gosh, this place really has vision. They're incredibly forward-thinking.'" In turn, she's working on attracting creative people to Wilson who work in fields that are generating jobs. She told me, "some are already here and we didn't even know it."

Like Chattanooga, Wilson is still in transition: standing near the Whirligig Park, I see empty sidewalks as well as construction projects. The progress that Van Dyck promises hasn't quite come into being yet, and it's not totally clear that Whirligigs are the answer. If Wilson can leverage downtown development and its fiber network into a place that feels dense and diverse and allows for proximity and a flow of investment capital, all of that together will create the difficult-to-measure flow of change and energy that prosperous, growing places have. Fiber alone is not enough, but it's necessary.

Greensboro, North Carolina, several hours west of Wilson, is quite a bit smaller than Raleigh, the state capital, and Charlotte, its finance hub. It's part of the Triad—not to be confused with the Raleigh–Durham–Chapel Hill Research Triangle—in the middle of the state: Greensboro, Winston-Salem, High Point. If you look at a map of the state, Greensboro appears to be both geographically central and central to commerce: it's right in the middle, where all the big roads run. Railway lines located their central repair yards here a century ago, and today several logistics and shipping companies have set up shop in the Greensboro region. Greensboro also is home to a long list of colleges and universities: University of North Carolina–Greensboro, North Carolina Agricultural and Technical State University (NC A&T), Bennett College, Guilford College, Greensboro College, and Guilford Technical Community College.

At the time of my visit there, I had just read George Packer's *The Unwinding*, a set of essays that focuses in part on the Piedmont region of North Carolina, where Greensboro is located, and how the collapse of the textile industry here affected peoples' lives. I wanted to be able to report that Greensboro's region was raising itself up in part by focusing on fiber. The story I found did not fit my narrative plan. Instead, it illustrates what can happen in places where both the state government and local inertia, intentionally or accidentally, support the incumbent-controlled status quo.

Jane Nickles, the instigator of the Triad consortium and the chief information officer of Greensboro, is a soft-spoken, well-coiffed, gently determined woman who grew up in Greensboro and was a dance major at the University of North Carolina. After a job during her college years introduced her to the puzzling glories of computer programming, she started working for the city's IT department. She worked her way up over decades and eventually found herself running the city's technology infrastructure. And when she became chief information officer in 2014, it troubled her that the Triangle was getting all the fiber attention: Google Fiber was showing up there, AT&T was issuing press releases saying it, too, would be building last-mile fiber in the Triangle, and CenturyLink was selling fiber services to Triangle businesses.[14] Nothing of the sort was happening in the Triad. "I was curious as to why Greensboro was left out," Nickles told me.

So Nickles quietly nudged the TriGig group into existence.[15] "We wanted to heighten interest around broadband in the Triad, and how to promote it, and how to get internet service providers interested in building here and encourage competition, and to bring services into low-income neighborhoods and things such as that," she said. A North Carolina law passed in 2011 at the urging of Time Warner Cable—in direct response to the success of the Wilson network—prohibits municipalities from providing communications services directly to customers.[16] But Nickles and her legal counsel in City Hall took the position that the state law doesn't prohibit cities from leasing city-owned dark fiber, or facilitating access to poles and conduit. Greensboro has about two hundred miles of its own fiber that connects up the city's traffic signal system and wires about ninety-three city buildings and facilities, and Nickles figured someone would be interested in using that fiber to serve customers; she was particularly interested in innovative ways of reaching low-income neighborhoods.[17]

The TriGig group issued a request for proposals in mid-2016 looking for companies willing to operate an open-access fiber network that would attract additional retail operators. In exchange, the municipalities and universities were prepared to lease their

own dark fiber for ten years and provide access to their own conduit, poles, and buildings. AT&T showed up at all the vendor
meetings that followed, and even asked that the deadline for responses be extended, but then declined to bid. A hundred-year-old
local company, North State, responded favorably, and during my
conversations with Nickles in early 2017 she told me that she was
working with North State on a series of pilots aimed at providing
Wi-Fi to poor East Greensboro neighborhoods. "Our role as local
government is to facilitate partnerships and bring people together,"
she told me.

Nickles stopped talking about the city's overall communications problems and suggested focusing on public housing and
United Way neighborhood comprehensive services locations,
called Family Success Centers, as targets for Wi-Fi services offered
by North State. "We think these are very promising pilots for
Greensboro." She told me she planned to look for grants from the
city's housing authority, or perhaps community foundations, workforce development programs, or other nonprofits that might support TriGig's pilot projects. Her plan was to say that these projects
were simply filling gaps; she did not want to trigger concerns that
the city's actions would disrupt the existing private market in telecommunications. Leasing Greensboro's dark fiber would have led
more directly to all residents of the region paying reasonable
prices for last-mile fiber, but Nickles didn't think the city was ready
to consider that step.

Even Nickles's limited first steps encountered problems.
Eighty percent of Greensboro's city fiber was on poles, but the city
didn't control the poles: the local power utility, Duke Energy, and
telco, AT&T, did. The city raised the question of having North
State, or another provider, attach its equipment to those poles, and
the pole owners told them, essentially, "No, we can't do that. We
can't put multiple carriers on the pole. There's just no way." If the
city went underground with its dark fiber network, digging those
trenches would be expensive—although potentially less expensive
than waiting for permission from AT&T and Duke Energy.

But no one seemed willing to make city money available for
any of this. The city council and mayor knew about the projects
but weren't sure whether to support them. "This is more like a

grassroots initiative," Nickles said. She pulled together a draft summary of all the benefits of her proposed pilot projects for her city council. She got the council's support.

In April 2017, Greensboro's city council approved Nickles's pilot project. The grand aspiration of leasing dark fiber throughout the city was substantially narrowed: now the plan was to wire up a single Family Success Center that would serve as a hub for high-speed Wi-Fi in one low-income neighborhood. Nickles's strategy was to use this pilot as a model for similar projects in low-income and underserved areas of Greensboro. She also made it possible for nonprofit agencies to buy used City of Greensboro computers at discounted prices and make them available to low-income Greensboro residents. June 2017 found her waiting for North State's attorneys to approve Greensboro's draft contracts.

The fiber story in Greensboro and its surrounding region, despite Nickles's best efforts, is less than a work in progress. It's a process toward a procedure that might someday result in a plan. At the moment, Nickles is filling gaps, not disrupting the region's broken marketplace. Greensboro may end up slowly withering—it is at risk of becoming a North Carolina ghost town that got only bits of fiber from monopolistic carriers, and only in the leafiest, richest areas of town. Nickles remains determined: "We're going to be the desert in between the Triangle and Charlotte, and we can't let that happen. We have to take an active role in this." But it is unclear what she can actually do without public money or the strong involvement of city leadership. I think the world of Jane Nickles. But in Greensboro, she's a lone ranger.

You have to wonder what happened to Greensboro. In 1895 the Southern Railway, the North Carolina, the Atlantic & Yadkin, and the North Western railroad tracks met there and triggered a boom in downtown development, giving Greensboro its nickname, the Gate City.[18] As a 1903 pamphlet, "Progressive Greensboro: The Gate City of North Carolina," put it, "Greensboro, altogether, is one of the healthiest and most desirable cities in the country," and "There is no question but that Greensboro affords an ideal location for the establishment of certain lines of manufacture." The city boomed in those years. By 1903, Greensboro had fifty manufacturing plants—producing textiles, carpets, furniture, lumber, metal goods, and tobacco, among many other things—and sixty trains came and went each day; today, Greensboro has an airport serving the entire Piedmont region.

So why is it that between January 2007 and November 2016, the Triangle added 383,000 net new workers, while the Triad added just 3,000?[19] Greensboro's population growth is slow and flattening, the percentage of people between ages twenty and thirty-four who live there is declining, its average wages are low and stagnant, and its poverty rates are stubbornly high—about one in five residents in Greensboro lives in poverty.[20] It is ranked tenth among American cities that lose the most jobs each day. Jeff Thigpen, a longtime civic leader who met me at a local diner, told me there's little intentional effort to keep young people here. "A lot of them leave. I'll just be honest."

Zack Matheny, a pugnacious man in his mid-forties working on downtown economic development, said the city has a history of lack of foresight and planning: "North Carolina National Bank talked about putting their headquarters here, and our forefathers said, 'We're good.' NCNB is now Bank of America. Probably weren't thinking ahead on that deal." He told me the city fathers were protecting the textile industry, just as those in Wilson once protected the tobacco industry. But when textile and furniture manufacturing left the city, a hundred thousand jobs were lost and never really replaced.[21] It was late on a Friday afternoon in his high-ceilinged downtown Greensboro conference room, and Zack was weary.

In Nickles's office, I met with Joe Magno, a man in his mid-sixties who struck me as a connector extraordinaire, a man of enormous energy and many overlapping projects, bald and straightforward, the kind of guy who, within five minutes of your meeting him, will have offered to introduce you to seven people. His role was to tell me how hard it is to get any large economic development project off the ground in Greensboro.

Magno tried for two years to launch a large new business in town—a biotech company—and was enormously frustrated by the lack of regional leadership. "The twenty-minute ride between Greensboro and High Point, or between Greensboro and Winston-Salem, might as well be going across the Atlantic Ocean," he said.

Leaders in the Research Triangle, he told me, accepted that they had to relinquish some power in order for the entire community to move ahead—and, indeed the federal government forced collaboration among Triangle-area universities as a condition of getting certain science-related funding—but that hadn't happened in the Greensboro region. Magno told me he eventually gave up: the more he got involved, the more he "realized that everything was very insular."

On all of my visits to Greensboro, I sensed its residents' amiable, unfocused hope for their city, as well as the lack of zeal among high-level leadership. The place was subsiding genteelly into poverty, with a few bright spots in downtown development not enough to stop the gradual, invisible decline. The lack of local energy for fiber, alongside the state's strenuous efforts to ensure that a Wilson-like network never happens again, is part of that overall slump.

Chattanooga is less dense than Greensboro and has a smaller population; the square mileage of the two metro areas is about the same.[22] Neither Greensboro nor Chattanooga is the biggest city in its state. Greensboro is not as famous, large, or well-resourced as either Raleigh or Charlotte. Chattanooga is the smallest, slightly, of the four large cities in Tennessee, and it doesn't have a major educational institution. But the growth story for the two places is strikingly different. Unlike Greensboro, Chattanooga seems to be a place of genuine economic hope.

Greensboro faces the problems many American cities are confronting: it needs downtown energy and new businesses, both of which will require great connectivity. Zach Matheny is working hard on Greensboro's downtown. But when it comes to connectivity, Greensboro's city leaders seem to fit into a long local tradition of failing to think of anything greater than themselves. The city hasn't yet cooked up a Greensboro Way analog to Chattanooga's purposeful approach to progress.

Wilson is a step ahead of Greensboro, because it already has fiber and it is attracting and retaining businesses. BB&T (Branch Banking and Trust), now one of the largest banks in the southeastern United States, was founded in Wilson and maintains a large office downtown with about two thousand employees. BB&T's presence is a feather in the city's cap, and the bank is the city's largest employer.

Bridgestone is also a major employer in the area, and the pharmaceutical companies BD, Merck, Purdue, and Sandoz collectively employ about a thousand people in Wilson County.[23] At any moment, at least five hundred well-paying jobs are unfilled in Wilson, and Wilson is a top-ranked small U.S. city in which to launch a startup.[24] But its downtown economic development is where Chattanooga's was twenty-five years ago: Wilson is trying to rescue its urban core and bring street-level energy to a faded set of sidewalks.

Inexpensive, ubiquitous fiber access, by itself, won't bring economic development and prosperity. Without it, however, a city is likely to be in trouble. Who will want to move there? Why will people stay? Why will new businesses show up?

CHAPTER SIX

Education and Fiber

C HATTANOOGA'S PUBLIC STEM (Science, Technology, Engineering, and Mathematics) magnet high school is in a former warehouse on the campus of Chattanooga State Community College, which was one of the first places connected to the EPB fiber optic network in 2010. So far, the coolest curriculum element using the gigabit fiber connection has been a biology project with a distant partner: the University of Southern California, located in downtown Los Angeles.[1] Professors David Caron and Richard Weisberg of USC had taken an advanced digital video microscope—called a "4K" microscope—and put it under the control of the Chattanooga students. From their desks in Chattanooga, almost two thousand miles away, the students observed live biological specimens swimming around in real time. The "movies" came across with zero delay or jitter, so the students were able to get the feel of actually operating the microscope.[2]

Keri Randolph, then the director of innovation for Hamilton County schools, told me: "The kids did experiments. They used Pacific Ocean water that we shipped back and forth, and they used Tennessee River water that we shipped back and forth." The experiments allowed the students to appreciate the complexity and beauty of the microworld on huge screens instead of tiny ones. There was something magical about having two 4K (ultra-high-definition) monitors in Chattanooga, with the USC scientists on one screen and the feed from the microscope on the other. The students were able to point together to the microscope images, and to talk to the scientists on the other screen—it was a fascinating collaboration.

At a work table in one of the STEM school "classrooms"— more like an area than a formal room, because all the walls move and none of them reach the ceiling—I sat down to talk with six STEM students who had been part of the USC microscope experiments. One student told me: "I didn't think you could see so much on there! And you get to do it yourself, hands-on." Another student, a bright senior named Erica who told me she was going to Howard University the following fall, said working with the scope made her want to major in biology. Inspiration, from eighteen hundred miles away.

Today it's a 4K microscope they're pushing and pulling; tomorrow, the operation of any form of complex equipment. Medical robots, radio telescopes, or power generation plants could be made available to students. Today the Chattanooga students are observing the world of microbes using their gigabit connectivity; tomorrow, because so much information can flow over fiber without any delay, they could be fully present in classrooms located thousands of miles away.

The only way the students were able to see microbes with 4K clarity and move the scope around in real time was with an enormous amount of data flowing back and forth between California and Tennessee, and that required Chattanooga's last-mile gigabit fiber connection.

Fiber alone, of course, doesn't provide an education. But when you use it to give students opportunities that will open up their lives, the transformations can be electrifying. Physical schools like the STEM school; schools in rural places like Nevada City, California, that aren't large enough to hire teachers for specialized classes; all-virtual skills-based courses taken by millions of people through the Coursera platform; hybrid physical/virtual schools like Minerva, which marries urban exploration with critical thinking skills; "hands-on" job training using devices and glasses that provide instant, realistic feedback to students—all of these models require last-mile fiber connections in order to function at their best and help humans thrive wherever they live. Upper-level education is changing rapidly, and mostly for the better. To be great, education needs fiber.

The Chattanooga STEM school was launched five years ago with seventy-five freshmen and now has more than two hundred ninth through twelfth graders.[3] The central hallway of its nondescript building, four miles up the Tennessee River from downtown, opens right into the classroom building at Chattanooga State Community College. Juniors and seniors enrolled in the STEM school can take as many of their classes at the college as they want, and they have the option to graduate with both a high school diploma and an associate degree. Every "ordinary" public high school in the county is allocated slots in each STEM school class, and seats are filled by lottery rather than academic achievement.[4] This is a key part of the charm of the STEM school for me: the same kids who attend Howard High could come here.

The school has a strict dress code, and a yearbook is handed out at the end of the year, but just about everything else about the school is nontraditional. The STEM school in Chattanooga seems to have figured out the recipe for student empowerment: focusing on projects instead of rote learning, weaving "content"—skills and concepts the school district and the state require—into quests that are drawn from real life and involve working with teammates who are different from one another. The school also places enormous emphasis on student engagement in running the school itself, subject to administrators' veto if a bright new idea might pose risks to students' physical and emotional safety.

When I walked in, assistant principal Jim David, a large and friendly man, greeted me. He's a booster: "I was in a traditional school for a lot of years before I came here," he said, "and you couldn't drag me away from here, not with ten horses." Many things about the STEM school represent a big upgrade to traditional schooling, and they're all connected to EPB's fiber. "It's not just about sticking fiber in a traditional school," David said. "We're fiber in a very nontraditional school."

There is a fundamental link between the school's abundance of data connectivity and its nontraditional educational model.

Upper-level students these days don't want to be talked at, but they do want to learn. Teachers can no longer hide facts—because everything can be found online—but they are still needed as coaches and mentors. An enormous amount of learning and mentoring goes on at the STEM school every day. And the advantage of the fiber connection is that it enables real-time, satisfyingly human interaction with distant resources (experts, cascades of data, other students) that had never been possible before.

Even the USC scientists had some trouble understanding that the STEM school firmly did not want them lecturing to their students. Keri Randolph said she told them, "We can give them some of those tools on our side. We want them to be scientists, not learn science." Erica, one of the students on the other end of the fiber connection to USC, said she feels sorry for her friends at other public schools. She told them, "'You have no idea what you're missing out on. I have so many opportunities that you will never know about. You missed out on being prepared for life. You missed out on an experience.'"

The school is looking for more projects that take advantage of very high bandwidth. Ken Kranz, a retired Air Force engineer, runs the school's Fab Lab ("the greatest part of the whole school, pretty much the beating heart!" said Angelica, the young student assigned to give me a tour) and wants to help students use drones to collect images of the STEM campus and make a miniature 3D model of it; processing all that data and stitching it together will take processing power that the STEM school computers don't have. Kranz wants to find a remote partner with the right computing center, and have that partner allow the STEM students to manipulate its computers from Chattanooga. The STEM school is mostly funded by the county, but many of its projects are built on partnerships with private companies and other funding elements.

One of the STEM students, Jeff, had long, messy hair and a frank way of talking. He told me that the Chattanooga STEM students recently teamed up with a school in Vermont that also had a fiber connection.[5] They had a concert: "And half of the people were in another state. And they were in rhythm, playing the same time. ... When they were actually playing and getting into it, it was like they were in the same room. It was like, wow, this actually

feels like we just created a portal connecting the rooms together."
He paused to reflect. "It was like we just stitched two parts of the
world together."

Two other schools in the district are taking a simpler approach:
they have a live stream from the aquarium downtown into a few
classrooms. It comes straight from the jellyfish tank, live, in 4K resolution, on enormous screens. It's quite a sight—a wall of jellyfish.
The students ask zillions of questions; the writing teacher brings
that view into her classroom. Their curiosity has been sparked—
a locution handed down to us from the time when electricity
was new.

There's another key connection between fiber and public schools
in Chattanooga: the availability of fiber is bringing in young tech
workers who will be working with startups that rely on Chattanooga's low-latency, high-capacity fiber connections.[6] Many of these
workers are also parents who want their public schools to be great,
and like many other parents, they will likely be engaged in their
kids' education.

Tiffanie Robinson's career was propelled by the arrival of fiber
in Chattanooga; she is an energetic, forceful, and tech-aware young
social entrepreneur. In 2015, as the parent of a five-year-old and a
toddler, she saw that the school system—the worst in the state,
chronically underfunded by the county and constantly threatened
with a state takeover—needed passionate people to get involved.[7]
And so she did: she ran against a long-time incumbent for the
county school board, and won by a hair.[8] Robinson is both the
youngest woman ever to serve on the school board and the first
white person to be elected to her particular seat.[9] She believes mid-
dle- to higher-income parents in Chattanooga don't know enough
about the schools: "There's a big trust gap, and it's really stemming
from, 'Well, that school looks like it's falling down. My kid will
never go there.' When, in reality, that school may be awesome."
She believes that if she can get young, involved, fiber-attracted parents active in the schools, she can turn the system around. "I've noticed that the lack of buy-in to our public school system creates a
lack of diversity in our schools. Which obviously creates this major
divide and huge issue whenever it comes to kids learning," she said.

Robinson, who said she knocked on just about every door in her area during her campaign, is worried about the connection between the poor quality of the city's public schools and Chattanooga's continued evolution. "If we don't fix this," she said, "we'll be trying to get better and there will be this big bump in the road. We'll just stay right here forever." For her, the tie between fiber and schooling is vital and pressing: Chattanooga is changing as it attracts businesses and people to whom a terrific internet connection is important, and those people need to be drawn into engagement with the city's public schools.

Rural educators see a direct connection between fiber and the classroom: with fiber connections, these under-resourced schools could share teachers with other similarly situated places. They could, in effect, open virtual portals to a combined, twenty-first-century one-room schoolhouse. Talking to a cheerful man named John Paul (everyone always uses his full name—he's never just John) and members of what he calls his "beloved community" in the foothills of California's Sierra Madre mountains led me to this story. Because John Paul himself has been through many of the twists of the local fiber narrative in America, it is worth pausing for a moment to introduce his community.

To get to Nevada City and Grass Valley, California, you drive east from Sacramento toward the Sierra Nevada. The sparkling late-winter morning I was there, ample rainfall had turned the flatland fields into fiestas of bright yellow forsythia; cows stood decoratively alongside the road. Route 49 winds up gentle hills covered with very tall pine trees (which play a major role in the area's connectivity challenges) into downtown Grass Valley. It's a small town of about seven thousand people, with some low-slung, ramshackle commercial buildings and a tall Art Deco movie house sign—the Del Oro.[10] Nevada City, with its charming narrow storefronts and Gold Rush atmosphere, is four miles uphill from Grass Valley and four times larger.[11] It was traditionally the place where the mine owners had their houses; the workers lived in Grass Valley. These paired towns are still somewhat at odds. In the little downtowns, Comcast is the dominant provider; right beyond those downtowns, it's copper DSL service from AT&T or mobile wireless. A lot of people complain about their internet connectivity. I chose to visit this area because it's relatively close to Silicon Valley and San Francisco and because it includes two small towns surrounded by rural, hilly, treed areas, all bundled up in a beautiful, desirable place for people to live—unless they need reliable access to data.

I turned into an empty, quiet parking lot as I waved to John Paul, a man I'd met six months before at a giant trade show in Nashville who had thrown all his energy into planning a fiber network for his area. He'd spent years grappling with both shady locals and the forces of AT&T and Comcast, and hadn't pulled it off yet; I had begun to recognize in him the optimism and half-newsy updates of someone trying to keep everyone in a boat that isn't quite seaworthy.

John Paul stood on that sidewalk in early March, waiting for me outside the South Pine Cafe in Grass Valley, a man in late middle-age with prominent upper teeth, bright-eyed and helpfully friendly, wearing a soft plaid shirt and a wide smile. He came up to Grass Valley/Nevada City twenty years ago from the Bay Area with his partner Chip Carman, both of them looking for a warmer place to live. Carman had been a networking guy, working for Mac-World and deploying the first high-capacity connection between San Francisco and Tokyo in order to deliver MacWorld content. John Paul's background was in media and advertising. Carman was more of a behind-the-scenes presence and often worked at home, while John Paul was the networker and the Rotarian. After they settled in, Carman was immediately furious about the poor internet access at their house.

It took a few years, but in 2006, Carman and John Paul launched a company they called Spiral that resells DSL internet access over copper phone lines from an office in downtown Grass Valley. Spiral was dedicated to providing first-name-basis customer service.[12] But without better lines than the copper wires over which they were reselling internet access, the service itself couldn't be any better than what AT&T was selling. So John Paul began his search for funding to support fiber.

At first, John Paul and Carman thought they might be able to bring better access to community members by hanging wireless equipment on poles that were themselves attached to fiber—cutting out the middleman of the badly maintained copper lines outside downtown. In 2009, when the Obama administration announced a grants plan supporting rural internet infrastructure, Spiral applied for funding.[13] The grant request wasn't successful; John Paul didn't notice that the local economic development agency had loaded its entire budget into the application, and a competitor, Smarter Broadband, told the federal government it could provide equivalent service at a far lower price. (Smarter Broadband, selling fixed wireless services in the area, has not been successful; the very tall trees and hills surrounding Grass Valley and Nevada City make wireless service unrealistic.)

In early 2010, Google announced that it was looking for cities to apply for Google Fiber wired connectivity—last-mile fiber optics running all the way to homes and businesses. John Paul had the idea of throwing a community parade to try to attract Google's attention. The parade led off with a visual demonstration to the crowd of just how much better fiber optic connectivity would be than what was already in place: "We had a juggler with a tennis ball, a basketball, and then this huge beach ball," he told me. "We said, 'The tennis ball is DSL, the basketball is cable, and the beach ball is gigabit fiber.' These big beach balls came out, and it was really exciting. Then we had a party; we had three bands and everybody danced." John Paul was excited and laughing as he described the goings-on, and on the wall of his office behind him was a picture of him with Carman, both dressed in Google colors. Five hundred people marched for fiber that day, but Google Fiber ultimately didn't come to Grass Valley/Nevada City.[14]

John Paul changed direction again. Fiber-to-the-home remained the goal. Spiral applied in February 2013 for state California Public Utilities advanced network funding that hadn't been used up when it was set aside to match the Obama program grants. The company was looking for $16.2 million in grant funding plus a half-million-dollar loan, and John Paul would have to raise an additional $10 million to get the network built. He brought CPUC staffers to the area to see just how tall the trees were and why a wireless network wouldn't work. Finally, in December 2015, after an arduous three-year process during which Spiral's application was challenged by Comcast, AT&T, and local fixed wireless entities that didn't want anyone else coming to the area, Spiral won the CPUC grant.[15]

In May 2014, Chip Carman was diagnosed with stage-four lower esophageal cancer. He was gone six months later. John Paul told me he promised Carman before he died, "Don't worry, I'm going to make this network happen." John Paul is still working on raising the remaining $10 million from private sources to build fiber in Nevada City/Grass Valley. He told me, "It's the Chip Carman fiber network. His name is going to be on all the cable."

One of the people I met in Grass Valley/Nevada City was Stephanie Ortiz, the dean of Sierra College, the local community college. She has more than thirty years of experience at the community college and university levels and was sporting a few streaks of purple mixed into her short black hair. Ortiz has been the executive dean since 2009; before that she was a divisional dean and a teacher of business, after a career in human resources management for the *Fresno Bee* newspaper and General Dynamics. The Grass Valley branch of Sierra College, founded in 1936, has an attractive, well-maintained hundred-acre campus and is part of a well-respected countywide system that includes three other community colleges offering more than 125 degrees and certificates—in everything from administration of justice to welding technology. About 1,600 two-year students go to classes on the Grass Valley campus, and the website says course work at that campus "is available in most degree and certificate areas, with some exceptions."[16] The problem is that Ortiz's campus can't offer what she believes her students need.

A true believer in the power of education, Ortiz told me that by sheer number of students educated, the California community college system is the largest system of higher education in the United States. Over two million students a year enroll in its classes.[17] It's an "amazing springboard," she said, for people who "do not have silver spoons in their mouths." She's convinced that the availability of high-capacity, no-delay data service "is a social justice issue that goes right to the core of how education is being delivered now and in the future."

Here's Ortiz's problem: she's in charge of a small campus with a tiny budget, and she often has to cancel classes when not enough students are enrolled to take them. Recently, she's canceled tech classes—classes on coding or on particular computer applications—because of thin student populations. She desperately wants to provide engineering courses that then transfer to the baccalaureate level. Her dream is that if the much larger Rocklin campus thirty-seven miles southwest of Grass Valley had a class, her campus and the Truckee campus (an hour in the opposite direction) could each contribute two or three students to it, sharing the cost of the teacher. With fiber last-mile connections to all campuses, she said, "we could then live-stream to all three campuses and have kind of a one-room schoolhouse."

Unconstrained internet connectivity could also help her students plan for their post-college future—something that Ortiz says few know how to do—by opening their eyes to other worlds. "Our younger people need more career guidance than they receive, and they probably don't receive enough guidance, the vast majority of them." So students end up doing, by default, what their parents or grandparents did. "It's a part of their education that's really missing." She's particularly concerned about the young men up here, who are often hopeless and jobless, and she wants structures to help them find work. "They deserve guidance," Ortiz told me, "and they deserve it from society, and the best place to get it at this juncture, I think, is from their educational providers."

Twenty miles farther east in the canyons and hills above Nevada City is the even tinier community of Washington. It's all tall trees and rivers. Rorie Gotham, an ethereal older woman with white ringlets and large brown eyes, told me Washington has "only 166 registered voters and 12 kids in our little two-room schoolhouse." She loves living there, she told me, on a street called Alpha Loop with the constant noise of water around her. "The view from the stove and the living room is of the river and the mountains off in the distance, and I don't see another house."

But she's worried about the downside of that isolation, namely the effect her community's poor internet access will have on those kids: "Our school is disadvantaged because we're a two-room schoolhouse. If we could get high-speed internet down there, we could improve the educational process. Right now it's one teacher with an aide trying to accommodate K through 8. The students could get materials that are a lot more conducive to their learning and the grade that they're in." Where Gotham lives, you can't even buy a DSL subscription; until very recently people were using dial-up connections.[18] People try to get by these days using satellite internet access, but it's extremely expensive and you hit your data limit very quickly. "If you want to have movies or music or something like that, then you're paying 120 bucks a month," said Gotham. That's far more than people in the area can afford. And you can't do anything that requires immediate response from a remote computer, like make a two-way video call.

For someone who looks like a delicate sprite-child, Gotham was surprisingly firm about this: "We must educate our children," she said. "If we don't educate our children at least to take care of themselves, we make the biggest mistake ever. I mean, there's no reason to dumb down an American citizen. This is a land of opportunity, right? Every person deserves to have information. Who is this group of people who chooses to ignore basic things at the biggest level? That's wrong." She glared at me, her be-ringed hands and immaculate nails flashing.

Although the federal government has tried in its $3.9 billion E-rate program to subsidize internet access over fiber to schools across the country, students in Washington, Grass Valley, Truckee, and Nevada City are among the 1.2 million Californian students who don't have access to that bandwidth. More than 11 million students across the country don't have the internet access they need for learning while they're at school, and tens of millions more don't have the access they need to do homework from home.[19] Singapore, by contrast, made getting gigabit access to 100 percent of its schools a goal for 2015, and did it. New Zealand has committed to getting fiber to 99.9 percent of students by 2017. Finland makes 100 Mbps access for students a basic right.[20]

In my travels, I kept hearing about non-college alternatives aimed at getting people into good jobs with local businesses. I started with a bias toward traditional colleges. Both my father and his father taught at traditional universities and loved that life.

But the more I listened to people around the country, the more I became convinced that a college education isn't for everyone. It isn't for Americans who don't enjoy thinking about abstract concepts. As time goes on, I've grown less and less sure what a university is good for.

I met Stephen Kosslyn during the fall of 2012, when he was considering leaving the Stanford Center for Advanced Study in the Behavioral Sciences to start an entirely new and mostly online educational venture. He had already left Harvard after thirty years and was clearly in an intense mulling period. Several months later, in April 2013, the news broke that he had made the leap and become dean of faculty for the Minerva Project. He replied to my note of ebullient congratulations: "I decided to roll the dice. It's unlikely I'll ever again have the opportunity to 'make a dent in the universe,' and the team here is fabulous. So far, so good."

Things have gone extremely well for the Minerva Project. They handle about three hundred students a year who rotate through term-long stays in dorms in various global cities—San Francisco, Berlin, Buenos Aires, Seoul, Hyderabad, Taipei, and London—and are expected to immerse themselves in these cities while studying.[21] Each class, of the more than seventy on offer, has no more than nineteen students, and all those classes are conducted online using an active learning platform (they call it the Active Learning Forum, or ALF) developed by the school. ALF records every seminar and provides an enormous amount of data about students' participation to teachers in real time, making immediate, frequent feedback possible as the students move seamlessly between discussion, breakout groups, debates, simulations, quizzes, polls, and team presentations.[22] The Minerva belief, supported by a 1972 study, is that memory is enhanced by "deep" cognitive tasks: applying material and talking about it rather than reading it quietly.[23] There's much feedback, personal attention, and no lectures—just what the Chattanooga STEM students told me they wanted. Very few students leave the program, and more than twenty thousand apply each year for the three hundred spots.[24]

Minerva uses the "flipped classroom" model, in a sense, for foundational courses: before they start classes that require background knowledge in things like calculus and economics, Minerva students take large online courses (known as Massive Open Online Courses, or MOOCs) on their own time. As Kosslyn put it,

"MOOCs are for information transmission. We're about information use, which is a different thing." Once they demonstrate mastery of the MOOC material, students are ready to participate in the Minerva seminars. Minerva professors are trained at length to understand the science of learning and map that into active discussion and participation by students, and they are expected to be educators, not cross-subsidized researchers. Many professors are interested: Minerva had more than sixteen hundred applications for nineteen teaching positions in 2017. The project will measure success by the quality of opportunities their students have when they graduate.[25]

One key metric says the project is doing well: student retention is north of 90 percent.[26] All of the employers, including Apple, Twitter, and Ashoka, who have had Minerva students as interns have said they would be happy to have them again. The annual cost is about $30,000, far less than the price of tuition for a year at Harvard or Stanford.[27] And a great fiber connection is unquestionably necessary for the Minerva model to reach its full potential.

It's a two-hour drive from Greensboro to Wilson, North Carolina, and Durham is in the middle, so I stopped at Duke University to visit a college friend named Daniel Egger. I'd never been to Duke before, and the uniformity and promise of the grand Collegiate Gothic buildings made me wonder why anyone would want to go anywhere else. Egger, now the executive in residence in Duke's Master of Engineering Management Program, wonders why people are spending so much time at universities at all.

One of the MOOC sources for Minerva basic learning is the battery of Coursera courses available online. Egger developed one of Coursera's most popular courses, Mastering Data Analytics in Excel.[28] It is one of five, all developed by Egger, that students can take to get a specialization certificate in data science from the University of Illinois. He tells me that people routinely list Coursera specialization certificates on their resumes—they're just as proud of them as they are of any other degree, and Coursera certificates have become a widely recognized informal credentialing system. Videos must last no longer than eight minutes, Egger told me, on the theory that "most people are doing the course in their little

snippets of free time"; all learning objectives have to be fully operational, as in "You will know how to calculate the optimum value
for the certain price of a good when there's a demand curve." "It's
very concrete," Egger said. "For a lot of people, the basic nuts and
bolts skills are incredibly valuable." Online learners can watch all
the videos for free; only those who pay can take the graded quizzes.

Until recently, Coursera's CEO was former Yale president
Richard Levin. Coursera reaches tens of millions of learners—
note, these are "learners," not students—around the globe, offering
thousands of courses. As of mid-2017, 164 universities around the
world had deals with the company, and hundreds of businesses are
starting to ask for skills content customized for their needs to be
made accessible through the platform.[29] You can offer a Coursera
course only if you are a faculty member at a university with which
Coursera has a master agreement, and your university has to back
you to do it. That's a pretty good filtering function for quality control. Although you can get an online degree through Coursera,
such as the master of computer science in data science offered by
the University of Illinois, I'm more interested in what Levin calls
"micro-credentials" and the courses sponsored by businesses.

The physical campus of Yale, I'm confident, will still be here
and still be valuable five years from now. What Yale and a handful
of other great universities offer is what a healthy, thriving city offers: proximity, density, fizz, resources, beauty, and interesting people; what Levin calls "education outside the classroom." But not
everyone wants or needs or can spare the time or money to gain
that experience. Millions of people want skills, techniques, and
learning that can be acquired in a classroom—but without also
buying everything that is currently bundled with that classroom.

Coursera, through its relationships with businesses, is learning
a great deal about what it takes to bring a learner into an actual
paying job. Its partner businesses can help Coursera identify the
skills considered necessary in today's business environment, and
someday, with adequate two-way connectivity, Coursera mentors
could help students directly as they go from goal to goal and move
toward employment. Without fiber, genuine eye contact and full-
size, fully human assistance—akin to physical presence—won't flow
easily among these teachers and mentors and students. To fill large

screens with real-time, real-seeming images and be able to respond and interact in real-time, real-seeming ways, you need last-mile fiber. "For the promise of barrier-less access to the world's knowledge and to great teachers," Egger said, "you've got to have great connectivity."

Certificates, skills, adult education: that's the workforce development model that mayor Andy Berke of Chattanooga is focused on, and the one Nevada City/Grass Valley and Greensboro don't seem to have. It's working well in Chattanooga, but students must physically go to a center, with its high fixed costs for buildings and grounds, in order to access adult education opportunities. Once they get there, they are able to step into jobs. Berke points out to me that although the local community college, Chattanooga State, has a graduation rate of only about 10–11 percent, the Tennessee College of Applied Technology (TCAT), which is located on the same campus but is not part of the community college, has about an 80 percent completion rate and a 94 percent placement rate. It provides certificate training in computer technology, machining technology, and a host of other job-focused skills.[30]

TCAT works in partnership with local employers. Volkswagen, for example, which is doing a large hiring push in Chattanooga and now employs more than thirty-two hundred people, has set up a five-week Volkswagen Neighborhood Talent Pipeline program that rewards its graduates with a Chattanooga Manufacturing Excellence certificate from TCAT. Jared Bigham, the executive director of Chattanooga 2.0, a foundation-funded effort aimed at improving educational opportunities for all Chattanoogans, said the Talent Pipeline program was launched after he got fed up with people saying "Volkswagen can't fill jobs." He asked, "Well, does TCAT know what Volkswagen is looking for?" He got vague responses, so he drove to Volkswagen and asked for a page of bullet points listing what the company wanted in entry-level employees—which turned out to be not so much skills as traits, dispositions, and affinity for the jobs available. Bigham took that list and brought it to TCAT, which created a program that has now been widely deployed. Seniors in their spring semester can take this program for free, and graduate with both a high school diploma and a credential that guarantees them a well-paying entry-level manufacturing job at Volkswagen's Chattanooga plant. Both Volkswagen and the city knew in setting up this program that they had to reach students where they are, so students can go to a neighborhood center—the Brainerd Youth & Family Development Center, located in a high-poverty area of Chattanooga—rather than the distant Chattanooga (Chatt) State campus.

Similarly, in partnership with Chatt State and the local school district, Volkswagen has launched what it calls a Mechatronics Academy. High school graduates can simultaneously apprentice at the VW plant, working in robotics or on welding, and in three years earn a specialized technical associate's degree from the community college as well as a certificate from the German-American Chamber of Commerce allowing the graduate to work abroad with Volkswagen. It's a wildly popular program, as are the many industry-specific certifications offered by TCAT.[31]

What if people looking for high-paying entry-level advanced manufacturing jobs could get safety and expertise training at home? Going to college may not be for everyone, but getting a credential that employers will value is enormously popular. And it can be a way of helping students figure out whether they actually want the jobs for which they are being trained. Many people don't realize they've made a bad decision until they've actually taken a job; churn in advanced manufacturing jobs is alarmingly high— around 40 percent, Jared Bigham told me.

There's a chicken-and-egg quality to the certification narrative: to go beyond talking and pointing, toward actually getting a feel for the job—touching the controls and wielding the machines—you need haptic (touch-sensitive) controllers and augmented reality or virtual reality glasses. The word *haptic* comes from Greek words meaning "suitable for touch" or "palpable." "Haptics" allows humans to interact with the digital world through touch; the device, in turn, gives the user feedback in the form of force or vibrations that create the sensation of physical connection. "Virtual reality" glasses immerse the user in a digitally created 360-degree world (that feels absolutely real to your stomach and brain); "augmented reality" glasses allow you to see a layer of digital information on top of the physical world. Add these things together and you can have students exploring new jobs. Veterinarians are already using a Haptic Cow and Haptic Horse to train students about their future patients' internal organs.[32] There's no need for any of this to be isolating: with enough bandwidth, anyone can work in a team to learn new skills.

But to be available to everyone, those devices and glasses need to be inexpensive. That in turn requires a big market for them, so it is worthwhile for manufacturers to invest in the research and materials development needed to make them cheaper. Which, in turn, requires fiber everywhere: without very high bandwidth flowing almost instantaneously between these devices and the remote computers that respond to them, they will remain wacky and unfamiliar one-offs. You may scoff, but you shouldn't. Haptics and VR/AR devices are just appliances.

People used to think that refrigerators were extraordinary luxuries not needed by everyone. A 1926 Frigidaire electric refrigerator from General Motors cost $285, the equivalent of nearly $4,000 today, and an ad for it shows a Wall Street man in a formal golf outfit and his extraordinarily well-dressed wife gazing into the open doors of their miraculous new Frigidaire with anticipation and wonder. A salesman had visited their house to consult with them about having a refrigerator, because that's the way it was done in those days, and the couple has clearly just come in from a morning of golf (there's a magnificent touring car drawn on the border of the advertisement, and a set of golf clubs lie at the couple's feet) to admire the new thing that invisible hired hands have installed while they were out. The ad copy reads: "Satisfaction . . . *that only Frigidaire can give.*" It's called an "Electric" refrigerator because electricity was still a glamorous item.[33] (Just as in the early 2000s "e-commerce" was still a thing; today it's just commerce.) The ad is aimed at women, because they are the ones who will persuade their husbands to buy these devices, and the wife in the ad is tightly clasping her hands in front of her throat and rising to her toes in her high-heeled shoes with amazed delight: her dearest desire has been fulfilled. Today we can't imagine life without refrigeration. The same reasoning goes for haptics and AR/VR glasses.

One piece of great news for education, human relationships, and every other realm of human endeavor is that when haptics and glasses become cheap, we will stop looking down at our phones. True, we will all be wearing glasses. But the stooped-over, lost look of gazing at a phone will seem just as strange to us as this 1926 electric refrigerator ad looks today, with its well-dressed man bending his knees and leaning forward to examine the interior of this amazing new device.

To ensure that every American has the opportunity to thrive, we desperately need these advances in adult certification and training to be put in place as soon as possible. We need to do a far better job preparing young people for a successful launch into the labor market. The kind of adult education program Chattanooga is working to provide is sorely lacking in parts of the United States where adult education was decimated budgetarily during the Great Recession. Adult training can step in and be a delivery mechanism for younger males, in particular, that don't take to school. We could do this, at a distance, with great communications connections, for everyone who wants it in every corner of the country.

Many important elements of America's education story require fiber connections. With more last-mile fiber everywhere, more students at every level can have exciting, hands-on engagement with great educational resources, both conceptual and applied, wherever those resources happen to be located—as the STEM Chattanooga students had with the microscope at USC—and more students will be able to do their homework online. With fiber, local institutions can share the cost of teachers. More students who want to go to a great university but can't afford it can study online; if Minerva scales, it will provide excellent seminar-like education for thousands of students. Many more students who don't want to go to college can find and pursue certificate training, either through an all-online model like Coursera or, even more promisingly, a hybrid certificate model that is done in conjunction with local businesses and includes some online-only content (like the TCAT model). And once haptic and VR/AR devices become commonplace, "hands-on" training can become standard wherever you happen to be.

With fiber connections, the kind of personalized mentoring and goals-discussion young adults need could be made possible by older people who are not nearby—a whole new job category. The dispossessed young men Stephanie Ortiz worries about and any student waiting for the clock to tick in his or her middle-school classroom all need this.

For students—or rather, *learners*—this is a good moment. If we insist on excellent, equal fiber connectivity everywhere, plus general support for dynamic forms of common education to spur workforce development, learners will have many more possible paths to follow.

A structural, seemingly immovable obstacle in the way of this student-centered future is the same one we stumble over for the fiber discussion as a whole: how much does it matter to Americans in any given community that all children, and not just their children or their relatives' children, have similar opportunities? Insufficient government support for public schools has many causes. Communities have different ways of funding their school systems, and the balance of power among local, county, state, and federal actors is constantly shifting (and again is different in different regions). But the disparity and equity problems are real and getting worse, triggering limited opportunities and cramped social mobility for increasing numbers of Americans.

Bernadine Joselyn, of Minnesota, ties everything together—education, fiber, a caring community—into a message of hope. "The connection is really about helping people feel hopeful about what's possible," she told me. Joselyn spent part of her life living in Russia, and saw a deep contrast with the United States during her time there. In Minnesota, you assume that things work and that you can trust the system. "In Russia," she said, "it's very much not that way. It's a deeply broken system, where people are cynical and checked out. And they think that if you follow the rules you're a chump. . . . There's just an assumption that you gotta take care of your own first because it's a scary place out there." She goes on: "The infrastructure alone does nothing. The real endgame is really about people integrating the technology and harnessing it up to their dreams about equal access and equal opportunity for everybody."

I typed these words in the Rose Reading Room of the New York Public Library, one of the most beautiful public spaces in New York City. One day, walking into the grand marble ground floor of the library building, I looked up and saw these words carved on a pillar:

ON THE DIFFUSION OF EDUCATION

AMONG THE PEOPLE

REST THE PRESERVATION

AND PERPETUATION

OF OUR FREE INSTITUTIONS

The quote is unattributed, but it comes from a speech Daniel Webster delivered around 1837.[34] For Webster, the survival of liberal democracy depended on access to education for everyone. "Open the doors of the schoolhouse to all the children in the land," he said. "Let no man have the excuse of poverty for not educating his own offspring." He believed we could better prevent crime through education than through detention or punishment—education would "provide for its never occurring." It is a fine speech. It is part of the great American doctrine of fairness of opportunity. I think Webster was right, and every corner of this country will need fiber to make his words come true.

CHAPTER SEVEN

Health and Fiber

IMAGINE YOU'VE JUST FALLEN backward down two flights of stairs in your house and landed on your back, in terrible pain. Luckily, someone was nearby (or you were able to blink significantly through your digitally enabled glasses, which somehow stayed firmly on your head as you tumbled) to summon emergency assistance. Now two burly men are gingerly examining you and beginning to move you onto a board and then a stretcher for transport to the local hospital.

They have a tablet with them that allows the attending physician back at the hospital to be essentially present at the scene. It's your local geriatric care doctor, whom you have seen often in person, both in his office and, when you had home appointments, on your living room wall. The doctor supervises what the emergency medical technicians are doing and asks you questions. At the same time, he is accessing your records to check whether the heart or pain medication the technicians have on hand can or should be given to you right away. He is reviewing radiology results from an injury you suffered in a car accident six months ago. And he is scheduling scanning and surgeries in your local hospital and putting people and resources in place that will be waiting when you arrive. This is the kind of care you expect—it's been this way since you were a child, but this is your first fall as a frail eighty-year-old, and you are scared. The voice of your doctor, and a glimpse of his face when you can manage to open your eyes for an instant, are immensely comforting to you.

Or imagine you are a bright but lonely teenager in a remote area. Your parents are doing their best, but you have shut them out of your inner life. They chose a place to raise their only child that is peaceful and quiet, and you are grateful for that, but you are experiencing overwhelming anxiety that you do not understand and feel powerless to stop. You have friends at school, but they are busy with their lives and their own inner demons, and you'd rather not have them know how awful you feel each morning. The one light in this darkness comes several times a week, when you join in a group session with other kids your own age—facilitated by a skilled counselor hundreds of miles away from any of you—during which you all talk about whatever is on your minds. The weekly individual sessions you have with that counselor are also important to you. She can see every part of your facial expressions and body language while you sit and talk together; she can tell when you are hiding your emotions and gently call you on it; you can see her care and respect for you in her eyes. You trust her and you feel less alone.

These low-cost, high-quality health services are not a reality. At the same time, we spend more than $3 trillion each year on health care, upward of $10,000 a person, twice what most other developed countries spend. Health care spending is growing at a faster rate than the national economy. Something like 30 percent of our spending is excessive, because we pay such high prices for our fee-for-service reimbursement system—and suppliers have enormous market power. According to Bob Kocher, a partner at the Silicon Valley venture capital firm Venrock, "We waste the equivalent of the entire health care system of Spain annually." Yet Americans' life expectancies are shorter than those in other developed nations, and our rates of infant mortality and diabetes—on which we spend more than $240 billion a year—are higher. The largest share, 32 percent, of the $3.3 trillion goes to hospital care, followed by care from doctors and other clinicians (20 percent); most spending goes to about 35 million Americans who have multiple chronic diseases and are poor.[1]

Every part of the health care system could be vastly improved by eliminating distance, bringing data, doctors, and counselors where they're needed via communications networks, rather than making 330 million Americans travel to where these specialists and databases are. Preventive care for people living in at-risk zip codes needs to be revolutionized. Elder care needs to support people living in private homes and apartments. People suffering from chronic illnesses and mental health issues need ongoing support. What needs to change? The methods of helping—so that patients receive more timely, convenient, less expensive, and more personalized care. In order for patients to get the care they need when and where they need it, and feel a sense of engagement and autonomy, we'll need fiber everywhere.

Most U.S. states already require private insurers and Medicaid to reimburse for a wide range of telemedicine-provided services without discrimination. But the field is still in its infancy: often, "telemedicine" means either very-low-bandwidth remote patient monitoring (of blood pressure, for example), or simply a phone call with a provider. It's hard to imagine a doctor-patient relationship forming through just phone calls, emails, text messages, and online questionnaires. Several states have restricted or banned reimbursement for telemedicine services that fall short of full-bandwidth communications. That makes sense: the game-changing, cost-reducing developments will require the real-time, reliable, visible presence of health professionals in patients' actual lives; a human, two-way connection that can convey empathy and compassion as well as two-figure data updates. Those are the connections that can vastly reduce the country's spending on hospital and in-office care.

The problem is that the vast majority of Americans—upward of 84 percent of us—don't live in a house that has a fiber connection to the outside world.[2] And unless we upgrade to fiber as a country, we will never be the nation with the world's most advanced health care system. Instead, we will make more people unsafe and sicker, keep people waiting unnecessarily at medical offices and hospitals all over the country, and spend untold billions on services that are inadequately tailored to people's individual needs.

To look to the future, consider Sweden. The United States will never be a social democracy, and Sweden's health care system—fully government funded, paid for by taxes rather than through insurance—is completely unlike ours. But one element of the Swedish experience should be instructive here in the United States: in the beginning of the Swedish movement toward fiber optics, decades ago, they didn't really foresee its uses for health. Now that they are able to consult a doctor online or easily move enormous medical files around, Swedes see health care as necessarily powered by fiber communications.

I talked to Fredrik Jung-Abbou, a young man who has launched a Swedish business called KRY that allows patients to see doctors in real time over video. To book an appointment with KRY, you securely log into an app using your bank ID; you can upload images of symptoms if that's applicable. You ask for an appointment time, and then a doctor calls you through the app. The video is encrypted and not recorded, and the doctor keeps a record of the visit, which costs about $30. If you need a prescription or a referral, he or she can take care of that.[3]

The reliability and capacity of fiber make a huge difference when it comes to health. "If you are running a game on your cellphone over Wi-Fi," Jung-Abbou said, "it's not that important if it is an unreliable connection. Once you start running more important services that are more precious to you, like health, well, I think we will have a lot of pride that we did this [installed fiber in Sweden] ten years back."

Reliable health care at a distance couldn't happen without fiber, he said. "The countries that haven't invested in fiber before, they'll start seeing the pains now." He has launched his service in London as well as in Sweden, but it is text-based in the United Kingdom "because we don't know if the video experience is strong enough for the client. In Sweden, we can skip the text part any day because we know the video part runs so smooth."

Jung-Abbou thinks "it's the video part that makes it more interesting. The experience of talking and seeing and [the doctor] being able to really see your skin and eyes." The barrier in Sweden is not infrastructure but reimbursement; he's had to spend a great deal of time persuading Swedish county councils that KRY's services should be reimbursed. The first country council to budge was Varmland County, in central Sweden, which launched a pilot using KRY at the end of 2016.[4]

Based on the data he's seeing and the reviews KRY has gotten, Jung-Abbou said his customers think "this is better than going to the physical doctor." Customers "are exhilarated by the time they save, all the hassle, all the logistics, and the quality of the video meeting is great, so it creates a real-life communication experience." In Sweden, they think about fiber as electricity. "It's just there," said Jung-Abbou, in every remote corner of the country. "That's where the U.S. needs to move to."

In addition to imagining doctors' visits, consider fiber's benefits for old age and isolation. Again, there's a lesson from Sweden, which has no system of assisted-living centers; the only public-paid facilities are nursing homes, and they're hard to get into. "You need to be really sick," said Stéphanie Treschow, founder of a company called Villa Nest that will provide a new form of assisted living for seniors. At the same time, the population is aging rapidly: by 2045, according to Statistics Sweden, a quarter of Swedes will be over sixty-five, and the country's fully public care system probably won't be able to cope with their needs.[5] Treschow is negotiating with five cities in Sweden to place Villa Nest housing facilities for people over fifty-five that will provide a transition between the period they can still stay at home and the time they need to be in a nursing home. Those seniors will be using technology services that will allow them to push a button to call their doctor, schedule an appointment for the same day, and then talk to the doctor over video. Treschow told me, "I think we're slightly ahead of the curve because people keep saying, 'Well, the elderly, they won't understand technology. They don't know how to use this.' That's no longer true. They're absolutely super capable of managing technology. Especially when it comes to iPads."

When it comes to fiber, it's never about the fiber itself but rather what it enables. For example, iPads connected to a fiber network are ideal for an older person. The device is big but still capable of being held comfortably by an arthritic and trembling hand, the text on it can be big, and the interface can be really simple: just buttons saying, "Call doctor," "Call home health care provider." Or prompts like "Don't forget to take your medication." Wearables, tied into the same communications capacity, could augment this system, triggering warnings to both you and your doctor when your blood pressure goes too high. The home health care aide could visit by camera at times. That's already happening in Vasteras, a municipality in Sweden that has been a pilot site for experimenting with health care technology. Public care can be hit-or-miss. "Where I live, in a suburb north of Stockholm, we have 770 elderly using home care, and 11 providers," Treschow told me. A senior could wait a long time, feeling isolated and lonely, for someone to show up. Treschow plans to make her for-pay services quite inexpensive, so that she'll gain many customers. "I'm doing this a bit early," she said. "I do understand that, but in ten years' time or even in five years' time, everybody's going to be doing this."

Here in America we'll need to catch up quickly. Over the next fifteen years, the number of elderly in the United States will grow by more than 50 percent, at the same time that elderly people are becoming dramatically more willing to accept and embrace technology. Today's fifty-year-old is (relatively) technology-savvy and, whether he or she lives in a rural or urban area, will very likely want to age in place: a recent AARP survey showed that nearly 90 percent of Americans sixty-five or older want to stay in their homes as long as possible.[6] They'll need to be connected to fiber in order for their quality of life to be its best.

The obstacles in Sweden are not people like Jung-Abbou or Treschow. But as in the United States, an enormous barrier to success in telemedicine is the attitude of the entities reimbursing for services; in the United States, that's the private insurance market, and in Sweden, it's the government. But the structural barriers are the same.

In Stockholm, in the offices of the local county council, I talked to Daniel Forslund. He's a young, fast-talking man in a hurry who has been charged with leading the county's strategy for e-healthcare and government innovation. (Sweden is divided into twenty counties or regions; counties, not cities, have responsibility for health care and transportation, while cities are responsible for elder care.)[7] Forslund, the first county councilor in the country to be designated as responsible for innovation in his region, is focused on the county's pilot experiments to test the appropriateness of treating online services as reimbursable equivalents of in-person visits. In collaboration with researchers from the Karolinska Institute, four general practitioner clinics in the Hässelby-Vällingby borough of Stockholm are trying video-based visits for people with chronic illnesses or who otherwise need frequent care.

Forslund told me he is interested in reforming the county's reimbursement systems so that video conferencing is a "true and integral part of the health care offer" for all residents of the Stockholm region. Without reform, clinics have to resist providing services in the most effective way: you can't get services online because "you have to go through my door then I get reimbursed." He went on: "That created such strange incentives, because you are locked into the older ways of working because that's the only way you can do it."

Forslund is lucky; like all Swedes involved in health care, he's confident that his patients will be able to connect. "All of this requires good fiber connections, both in the clinic and to the home of the patient," he said. "I feel very comfortable doing this because we have such a great fiber infrastructure. In Stockholm City, about 96 percent of all homes have at least a 100 Mb connection. . . . The coverage of e-health services is much better [in Stockholm than in the United States] because no one is left behind on the digital level." In the future, Forslund predicted, "you will as a patient want to have access to huge quantities of data. You will want to see that film from your operation or from the MRI scan. You will want to see how everything is working with your tissues and joints, and you will want to produce live streamed data from your connected device—a glucose level, or your heartbeat, or anything else—and that will require very large data connections from the individual patient to the health care sector."

These connections will need to be extremely secure and reliable: "If I'm on life support in my home," he said, "I will really be dependent on my fiber cable into the home to be meeting top-notch standards." He pointed out that we would never accept the low-tech level of current health services—faxes! required in-office visits!—in any other part of society. We're simply used to a lower service level in health.

The pilot studies in Hässelby-Vällingby are designed to help researchers develop new ways to measure the quality of patient care—not just counting the number of sessions, but also looking hard at quality-of-life metrics and outcomes. Forslund is also interested in effects on medical staff quality of life. "We're putting a lot of emphasis on describing value created for individual citizens, individual health professionals, for society, and for tax payers," he told me. His studies are also testing the effects of increasing the level of reimbursement for home-care services for the chronically ill and elderly, on the assumption that paying more for at-home health care over video will save the county bundles of money while sacrificing nothing in quality of care. He has to start with small pilots to ensure he can answer all the objections that institutions always raise; he needs to pinpoint all the risks and have answers to them.

Forslund is particularly excited about focusing on e-health for elderly people, for whom getting to the doctor can be an ordeal. "People think that, 'Well, this is kind of cool, [these are] new ways of meeting health care needs for you and me who like technology and are fairly young and tech savvy.' Perhaps the most value will come when my grandmother doesn't have to go out in the snow in the mid-winter and fall on the pavement because she is going to the primary care clinic. Now she can sit on her sofa and have a dialogue with her doctor online."

Forslund told me that in the thinly populated north of Sweden, health care services over fiber have been routine for years, but mostly via connections between small local clinics and large regional hospitals. His pilot studies are forging the way toward individual services in homes, and he hopes to expand them to reach the general patient population as well as patients in more sparsely populated areas.

He's also interested in identifying the cost to society of *not* reimbursing fiber-based online services. "If we don't have it," he said flatly, "it costs us perhaps billions a year because we lose so much productivity in so many areas of health care." He's got the fiber; he just needs to change the reimbursement models.

In Chattanooga, Dr. Allen Coffman is leading an ambitious effort to use school clinics in elementary schools, and EPB's fiber connections to those schools, as central places for local families to get health services. Families in poorer areas often don't have the access to transportation needed to get basic preventive care, but everyone trusts the school nurse and can find his or her way to the school. He's focused on areas of concentrated poverty within EPB's service area—five zip codes where most of Chattanooga's black and Hispanic people live.

What he tells me about health outcomes in those five zip codes is terrifying. "We're on pace now to have, by 2020, a third of our adolescents finish high school obese," he said. "You look at the projected impact that's going to have on health, and it's just mind-blowing." Many kids already have type 2 diabetes or joint problems. Many young adults can't get jobs because they simply can't move. My face must have registered surprise at this, because Coffman went on to explain: it's not as if at one time these kids were active and then something happened. "These kids have been obese forever, always," he said. "It's a whole new adult patient population that's going to be coming out of the pipeline that our payment systems just can't handle." It's not just obesity, either, that dogs youngsters in these areas; they've got behavioral issues, attention deficit–hyperactivity disorder, anxiety, depression, and asthma, at rates that far exceed those in richer zip codes. Infant mortality in these areas is three times what it is in areas more populated by whites.

Everything maps into those five zip codes, he noted: low levels of school readiness, high absenteeism, food insecurity, high crime, lack of street lights, lack of public transportation. And in those five zip codes there are about 4,200 kids, out of a total population of about 11,000 school-age children, who don't have access to primary care services at all—often for logistical reasons.[8] "Parents working shifts, nobody available, grandma can't drive, mom is disabled," he said. "It's completely like we need UPS to come in and look at this issue."

Coffman is a very busy pediatrician. In his spare time, as a "hobby," he laughed, he has launched a plan aimed at asthma, "even though what we're trying to do is build better comprehensive health." (Everything from tulips to palm trees can grow in Chattanooga's climate, but the downside is that pollen seems endemic to Chattanooga's valley; the beautiful mountains that encircle the city trap the air, and the pollen combines with high ozone levels and particulate matter from car exhaust to create a lot of bad air days.)[9]

Coffman thinks he can short-circuit poor families' logistical barriers in getting access to care by bringing telemedicine services to the schools and helping school nurses act as care coordinators. Like Daniel Forslund, Allen Coffman is focused on a series of pilot studies; his are in five elementary schools, each of which provides free or reduced-price lunches to 99 percent of its students. He hopes that the pilots will be so valuable that people will ask, "Why aren't these in our high schools?"

School nurses are highly trusted, Coffman has learned, and many families rely on them exclusively for all forms of health care. "They're a part of the family, where the teachers are not seen as such," he told me. Parents in Chattanooga schools say, " 'When the teachers call me it's always something bad. The [school] clinic is a good place that I trust.' " He's been working on training the school nurses, most of whom are underappreciated by their schools, to use a telemedicine unit to consult with doctors in the downtown children's hospital. To the child who has come to her clinic office and, if available, a parent or other responsible adult, the nurse will say, according to Coffman, "You know me, I'm here with you and I'm here to help. We'll talk to the doctor through the computer, and then I can actually show them things about you. Then they'll help us figure out what's going on, and they can write a prescription and we can have it delivered. And you can get it. Isn't that great?" The school nurse's empathy helps the child navigate the telemedicine setup.

It's still too early to talk about outcomes. Coffman is midstream on a host of plans. He's also working on having a community clinic pediatrician see patients in her clinic office and then follow up via a telemedicine link to the school with the child, a parent, and the child's teacher all together on the other side. "So often," he said, "People don't get this as a systemic problem. There aren't resources right now. There's no way you could make this a short-term revenue-producing business model with a hospital system or within a county government." He knows the long-term payoffs of his approach will be enormous, even though the medical community he is in "is just not concerned at all."

At the same time, he's clear-eyed. He knows that the cultural obstacles, the logistical problems, the trauma experienced by the people living in those five Chattanooga zip codes make any easy answers impossible. As damaging as the medical establishment's indifference is what he calls "medical populism": doctors who resist treating their patients in new ways, and patients who want to "rule their bodies" yet take the position that "there better be something out there to help me later." He sees experimentation through pilot studies, knowing your population, listening to what they're saying, encouraging further development of plans that are working and killing off the ones that aren't, as the only way to make progress. Everyone needs to realize, he told me, that "we're in a system that goes to destruction. If everyone just takes care of their own and just gets theirs, over time it degrades."

Eventually, he said, we will have to see health as a part of a community's infrastructure, like streets, air quality, and recreation. Rural counties in particular will need to take a regional approach to health in order to remain sustainable. "Who's going to build a plant in a county that doesn't have birthing services, that doesn't have a pediatrician?" he asked. But in both rural and urban areas, schools can be community health hubs that serve every child and use tele-medicine links to connect them to distant resources—including, crucially, psychiatric services that can address mental health issues. "If you have no capacity to absorb bad stuff," he noted, "at some point your life is going to go horribly wrong. We live in a chaotic world. How do we build capacity into these kids, so that as they go on, they can roll with the punches and be resilient?"

Pediatric health systems are cheap: "It's a rounding error com-pared to what we spend on highways." Through these school hubs, parents could get affirmative (rather than reactive or opportunistic) information about their children's development so they could parent appropriately. Communities and regions that can take on the eco-nomic development challenge of pediatric care based in schools will be able to turn the tide, he thinks, giving everyone the opportunity to thrive. And a key part of the "organic progressivism," as he calls it, that will make these communities successful is the ability to "be open to new technology and look at how it pays off." In his view, that means two-way video communication. That, in turn, means these communities will have to have last-mile fiber connections to make two-way video a realistic and cheap commodity available to everyone.

There's a strong connection among education, health, and fiber. Consider the problem of sick youngsters who can't get to school.

Twenty-six-year-old Karen Dolva is one of three entrepreneurs who founded No Isolation, a Norwegian company that uses technology to address loneliness. She's a computer science graduate who began noticing that technology developed for the elderly "did not solve their problems, nor meet standards that you and I would expect." And then she noticed that other groups were being disrespected: "I have a friend who's a nurse, and she'd been talking to me about the children's department at the hospital she works at, and how sad it is that children just stay there. Nothing is going on." She was talking to friends over a beer about the effects of loneliness, on them and on the elderly, and then it came to her: What happens to those kids in the hospital when they're lonely?

On-the-ground research revealed to Dolva that the school connection with sick kids was a priority for parents. She decided she wanted to bring some kind of telepresence solution into classrooms on behalf of very sick kids, "because we can't physically bring them there." She also learned that "the teachers cannot be involved because they do not have the time to set up a computer, or to answer a Skype call." She wanted to give sick kids "who had stopped having the freedom of being a kid"—because doctors and others monitor every detail of their lives—a measure of power, and not really involve their parents.

Dolva and her colleagues came up with an adorable white robot to bring into classrooms, about the size of a basketball, with two eye holes that can light up and a ring of lights on top of its head. When the unit—called an AV1—is not on, it stands with its head tilted down and its lights off. When a sick child at home or in the hospital logs in using a tablet or a smartphone, the AV1's head goes up, and the LED lights in the eyes and on the head go on. By swiping right or left, the child can spin the AV1's vision a full 360 degrees and move its head up and down.

If the student is feeling sad or passive, she can turn the lights on the top of the AV1 to blue; to raise her hand, she can make the unit's top lights blink. It reminded me of WALL-E, the charismatic lead of the eponymous 2008 movie; sweet as can be, and equipped with a loudspeaker, an eight-hour battery, a microphone, and a camera. According to Dolva, it works for any age; she told me about a very grateful twenty-five-year-old Norwegian woman who after years of being sick had finally been able to finish high school by persuading the authorities that her attendance by AV1 could be considered presence.

There's a short video about the AV1, showing a young girl named Maja who has cancer but is present in her classroom because of the robot. "It's a bit weird, but also a lot of fun," she says to the camera from her home. "It's nice, because now I can be a part of society too." The little white robot, head down, eyes blank, sits politely next to her. "I can also be a part of the class, and I can keep up with the others when I return to school." Through the robot, she says, she joins in; "When something fun happens, my classmates bring me outside to join." Before the robot, Maja says she thought "it was very scary to come back to school." She shifts in her chair, awkwardly, remembering her fear when she spent so much time in the hospital. "Back then, it felt like nobody saw me." The video shows kids in her classroom smiling at the robot, talking to it actively, even dancing around it while its head swivels around. They're clearly comfortable with Maja's robot presence.

I ask Dolva what it's been like in the classroom, and she tells me the most frustrating problem is the teacher. The kids know it's "her," Maja, but the teacher doesn't trust the technology the way the kids do. Dolva hopes the teachers will begin to accept, if she keeps explaining it over and over, that there's a private, encrypted connection between the classroom and the home and only Maja is behind the device. The company will also add more emotional indicators to the next version of AV1, to comfort the teachers who want to know how they are doing with their robot students. No Isolation was surprised to learn how complicated it is to introduce new technology to the school system. "We underestimated the role that the school would play in implementing AV1. We always had the user's needs at the top of our minds, but never really considered the teacher's needs," Dolva confessed. The schools need to get with the program. Their students are way ahead of them.

A one-way use of fiber is already in place in the small town of Independence, Oregon, about an hour south of Portland. It's a "store-and-forward" teledentistry program, possible only because Independence built a gigabit fiber network ten years ago. The network, called

MINET, allows dental hygienists working in elementary schools serving fifteen hundred kids in the Central School District of Polk County to upload (that's the "store" part) and send ("forward") very-high-resolution X-ray images of kids' teeth to dentists in Portland or Salem. Independence is a "poverty hot spot," according to Linda Mann, director of community outreach for Capitol Dental Care. Few dental offices nearby will take Medicaid patients, and parents have to drive their children thirty miles for an office visit. As a result, many of the kids in Independence have never seen a dentist, and they all need preventive care.

With a grant of $112,000 from the Oregon Office of Rural Health, the hygienists were able to go right into classrooms and cafeterias with a laptop, a portable X-ray unit, and a camera.[10] Dentists in Portland could then see whether a particular child had a cavity; most of the children's cavities could be treated at the school by the hygienists using "scoop-and-fill" procedures with fluoride-releasing fillings, a method of care that is painless and doesn't need drills. A major consequence of the pilot is that the local dentist offices that do take Medicaid are freed up to provide restorative care rather than routine prevention. Mann says most of those offices are booked two to three months ahead for routine care due to the demand for regular dentist appointments.

Like Allen Coffman in Chattanooga, the leaders of Capitol Dental Care are focused on using schools as hubs of pediatric care. "Children are a captive audience. You can reach them in schools," said Eli Schwarz, professor and chair of the Department of Community Dentistry at the Oregon Health & Science University. In Denmark, where Schwarz grew up, school-based dental care has been available in every school since the 1980s.

Store-and-forward works for transmitting pictures of teeth, but to change minds you need two-way, real-time communication. In rural Minnesota, where the RS Fiber network will soon bring "fiber to the farm," Denny Schultz, the farmer who ran economic development for Arlington until that town decided it wasn't interested in fiber, mused aloud to me about fiber's potential in psychiatric care. "With high-resolution two-way video," he said, "you can do psychiatric diagnoses. You can pick up on the nuances of eye movement or facial expressions." Mental health care is a huge need in rural areas. "We're in so desperate need of that," Schultz told me. "If you can have somebody doing it remotely and cover more people, but cover them adequately and accurately, that's what we need. That's where a fiber application can come in."

It's not just rural areas that urgently need mental health services: we have staggering mental health problems in this country, and particularly in the young. As many as one in five children in the United States have behavioral health issues, but only 20 percent of those who need mental health services actually receive them.[11] And of that 20 percent, about half end treatment prematurely because of access, transportation, or money issues.[12] The problems continue: about 20 percent of adults, or 43 million people, are affected by mental illness every year, and most receive no treatment whatsoever.[13] The main barriers are stigma and cost.

Nationally, the number of "telemental health" visits is growing steadily, starting in rural regions that have shortages of mental health professionals.[14] Roger Root, whose title is "person-centered telepresence integrator" for the Minnesota state information technology agency, told a Minnesota newspaper, the Bemidji *Pioneer*, that telepresence is "opening . . . a whole new set of possibilities to get the right service to the right person in the right place at the right time." As the *Pioneer* reported, students at schools connected to fiber can stay at school while meeting with a therapist, and local emergency rooms can make therapists available to patients with mental health crises.

Fiber isn't the only barrier to providing these services. State law can also get in the way. For example, Massachusetts has taken the position that telehealth services will be reimbursed only in areas designated as having shortages of health care providers— meaning mostly rural areas.[15] The state perceives telehealth mental assistance as unnecessary except for people who would otherwise have to drive a long way to see a psychiatrist.

One of my students, Lin Wang, interviewed Omid Toloui, the vice president of digital health strategy at Caremore, an integrated health plan and care delivery system for Medicare and Medicaid patients. Toloui is focused on the potential for telehealth to transcend language and cultural barriers, by using video links to provide doctors with the language skills or cultural sensitivities necessary to assist poor minority populations in Boston for whom psychiatric care would otherwise not be easily available. Toloui pointed out that the Massachusetts stance on telehealth makes community clinics uninterested in providing these services, which means that telepsychiatry services aren't integrated into primary care for Medicaid recipients in Boston.

Not all public institutions take this approach. The Veterans Administration, for example, has embraced telepsychiatry. According to a recent article by Joshua Kendall published on the online site Undark, the VA has "already administered over 2 million video mental health sessions with patients," and the growth of VA telepsychiatry continues to accelerate.[16] New York State recently adopted a set of standards for telepsychiatry, stating that "in order for telepsychiatry claims to be reimbursed, videoconferencing equipment must be employed allowing quality synchronous video and voice exchange between provider and patient."[17] Both the VA and New York State are focused on hub-and-spoke models, in which the patient has to go to a clinic in order to access service. In the future, we'll want to broaden availability so that the patient can be served wherever he or she is.

It turns out that where telepsychiatry is available, patients are more than satisfied with it. A great deal of evidence shows that they are happy to avoid transporting themselves to and from appointments, and that they feel comfortable disclosing the same kind of information they would disclose in a face-to-face session. Parents seeking help for their children are especially pleased with telepsychiatry, because their kids are comfortable with screens and they are happy not to have to force a trip to an office that may be freighted with stigma for their child. Assessments of mental state by way of telepsychiatry appear to be comparable to face-to-face assessments, with higher-quality observations when video and audio quality is high. Overall, mental health interventions delivered via telepsychiatry appear to yield outcomes no different from face-to-face sessions. This form of treatment may be more cost effective as well. Telepsychiatry makes it easier for more people, especially in isolated areas, to access expert mental health care.

According to Mary Carpenter, a psychologist and CEO of the Range Mental Health Center in Virginia and Hibbing, Minnesota, teenagers actually prefer telepresence. She told the Bemidji *Pioneer* that telepresence "really is their mode of communication, so their defenses are down more so than in an office face to face."[18] Teenagers are used to connecting via screens.

Adults are getting there too, and with a high-resolution screen large enough to show us most of the body, not just the head, all the in-person cues of body language, tone of voice, nuances of facial expression, involuntary physiologic responses (shaking, sweating, blushing, blinking), gestures, proximity, posture, eye contact and avoidance, and eventually even touch (through haptic communication devices) will be available to us. All of this will add up to human connection and a genuinely helpful possibility of empathetic therapeutic assistance.

Eye contact is effective only over an extraordinarily high-resolution connection. Yet eye contact is fundamental to doctor-patient relationships, empathy, and mental health; its connection to psychological problems is circular and reinforcing. When we avoid it, we make less of a connection and are more likely to suffer from depression or feelings of isolation. The patients of doctors who make eye contact are healthier. We can all communicate more effectively, more richly with someone after we make eye contact with them: Atsushi Senju, a cognitive neuroscientist who studies the biological and cultural aspects of eye contact at University of London's Center for Brain and Cognitive Development, said that eye contact "amplifies your ability to compute all the signals so you are able to read the other person's brain."[19] Static pictures don't do that for us; we need the direct gaze of another.

For all of this nonverbal communication to come through without hesitation or delay (humans go nuts if we are more than fifteen milliseconds off with the person we're interacting with), we'll need tsunamis of data flowing back and forth—which will require fiber. I'm convinced that the convenience and user-centered-ness of telepresence for mental health purposes could someday feel standard, but only if we make the upgrade to light-filled glass everywhere in the country.

Just as "e-commerce" has become simply "commerce," we will someday stop attaching "tele" to health services. The stories I've told here are about pediatric health, elder care, loneliness, dentistry, and psychiatry. Their protagonists just happen to be using high-capacity fiber connections. We haven't yet scratched the surface of the health-related implications of a fiber upgrade.

But we have a very long way to go in America. A recent bill aimed at setting telemedicine standards in Montana failed because more than half of the state's residents don't have access—at any price—to internet connections that could support a video session.[20] Dave Trebelhorn, the former mayor of Winthrop, Minnesota, remembered with a chuckle a story about one of the Sibley County commissioners who, at seventy-one, was deeply opposed to any government involvement in fiber. The man—let's call him Bill—was in the real estate business, had never really spent much time online, and was well off. When he publicly expressed his opposition to RS Fiber, one of the nurses from the local hospital in Arlington said, "'you know, Bill, if you ever come in to Arlington Hospital, and we have to transfer you to Waconia'" (the nearest major hospital, twenty-seven miles away), "'it'd be pretty sad if we couldn't get the records there in time, because the ambulance beat the records there. Because we have to transfer all your records, because they're here.'" Given the region's awful data connections, taking the records in a thumb drive by ambulance from Arlington to Waconia would take less time than attempting to upload them for use by the other hospital's doctors. Bill still voted no, likely because he didn't understand the technical or medical implications of what the nurse was saying.

Imagine happier researchers, doctors, and radiologists, able to review and send enormous medical files, wherever they are. And if you can't put yourself in the shoes of a researcher, medical student, or doctor, imagine yourself as an older person, perhaps housebound or suffering from a chronic illness. Loneliness and isolation are major risk factors for premature death, coronary heart disease, and stroke. But there is little evidence that public health professionals are doing anything about the connectivity side of this issue.

What if empathetic people could easily visit others via a large screen, just to chat? What if home care providers could check in briefly with you, when needed, as needed, to foster connection? What if you could reach others to serve them? Yes, an in-person visit would be better. But when that's difficult, you'd be happy if you had a fiber connection.

CHAPTER EIGHT
Inequality and Fiber

I
N MID-2017, THE Federal Reserve banks of Atlanta, Boston, Chicago, and New York, together with a large group of private foundations, released a report assessing the revitalization they had seen in several American cities—including Chattanooga— after the Great Recession. The report's central finding was that economic growth alone does not lead to opportunity or fairness; somehow, the authors suggested, "the arc of growth" needs to be intentionally connected to "the arc of opportunity." Places that successfully connect these arcs by, for example, ensuring that the benefits of downtown redevelopment and recruitment of new high-tech businesses reach low-income and minority residents will emerge as inclusive, prosperous localities that, in the long term, are better places for everyone to live.[1]

Last-mile fiber should be part of this intentional connection. By itself, fiber won't fix the staggering, interlocking problems of inequality that America confronts, but without fiber we stand little chance of taking on inequality at all. And if we do not address inequality, we risk the future of liberal democracy, in which responsible, self-governing people are committed to everyone's individual freedom. Every policy choice that will support liberal democracy—adequate education, health, transit, and employment opportunities, which together make an informed and engaged citizenry possible—requires the bedrock of fiber everywhere, reaching every home and business, in order to be effectively and fairly implemented.

We have a distance to go to get there.

Digital inequality in America is on a dismal trajectory. Poorer, rural, disabled, and minority Americans are far less likely to have wired high-speed internet access at home than rich people in urban areas, just as, a hundred years ago, they were far less likely to have electricity—or if they had enough electricity for a lightbulb, they were still unlikely to have electric heating, cooking, or refrigeration. Today, these left-behind populations are often forced to rely on the data plans of wireless carriers, which are more expensive and less reliable than wired access—or to rely on satellite access, which is also hugely expensive and full of delays. This reliance on a third-rate form of access (first rate is fiber; second rate is cable) has enormous consequences for their opportunity to lead a thriving life.

The trouble in all this—a trouble even deeper than the travails caused by treating electricity as a luxury—is that inadequate fiber connectivity and the expense of connectivity generally both amplify and entrench existing patterns of inequality and make it less likely that we will remain the world's beacon of democratic and economic opportunity in the future. All of these relationships intertwine in a vicious downward spiral: we risk dumbing America down.

This is a particularly painful problem in rural areas. Rural Americans are ten times more likely than urban Americans to be unserved by *any* connection that meets the FCC's not-very-aspirational standard for high-speed internet access—currently 25 Mbps download and 3 Mbps upload.[2] Even where these connections are available in rural areas, only about one in eight residents have a choice of more than one provider.[3] About 24 million rural Americans can't buy a 25 Mbps connection at any price, and most of the rest are stuck with an unregulated monopoly provider. The same problem faces rural schools. The situation is even worse in tribal areas, where 70 percent of residents can't buy such a connection even if they had all the money in the world—which they don't.[4]

As we've already seen, many communities aren't waiting for their states or the federal government to reach out. They're tackling the fiber problem themselves. There is an enormous payoff for this effort: areas in the United States that have taken on the question of utility-style fiber access are not only ready to close the digital divides that are making inequality worse, they are also in a better position than most other places to take on other structural aspects of inequality—to intentionally connect the arcs of growth and opportunity.

This capacity story can be told by looking closely at three places: Chattanooga, Tennessee, and Greensboro and Wilson, North Carolina. Chattanooga's fiber network has given it the capacity and vision to see the next set of issues that need addressing. Greensboro hasn't been able to confront its communications issues and isn't ready to take on its similarly staggering inequality. Wilson's fiber, and that city's choice to make access to fiber available in public housing units and apartment buildings at a genuinely low price—$10 a month—helps it address the social justice and workforce development issues it needs to confront. The rural framework of this capacity story is revealed by comparing Nevada City/Grass Valley, where local government refused to get involved in fiber, to the RS Fiber region in Minnesota, and to Otis, Massachusetts—two places where local government did all it could to bring fiber to town.

Chattanooga greets arrivals at its airport with an enormous sign reading WELCOME TO GIG CITY. In many respects the city's prospects look bright. Volkswagen is expanding and hiring in Chattanooga; new midsized businesses and startups are showing up; there's a brand-new Innovation District of which City Hall is justly proud. Economic growth in the city is holding steady or ticking upward, a sharp contrast to many similarly sized places in America. In the past five years, Hamilton County has added jobs at a faster rate than the state of Tennessee as a whole, and Chattanooga is second only to booming Nashville in job growth.[5] The revved-up ecosystem is attracting well-paying new jobs in advanced manufacturing, logistics, and health care. City leaders will tell you that Chattanooga is now one of the best places in America to live, work, or start a business, and the EPB fiber network has clearly played a significant role.

But these developments don't tell the whole story. The corrosive effects of concentrated poverty in Chattanooga continue unabated. At least four out of ten students in Hamilton County live in poverty.[6] More than 80 percent of Chattanooga's good new jobs in the coming years will require some form of postsecondary training, but unless something changes, just 35 percent of students in the county will get that training.[7] The buzzword driving the discussion is "advanced industries." Over the past five years, spurred at least in part by its great communications capacity, Chattanooga has seen a huge leap in the number of automated manufacturing jobs. These, in fact, account for almost all of the city's job growth. But they require skills beyond what kids learn in a traditional high school curriculum.[8]

Several of the city's public schools fall in the bottom 5 percent of schools statewide based on academic achievement; students there can't get the fifteen thousand jobs in Hamilton County that are open but unfilled because people lack the training, skills, and education they require.[9] The problems start at birth and in early childhood: in 2017, only 42 percent of the county's kindergartners were ready to learn when they arrived in school; only 38 percent of third graders were reading at grade level; in middle school, less than 50 percent of students had reached literacy and math benchmarks for their grade levels. Some county high schools graduate no students that meet all the benchmarks for college and career readiness.[10] A black child in Hamilton County is thirty-three times more likely than a white child to attend one of the lowest performing schools in the state.[11] Although most future jobs will require specialized post-high-school training, just a quarter of the local community college's students graduate with a degree. A decade ago, 62 percent of the jobs in Hamilton County's top industries were held by Hamilton County residents. Today, just 57 percent of those jobs are—equivalent to ten thousand jobs leaving the county. "We've got the jobs," said Jared Bigham, executive director of Chattanooga 2.0, the revitalization effort that began in 2015. "We're just farming them out to people who don't live in Chattanooga."

Concentrated, intergenerational black poverty and stunning inequality are part of the city's fabric. It's not just an education issue. Five zip codes near the base of the mountains surrounding Chattanooga have very low incomes, very high crime rates, very low educational attainment rates, and very poor health outcomes.[12] Public transit to these places is awful; 84 percent of counties in America have shorter commuting times than Chattanooga does. Commuting time has emerged as the single strongest factor affecting the likelihood of escaping poverty.[13]

Keri Randolph, the former director of innovation for Chattanooga's public schools, is dismayed by the city's Gig City brand. "This whole Gig City thing?" she said to me. "I remember thinking if I could draw, I would draw a political cartoon that had kids in a school looking out the window and it said 'Gig City' and they're beating on the window." She's thinking about Howard High School, the historically African American school just beyond the freeway that loops past Chattanooga's gentrifying South Side: "Our schools are so isolated. We have kids that go to Howard and haven't seen the river which is a mile and a half from where they live." That isolation has consequences; the "pretty incredible poverty" in West Chattanooga, where Howard High sits, is often invisible to richer Chattanoogans—many of whom live above the city on Lookout Mountain or Signal Mountain. "We have a profoundly segregated community," David Steele, now the director of civic engagement for the University of Chattanooga, told me. "There's so much that goes along with that segregation, so that even if you have people of good will on both sides of the river, or both sides of the railroad track, the mere fact that you're not in a persistent, productive collaboration is its own pathology."

Randolph told me she went through a leadership program in Chattanooga a few years ago with a cohort of fellow trainees, most of whom had grown up in town. "They had no idea that the West Side exists," she said. "We met over there on the second or third day we met as a class. I can't tell you how many of them said, 'I had no idea.' How can you breathe in Chattanooga and not know that this was here?" Brandon Hubbard-Heitz, who teaches at Howard, sees the inequality every day: "The haves have quite a bit, and the have-nots are dodging bullets from gang violence while trying to get through school. That's Chattanooga." He sounded grimly cynical. "We were named in 2015 by *Outside* magazine the 'best town ever,' largely because of our lovely proximity to plentiful outdoor adventures.[14] Most of which none of my students have access to."

Chattanooga's profound inequality makes many Chattanoogans I met feel jaded or worried. The African American cab driver who took me to my hotel after my arrival at the airport was immediately dismissive of the city's fiber project. "It's just for the rich guys," he said. "Doesn't help me at all." Tiffanie Robinson, who now sits on the Hamilton County school board, told me: "We just have a big divide between the haves and the have-nots in Chattanooga. ... I've watched us grow so much, but I'm actually really nervous right now. We've built a lot of hype around our success. And I'm worried that we're running on those fumes." Chattanooga's success is not sustainable, she knows, if it doesn't involve everybody. The city's leadership is forthright about the city's searing inequality problems. "We have to be honest that there are people left out of the growing prosperity," mayor Andy Berke said at a downtown forum on diversity. "Yes, even in the best town ever."

Today, the Patten House, a former hotel turned Section 8 public housing apartment building, stands directly across the street from the Edney Building, the anchor of Chattanooga's new Innovation District. Its 231 units house elderly and disabled people, mostly African American. Ken Hays, executive director of the Edney, told me the Edney had worked to have neighborhood events with residents—health fairs, Bingo games—and he's convinced that the Edney has helped Chattanooga businesses take "more of a 'They're our neighbor'–type attitude." But it's hard to miss the contrast between the worn public housing complex and the shiny development nearby: Chattanooga's rising tide has not lifted all boats.

Sarah Morgan, the leader of the Benwood Foundation in Chattanooga, came to the city thirty-four years ago. "When I got here it was horrible, it was broken," she said to me. "So I participated in the long run of renaissance around the city. Now we've gotten to a place where we can be more courageous. We're so proud of all our big stories, but we don't want to be two Chattanoogas." The jobs going unfilled in the county serve as a useful catalyst for collective action, I was told by many people I interviewed. But it's not just about jobs: "We started with an economic imperative," said Bigham. "As we started sharing the data, and talking to people, and engaging with stakeholders, that economic imperative started moving pretty quickly into a moral imperative." Groups across the city are thinking not just about economic growth but about how to ensure opportunities and fairness—social justice—for every Chattanoogan, including those in the five zip codes of concentrated poverty. These are tough discussions; these patterns are connected to race and poverty issues that have been around for a long time in the South. But without fiber, the discussions wouldn't be happening at all.

Morgan and Bigham are at the heart of the Chattanooga 2.0 redevelopment effort. It is the latest flavor of the Chattanooga Way: now that the physical infrastructure is in place (the riverfront, the downtown, the South Side, the fiber), the question has become what Chattanooga can do to address Hamilton County's glaring disparities. Old-fashioned civic competition had something to do with the timing of the effort: Memphis passed Chattanooga in school achievement in early 2015.[15] Business leaders, in particular Bill Kilbride, the head of Chattanooga's Chamber of Commerce, began to realize that if the area didn't prepare its people better, it wouldn't continue to attract investment from new companies. Kilbride and Morgan decided they needed to act in concert with the county, which runs the school district, bringing everyone along by the force of their logic and the breadth of their coalition.

Put in motion by the Benwood Foundation, the Chattanooga Area Chamber of Commerce, the Hamilton County Department of Education, and the Public Education Foundation, Chattanooga 2.0 began by issuing a report laying out the early-childhood-to-job picture in the city. The data were sobering; the problems were awful. "One of the things that I'm so fond of [about Chattanooga] is the community's relative willingness to be candid with itself," said David Steele. "I think that we are trying to solve, in many ways, the problem of the South." For the first time in Chattanooga, businesses were thoroughly engaged in these difficult issues.

Rather than make suggestions for reform, that initial report ended with a set of questions, including "Do we have the will as a community to do something about this?" and "What happens if we don't do something?"[16] With a staff of just three people including Bigham, Chattanooga 2.0 quickly acted to convene a huge number of meetings and form action teams—more than 150 volunteers, decisionmakers drawn from a diverse range of groups, meet every single week—all focused on aligning their efforts to reach two major goals, reflected in the coalition's second published report: by 2025, the plan is to have 75 percent of Hamilton County residents have a workforce credential or postsecondary credential of some kind, and to double the number of high school students with a postsecondary credential within six years of graduation.[17] Several people ran for four open seats on the county school board with the 2.0 goals as their platform, and three of them won, including Tiffanie Robinson.

Several funded programs have already been launched that are aligned with these two goals. The work is not aimed just at education reform. In those five zip codes, the neighborhoods are often just as broken as the schools: housing, health, food, students constantly moving, crime, and general insecurity are all issues. As Bigham told me, "You can have the world's greatest teachers, the best principals, but if you don't address the wraparound supports of what students are facing outside of school, we are not going to improve academic gains. We have to address some of those social issues." Grants for transportation, housing, and just staying in school; opening the schools to serve as community hubs for all parts of the neighborhood, not just education—these are the kinds of steps that Chattanooga 2.0 is taking, funding, and advocating for.

It's not a top-down initiative—the community is all-in—but they're just beginning. It will take decades of steady work for Chattanooga 2.0 to be successful; its alignment of funding and policy decisions needs to serve people who are being born in Chattanooga today. Its leaders are proud of the physical infrastructure that was planned—including, importantly, the EPB fiber network—and are saying that it is now time to pivot to people.

According to Keri Randolph, the change of focus is real: "People talk about the Chattanooga Way all the time," she told me. "They talk about revitalization of the waterfront. The Chattanooga 2.0 process, this second wave—where we've come to is, it's not about place, it's about people. Going from the dirtiest city in the country to what we have now gives people hope that we can do this. There's this sense of, 'This is really hard but we can do this.'" David Belitz hopes Chattanooga 2.0 will help break the intergenerational cycles of poverty and joblessness in those five zip codes next to the mountains. He would like students at Howard High to be ready for jobs paying $50,000 a year by the time they finish high school. "Without even having to go to a two-year college," he said. "That changes the world."

Once again, local philanthropy is playing an important role in catalyzing change. Sarah Morgan, leading the Benwood Foundation, is funding Chattanooga 2.0's coordination with Hamilton County and the State of Tennessee as they work toward placing troubled schools inside the city limits under the control of a jointly run nonprofit, with increased resources, focused accountability, and greater autonomy. They want to avoid having the state itself take over the schools.

The coming of fiber to Chattanooga had several related effects that made Chattanooga 2.0 possible. First, the gig helped the city imagine its postmanufacturing future. As Mayor Berke put it, "I grew up in a city that had way too much concentration in manufacturing. . . . When the jobs of the past left, so did our city's energy and vibrancy. The fiber has allowed us to reimagine what our city could be. To think of ourselves as a city that can invent things again. We didn't have that self-conception five years ago." Now the issue is ensuring that this upward trend of wealth creation and job creation continues, and that its benefits are felt by everyone. "We need to continue to grow our own people," said the mayor. "The equity piece is important from a moral standpoint, but it's also important from a development standpoint." He envisions the city as a place "where each person can live the life of his or her own choosing." He knows this is a big job: "We're at a point now where we have the chance to give people that hope. It's going to take hard work."

Chattanooga 2.0 wouldn't have happened without the fiber. "Fiber brings that entrepreneurial spirit," Bigham said. "It's a culture that is conducive to trying to be a little bit outside the box, like [Chattanooga 2.0] want[s] to be. Because we know there is no silver bullet in this; I keep telling people it's going to be a silver buckshot approach. We'll have to do dozens of things. Because if we don't do something different, we're going to get the same results." Steele agreed: "Whether it is how we ended up revitalizing downtown and getting the aquarium here, or how we got the gig, there is a relentless optimism and a willingness to act collectively that is fundamental to our identity as a community."

Fiber brought or encouraged the creation of jobs—the economic imperative—that Chattanooga wants to fill with its own people. Fiber will also lead to more opportunities for all Chattanoogans. "Automation is changing America faster than our education system can keep up with it," David Belitz, who runs the Lupton family investments office and has quiet influence in a host of civic arenas, told me. "Unless we figure out how to deal with that, we're not addressing the problem."

On a more immediate level, the coming of fiber brought new and different voices into the discussions about inequality. Eight years ago, said Mayor Berke, "there wasn't a tech industry in Chattanooga." Today, drawn by the fiber, hundreds of startups are churning away, hiring, seeking capital, and working in the city's Innovation District. *Fortune* magazine has labeled Chattanooga "one of America's most startup friendly cities."[18] Startup employees are often millennials. And for millennials, you can talk about economic development until you're blue in the face, but they also want to hear about social justice: "Caring about social justice," Ann Coulter said to me, "may ultimately be [the millennials'] most valuable contribution to this country. It's what they do after five o'clock." "The most important thing about the gig," David Belitz said, "is that it attracted people who think. They are practical people who want to do things that are good for Chattanooga." Belitz, who calls himself a "right-leaning conservative guy," says these new arrivals are joining many in Chattanooga who, like himself, thoroughly approve of the idea of addressing inequality: "What's good for the least is good for your city," he said, "because you're growing."

Jack Lupton, the Coca-Cola bottling heir who drove the downtown redevelopment effort, died in 2010, and his descendants have mostly left town. But a new generation of under-forty philanthropists, whose success has been fueled by the fiber network, is ascending: Ted Alling, one of the founders of the Lamp Post Group, a startup incubator in the Innovation District, made his money in transportation logistics companies. Now Alling and his wife are launching a leadership academy for boys called Chattanooga Prep that will recruit its students from those five troubled zip codes.[19] Chattanooga Prep will be a charter STEM school modeled on a successful girls' school next door, the Chattanooga Girls Leadership Academy, that is posting large academic gains. Fiber is playing a role in focusing the city's attention on solving its problems and informing the city's vision of its future: based on what I heard in Chattanooga, it seems to me that the sense of civic purpose and, frankly, excitement associated with the EPB network are contributing mightily to the city's collective capacity to confront its long-standing demons: isolated poverty and hopelessness.

Greensboro is like Chattanooga in many ways. Race-based inequality is an enormous problem in both places. The racial segregation and income segregation found in each city is in the top 10 percent of all U.S. communities: rich and poor, black and white live separate lives.[20] Economic inequality is also spectacularly high; the cities' "Gini coefficients," or comparisons of distribution of income compared with a society in which everyone earns exactly the same amount, are in the top 5 percent of all U.S. areas.[21] And in both Greensboro and Chattanooga, the share of income held by the top 1 percent of the population is, again, in the top 10 percent of all U.S. areas.[22] When you get off I-70, the huge highway running west across North Carolina from the Triangle toward Virginia, East Greensboro is what you drive through to get to downtown. It is a traditionally black area of Greensboro that, like the five zip codes that worry city leaders in Chattanooga, is struggling with concentrated poverty and lack of opportunity.

But Greensboro is experiencing none of the energetic cycles of broad-based planning, rebirth, renewal, and opportunity creation that make Chattanoogans so proud of their trajectory. Greensboro in recent years has had a tiny fraction of Chattanooga's rate of job growth.[23] Zack Matheny, a former City Council member now encouraging Greensboro's downtown economic development, told me that he is still upset that city leaders rejected businesses like NCNB long ago—protecting the textile industry, he told me—and allowed existing corporations to simply decamp from downtown to the rich western suburbs. The city has no broad plans for fiber, although Jane Nickles is doing her best to nudge things along— mostly on her own. And it has no broad plans for workforce development. Although the downtown is seeing some new investment and new restaurants, there are still many empty storefronts.

Most importantly, the sense that the mayor, the business community, and a broad group of civic leaders are all in the same boat and rowing together—so palpable in Chattanooga—was absent, as far as I could tell, in Greensboro.

I asked Matheny what the workforce development plan was for East Greensboro. His frustration, never far from the surface, bubbled up: "We've worked on that for, I think, a lifetime. I don't know if we have a firm response for that question. We talk about it." As he was talking, a train went by, sounding its horn—many notes at once, a major third at the top—a gorgeous noise and a reminder that Greensboro has been a divided city throughout its history. Matheny works on the east side of downtown: from white Greensboro's perspective, the wrong side of the tracks.

The day we met, Matheny told me he had spent the morning in an economic development meeting where there was a lot of talk about strategy. He was a City Council member for twelve years before he took the downtown economic development job, and he was disappointed by the circular, inconclusive discussion he heard: "They do it every four years. I said, 'This is the same strategic plan that I've seen for twelve years. This isn't right. We have to make changes.'" He broke down, just a little: "It's amazing, the people that will come up to you and just say, 'Keep going, keep fighting.' I think our community . . . you are gonna make me cry. You're catching me at a tough time."

Jeff Thigpen, a local civic leader, talked to me about the intergenerational poverty and unemployment experienced in the 27406 zip code—East Greensboro again, at the edge of the downtown area. There are many layers of problems in 27406, including high crime, public infrastructure that is in bad shape, very low levels of voting, and few retail stores.[24] Unemployment rates for blacks in East Greensboro are far higher than for whites in West Greensboro, and their median household income is far lower.[25] Thigpen told me he'd been on the city's economic development committee for years. "All the white men," he said, adding, "There's one white woman. We ended up helping expand that group at the time and we put two African Americans on it." Thigpen did not think the Greensboro group was thinking about structural economic changes that would help 27406. "They're not thinking about those communities. They're not. They're thinking about how they can bring jobs and capital investment, and there's a certain playbook they all go by, and back then it was, 'Greensboro doesn't have a hook. If we had a hook we'd be okay.'"

The hook was usually a whale: a huge company that would come in and change everything. There was great excitement about getting FedEx and Honda Jet to come to the west side of town. But then the whales started asking questions. "So how's your transportation network?" Thigpen said. "Because you want to get people from these poor communities to those jobs." Within East Greensboro, people don't have assets, opportunities, or strong public transit, and Thigpen is frustrated that Greensboro isn't cutting through "this cyclical stuff that keeps happening." "What does a just community look like?" he asked. He's looking for structural, long-term planning that incorporates a "common understanding of the needs of a community," including, particularly, 27406 and places like it. He says he'd be happy to step right into "the really difficult discussions," which clearly include race and racial tensions. But it's hard to see when and where those discussions would occur.

Thigpen wants me to understand that, especially for young people, economic growth issues shade into social justice requirements. "The under-thirty-five generation, you can't come at them and say, 'We're just gonna improve our economy and blah, blah, blah. You've got to deal with the social issues. You've got to deal with it, because they're trying to deal with it, and they're so over, as one of them said, 'so over y'alls junk.'" And they need support, focus, vision, and opportunity. He thinks the city's consensus-based traditions, rooted in the Quakers who founded Guilford College in Greensboro in 1837, allow the city "to be positioned over the long term to do the convening to do the work" of social justice, as well as economic opportunity. That sounds to my ear like a very slow process.

"Greensboro has continued to portray itself as moderate and progressive," Duke University professor William Chafe, author of *Civilities and Civil Rights: Greensboro, North Carolina, and the Struggle for Freedom*, told CNN in 2011. "But the realities of it are that it has not changed that much because the underlying issues of seriously listening to black concerns have not really infiltrated the political process."[26] Zack Matheny was blunt: "We have got to make changes," he said. "I believe in bridging those lines and gaps [between black and white], because I know the more success [East Greensboro] has, the more successful the whole community." It was a Friday afternoon, and he was worn out. "I'm hoping that's in the works." He didn't sound optimistic.

I hope I have made it clear that Chattanooga is not the promised land. For example, although the process of wiring Chattanooga with fiber has unquestionably built the city's capacity to take on its intergenerational challenges of poverty, racism, inadequate education, unemployment, and gun violence, it has not led to digital equity. The Section 8 building across the street from the Edney is wired with fiber, but few of that building's residents have internet access. Most can't afford it. Right now, EPB, the public utility that runs the city's fiber network, takes the position that state law does not allow it to sell fiber access subscriptions for less than its cost, which it conservatively calculates to be about $27 a month per household.[27] (EPB is trying not to attract further attacks from the legislature or litigation from cable or phone providers.) Families living in poverty are unlikely to want to pay that much for communications capacity. "Nationwide, we so do not have a handle on something [digital equity] that gets bigger and worse every day," Ann Coulter said to me. "It is painful," Keri Randolph said. "We've tried several things, but I can't say any of them have been super successful." The STEM school in Chattanooga, for example, makes sure that every student has an iPad.[28] But when those students leave the school grounds, most join the ranks of the unconnected—or they have to rely on smartphones tied to expensive mobile data plans. If they use too much data, the overage charges can be overwhelming for a poor family.

This element of the Chattanooga story, like so many others, is echoed across the country: having a wire at home is closely correlated with socioeconomic status and, often, race. If you are low-income or African American, you are far more likely than a rich white person to rely on a smartphone for internet access—which means you will have trouble applying for a job online, getting health information, or doing anything that requires detailed production of large amounts of information rather than consumption of low-bandwidth entertainment.[29] The problem is cost: those who can afford it have high-speed internet access at home, and two-thirds of Americans say it is a major disadvantage not to have this kind of data access.[30]

This is the additional hammer of inequality: not only is a five-year-old likely not to be able to better herself if she is born in one of the troubled zip codes, her inadequate internet access will also amplify the other unfairnesses lined up against her. Her mother can't sign up for SNAP or social security benefits online. She can't get access to the materials she needs to do her homework, and there are no buses to take her to the library—if the library is open.

The problem of socioeconomic and racial inequality in digital access mirrors the history of electrification: absent government involvement, change does not occur. Greensboro's electric trolley lines, launched in June 1902, didn't run to East Greensboro even though the city government tried to require it. The city had little leverage: its trolley system was run by a private company, the Greensboro Electric Company, whose president lived in Hackettstown, New Jersey, and treasurer in Pittsfield, Massachusetts.[31] The company had no particular incentive to serve poorer areas of the city, presumably because those people wouldn't be able to pay the same fares that richer people could.

Electricity itself came much more slowly to the poor, black parts of Greensboro and the surrounding rural areas than to the richer white sections: a 1940 real property survey of Greensboro shows that blacks were far more likely than whites to live in houses without refrigeration or electric cookers.[32] They had electric lighting, but that was all. The private electric companies serving Greensboro did not consider it worthwhile to provide electricity for powering more than lightbulbs in black areas.

The same was true in Chattanooga: in 1933, nine out of ten families didn't have electricity.[33] "There was not much of a middle class in Chattanooga," Jim Ingraham of EPB told me. The rich families had electric refrigerators, but if you were a factory worker you were still lighting your house with oil or kerosene. Six months after EPB was chartered in 1935, as a public distributor of electricity with a mission to keep prices low and act like a utility (following the creation of the Tennessee Valley Authority as a generator of electricity in 1933), rates came down enormously, and "everyone in our 600-square-mile service area had signed up for electricity," Ingraham said.[34] Everyone had it: all the factory workers, all the African Americans. "We offered refrigerators out of our office," he said, "and we had a kitchen. We showed people, here's what these appliances can do for you."

Today's attitude, that relying on smartphone access using expensive mobile data plans is good enough for poorer people, comes from the same market-driven ethos that preceded EPB. Wired internet access in East Greensboro is rare and expensive; Spectrum, the local cable company, has 80 to 90 percent of the market for the whole city, but only a few households in the 27406 zip code subscribe to a modern internet connection.[35]

Jeff Thigpen and Zack Matheny are worried about the city's extraordinary inequality, but they don't see a realistic prospect of change. Tiffanie Robinson, Keri Randolph, and Sarah Morgan are similarly worried about inequality in Chattanooga, as is Mayor Berke, but there's a crucial difference between the two cities. Chattanooga, aided by what it has learned from its shift to being the Gig City, is doing something about it.

Here is a two-part coda to this difficult story of inequality, capacity, and opportunity. Areas of the country that are considering fiber installations often consult with one another. Fiber enthusiasts are a generous bunch. Wilson, North Carolina, went with fiber in 1997 because Chattanooga's EPB staff shared research and thinking with Wilson employees.

Now it may be time for the knowledge to be shared in the other direction. Wilson has the most innovative, helpful fiber access plan around for low-income residents. If you are living in an apartment building or a public housing unit, Wilson will sell you 50 Mbps symmetrical fiber service for $10 a month.[36]

Tiffany Cooper, an African American single mother of three teenage boys living in public housing in Wilson, could not wait to tell me how excited she is about having a city fiber connection to her unit. The $10 monthly price of her subscription is added to her rent bill. "It's the best thing that could have happened to me," she said. Cooper is working several jobs. Already a certified nursing assistant, she's been able to work toward certificates in medical technology and phlebotomy, all using the fiber connection that was turned on a few months before I met her. "And I'm not going to stop," she told me. Her next online program will certify her to read electrocardiograms (EKGs).

Before Cooper got her fiber connection at home, she had to go to the library to do her weekly homework assignments; the community college used Blackboard course management software that could be accessed only with a high-speed connection. And getting to the library was hard: "I don't have any transportation," she pointed out. Now she can look up new programs and participate online, from home.

The best part, the really important part about having this connection at home, is that her sons' grades have improved. "I noticed it and I couldn't believe it!" she told me excitedly. Before she got fiber, "I was getting phone calls from teachers, and letters, because there were a lot of things they could not do at school because we didn't have access to the internet." She was emphatic: "Their education comes before anything." The fiber connection "is doing a whole lot of good in our home."

Christopher Richardson, Cooper's shy, polite fourteen-year-old son, her youngest, was on the couch next to me, listening. His mother sighed and told me Christopher wanted to be a pro football player. I asked him what he loved about school these days, and he talked about the grading system: "I'm shooting for all As," he said, proudly. Cooper said that if she were queen, she would give fiber internet access to everyone, "especially if the price is good. I think it's the best that Wilson County, whoever discovered this idea, it is the best thing that could have ever happened in life with these children. Honestly, it really is." For its part, Wilson views the unused fiber already installed in public housing buildings as a sunk cost, and figures that some revenue coming in is better than nothing; if the city charged more, residents in public housing and apartment units would likely default.

In its efforts to become a stronger, fairer city, Wilson hopes to attract more than just "creatives" and white millennials. Almost 50 percent of its residents are African American now, and there's a large Latino population and many migrants.[37] They have one of the largest advanced manufacturing bases in North Carolina; the number of these businesses—all needing fiber—is growing, and jobs in that sector need to be filled.[38] Those jobs need to be available to everyone, black, white, and Latino. City manager Grant Goings said the fiber network had given Wilson "a tremendous amount of hope, and I would argue even momentum."

I told the story of Wilson's $10 per month service to people I met in Chattanooga. "That's what we need!" Keri Randolph immediately responded. She was upset that EPB's lowest-priced product is $27.99 a month, and she didn't understand why they couldn't do better. "These aren't your customers that are switching to a low-cost option," she said wryly. The mayor was interested; so was the head of EPB, David Wade.

So far, we've been discussing midsize towns and their efforts to ensure fairness and opportunity. Digital inequality in rural areas also produces severe democratic deficits.

Rorie Gotham glared at me when she started talking about internet access in Washington, California, her tiny town twenty miles east of Nevada City in the Sierra Madre mountains. She's relying on a satellite connection that doesn't work all the time, and yet it seems to her that every transaction with the world requires going online—yet she can't reliably be online at all. "When rural communities can't apply for a job, and they can't get their birth certificate, and they can't apply for a passport, and they can't pay their taxes online, there's something wrong with that," she said. "There's something wrong with our leadership. There's a fairly substantial number of citizens of this country that can't communicate, so what that requires is that you have to go drive to these places, and fill out forms, and then wait." She's especially annoyed when people say, "You chose that rural lifestyle," with its implication that rural people are not entitled to modern-day internet access. "This is America. It's just wrong."

All people, wherever they live, she said, "deserve to have equal access to information." She thinks internet access should be a required part of getting a building permit: "It needs to be part of moving in, part of growth." Laissez-faire is not working for rural

America, particularly in areas like Nevada City/Grass Valley where the local authorities are uninterested in intervening to ensure that their people have communications capacity.

Gotham fled San Francisco for a rural retreat, and many of the people around her are retirees who live in Nevada County for the same reason. It's a different story for the people in the RS Fiber area, in Renville and Sibley counties southwest of Minneapolis–St. Paul, many of whose families have been farmers for generations. In their view, the unregulated marketplace for internet access has stifled innovation, artificially depressed economic development, and brought inequality of opportunity. Their vision, as Bernadine Joselyn of the Blandin Foundation put it to me, is to "integrate the technology and harness it up to their dreams about equal access and equal opportunity for everybody." Fiber is "right behind sewer, water, and electricity," Denny Schultz, former economic development officer for Arlington, Minnesota, told me. "Maybe [fiber] is even ahead of those others." A rising tide floats all boats, the people of rural Minnesota—including their local government leaders—think, and they point out that "you made your choice" to live in a rural area is not a responsible argument. As Bob Fox, a civic leader in Franklin, said to me, "Some of the people who are living out here are also feeding the world. If you expect the world to be fed, the way it can be fed through American agriculture, you have to have the technology that makes that possible."

Much of the agriculture of the future will be data-driven. Sensor networks will record data like soil moisture and temperature, while video drones collect high-resolution images for analysis. Tractors are becoming GPS-enabled sensor platforms keeping track of inputs (seed, fertilizer, herbicides, and water) and outputs (yields). A large farm might generate hundreds of terabytes of data, especially with video involved. Every farmer's goal will be to identify optimal timing and types of crop rotations, maximize yields, and minimize resource waste and crop losses. Cloud analytics will take advantage of other databases, like historical weather and yields, and maybe even seed genomic data.[39] It's a big vision. Climate change threatens agriculture with heat stress, drought, pests, and brackish groundwater intrusion at the same time that the global population is set to jump from seven billion to nine billion over the next forty years.[40] And while yields per acre have grown tremendously, agriculture is still relatively dumb; farms attached to fiber will be better able to take on this problem.

The people I met in the tiny towns and farms that make up the RS Fiber region kept reminding me that cities and rural areas are interdependent. "If it wasn't for these farmers, we wouldn't have the cities. And if it wasn't for the cities, we wouldn't have the farmers," Dave Trebelhorn, the former mayor of Winthrop, told me. The RS Fiber project was aimed at helping not just the members of the cooperative but the wider community. Farming is big business, and farmers need fiber as badly as people in urban areas.

People I talked with in rural Western Massachusetts often had the sense that political people in Boston and the cable companies uninterested in running lines to them didn't care how the rural small towns were treated, and certainly didn't want those little towns to make the leap to fiber. "We have cable, why should they have something better?" Chip Bull, who has been spearheading the town of Petersham's move to fiber, told me, paraphrasing what seemed to him to be the eastern Massachusetts establishment's sentiment toward modern internet access. But young people in Petersham, and new small businesses, were miserable at not even being able to get DSL. "Small communities out here in the hinterlands are really having a hard time getting into the digital age," Aaron Bean of Westfield Gas & Electric said to me. And when people in Western Massachusetts traveled to Tibet or Katmandu or Ukraine, they'd find better internet access than they had at home. Eight years of effort to get state grants supporting their fiber builds had brought little progress, and the money allotted for those grants was never enough to support fiber access anyway. That's why Otis pushed ahead on its own.

Otis, Massachusetts, one of the many localities I visited in connection with the country's fiber story, is a small town a few hours west of Boston, in the rolling hills of the Berkshires. Houses surround a lake, there isn't much of a downtown, and the city hall is located in a renovated former elementary school. Although Otis is a rural place, unlike Winthrop and the RS Fiber area of Minnesota, it is a magnet for second-home buyers, who generate about two-thirds of the town's property tax revenues.[41] Those monies will pay for Otis's new fiber-to-the-home network.

Otis's planned network is yet another variety of community-based fiber: like Santa Monica's City Net, it will be primarily funded and ultimately owned by the town. (The Commonwealth of Massachusetts is also putting up about $1.7 million of the $5 million cost of the fiber build.)[42] But the network will be built and operated by a nearby municipal electric company, Westfield Gas & Electric—a public utility, like EPB in Chattanooga—that is interested in helping other communities have fiber and isn't interested in making a huge profit. "We're not looking at this as a money maker," Aaron Bean, Westfield's operations manager, told me.[43] "We're looking at this as trying to provide a much-needed service out here as cost effectively as we can. Small communities out here in the hinterlands are really having a hard time getting into the digital age." Comcast doesn't wire areas that have fewer than forty households per mile of road, so Otis has no cable access. It relies on DSL and, sometimes, on extremely expensive mobile wireless data plans.

But that will change: soon every house and business in Otis will have its own dedicated fiber strand, as in Wilson. It's taken several years for the Otis network to take shape, and Westfield's involvement has been crucial. Westfield, in turn, learned a great deal from Wilson's Greenlight network. "When we were developing our business plan," Aaron Bean said, "We went down to Wilson, met all them. We had people over at EPB Chattanooga as well. We've talked to all of them and picked the best ideas from that." From that due diligence, the municipal utility gained the expertise to start installing fiber in its own town of Westfield.

Aaron Bean studied the history of public electrification in Massachusetts for his MBA at the Rensselaer Polytechnic Institute in Troy, New York. He's proud of Westfield Gas & Electric: "We are a 117-year-old organization," he told me. "Our roots go back to the 1860s. When the town bought out the incumbent electric and gas plant, that was in 1899. We've been operating ever since. We know how to string wire, we know how to operate electricity." WG&E had planned to be a cable TV provider, but then switched to selling fiber connectivity to larger commercial and industrial customers in Westfield. It found that its services were much cheaper and far better than what any incumbent was selling. "The townspeople are tired of Comcast," Bean told me. "They're tired of seeing their bills go up. They're tired of threatening to cut the cord, or reduce their service, and then hearing about the next best deal." For the utility, the price is the price, and the price is the lowest one they can offer responsibly. "We're operating at just the minimum we can to support the organization and have enough room for growth to keep it as an ongoing concern," Bean said. WG&E saved money and got a modest bond issued by its city council, and it's ready to build fiber to 70 percent of the residences in Westfield. A 2015 pilot in a few hundred homes showed its managers that the company was more than capable of doing so.[44]

Now they're interested in helping Otis do the same, by being the project managers for Otis's fiber plans. Chris Morris, then Otis's town manager, told me that "they're hoping to make some money over from our project that will help them finance the expansion of their network in Westfield."

It's very important to both Otis and Westfield that this arrangement is local: "That money is staying in the region," Morris said. "Half our money is going to turn around and help the people in Westfield. The money isn't going off to the Cayman Islands." It was also important that Otis not wait for someone else to build its fiber network: "It's, in the best sense, sort of the old Yankee feeling, like 'I'm not going to put up with this any more and I'm going to do something about it.'" They're not expecting that the network will pay for itself; they see it as a public good that isn't designed as a revenue stream. "We're going to have to pay for it, just like we pay for the fire trucks and the maintenance guys," said Bill Hiller, an Otis town selectman.

They're on a twenty-year payback schedule, said Hiller, which will give the town maximum flexibility: "What are the demands going to be in twenty years? We're putting in extra fiber for stuff that we don't even know what there's going to be. . . . But everybody thought, three years go, DSL, three megabytes . . . Wow! I'm never going to need anything faster than this. And now, it doesn't work. It doesn't work."

Otis held town meetings to vote on the fiber plan. The meetings were uniformly well attended. "Hundreds of people," said Morris.

The summer people can't vote, but they're furious about the lack of internet access in their houses and can't wait for fiber. Whether or not a resident actually signs up for fiber won't matter, because a line will be run to every house. To avoid inequality, Otis decided to treat the service like a utility and wire every house whether its current inhabitants wanted fiber access or not. They were, after all, doing the build with taxpayers' money. "We're going to have 100 percent coverage," said Morris. "Our feeling was, you're [everyone in town] all paying for it. And it could be, whatever your situation or your life or, like, 'I hate the damn internet.' Okay, you don't want the service, but the fact is, ten years, fifteen years down the road, you go to sell your house, the fact that the new buyer can, for a reasonable fee, tap into the network—that's going to be good for the value of your real estate. And if you're paying, you should have that benefit like everybody else." Westfield Electric will construct the Otis network in phases, connecting homes and businesses one neighborhood at a time so as to ensure a steady stream of revenue to support its operations.

The level of wealth inequality in America, already staggering and continuing to worsen, feeds into other patterns of inequality: of transit, of opportunity, of access to knowledge and skills, of health. These multiple inequalities, arbitrary and demoralizing to those experiencing them, aren't consistent with the values on which a liberal democracy depends. Although sustainable, effective interventions are unquestionably difficult, it's clear that ensuring reasonably priced fiber internet access to everyone deeply affects the ability to address these other inequalities.

Inequality, after all, is not a side issue: it causes and worsens a steep loss in social cohesion and trust. Wealthy people sense they must fence out less fortunate people and treat them as objects, and the less fortunate feel a deep sense of hopelessness. This loss of a sense of brotherhood and community triggers extreme uncertainty that, in a barbaric circle, triggers fear and lack of trust in civic institutions, at the same time that those civic institutions and ideals are systematically being undermined, underfunded, and hollowed-out.

Once we tackle fiber, many of the other problems we need to take on will become more tractable. The arcs of growth and opportunity may begin to intersect to support democracy itself.

CHAPTER NINE

Lessons from American Communities

I N APRIL 2017, EPB, Chattanooga's city-owned electric utility, announced that its fiber optic network had more than 90,000 subscribers.[1] When the utility launched the network in 2010, it thought it would need about 35,000 customers to break even. Just seven years later, it had nearly tripled that number and paid back all the debt it incurred in building the system. The fiber part of EPB now pays for both electrical and fiber services, plus about 50 percent more than what delivering those services costs. EPB also announced in June 2017 that power rates were *lower* by 7 percent as a result of its vastly increased fiber revenues: "The amount of increased revenue coming in from fiber optics as a result of now more than 90,000 subscribers has been a huge benefit to us and we estimate [that it] has helped to keep our electricity rates about 7 percent below what we otherwise would have to charge if we didn't have the money flowing from our fiber optics side of the business to our electric system," EPB's Joe Ferguson told the *Chattanooga Times Free Press*. "We've been extraordinarily pleased by the acceptance of our fiber optic services."[2]

Electrical grids need data too, as they move to more distributed power from many smaller sources of generation—including renewables—and begin to price their products at different rates during different times of the day and season. EPB's use of thousands of intelligent switching devices responding to data carried over its fiber network to detect and address power outages saved the area more than $130 million in just the network's first three years of operation, according to professor of finance Bento Lobo of the University of Tennessee at Chattanooga.[3] EPB used to generate 11 million data points a year from reading meters, but in 2017 it generated more than 2.3 trillion data points about energy usage and efficiency for buildings within its service area, all carried over its fiber network.[4] Using that data can help consumers and businesses manage their electricity use by moderating consumption during peak hours—a third of all the electricity we use is wasted— as well as look for outages.

PC Magazine rates EPB the best-quality internet service provider in the country.[5] Standard & Poor's upgraded its bond rating in 2012 to AA+ based on the strength of its fiber service.[6] The utility's payments to Hamilton County in lieu of taxes—equivalent to what it would be assessed if it were a taxpaying entity rather than a nonprofit founded by the city—make EPB the largest taxpayer in the region; roughly half of its payments go to the school system.[7] All of its revenue is staying local. As Adam Kinsey, developer of the Chattanooga Choo Choo, told me, "I have several friends who work at EPB, so I know when I go pay my EPB fiber bill that they're getting paid. That dollar isn't going out of town. Those dollars are staying in town, which should just raise everyone else."

Nonetheless, EPB has attracted much criticism from Comcast and AT&T. Part of what has made it such a model for the country is that its community, its subscribers, have stood up successfully to those companies. In August 2007, weeks before the city council was scheduled to vote on EPB's plans, 2,600 commercials were run locally telling people to "'call City Hall and stop EPB.'"[8] DePriest remembered that someone wrote a letter to the local paper saying, "Look, they want us to call City Hall to stop this. Why don't we call City Hall and say we support it?" In two weeks, six hundred calls were made to city council members. "That absolutely solidified the city council in their support of it," said DePriest. A few organizations, including one hired by Comcast, ran surveys; the *lowest* level of support for EPB getting into the fiber business was 80 percent of those asked. In the end, EPB had to do very little marketing: people wanted its fiber service.

Wilson, North Carolina, has also faced substantial opposition from incumbent providers, in the form of badmouthing from local cable installers asserting that the city's Greenlight internet service was unreliable and would be a flash in the pan. Wilson city manager Grant Goings remembered getting "the Time Warner letter" announcing the yearly price increase—except that the price increase for Wilson had been changed to zero. He laughed as he told the story. "It was not even a letter that was corrected on the computer and printed, it was a letter that had been white-out-changed to zero, but it was mailed in the same batch that went out with everybody else's, except mine had been whited out with a zero on my percent [increase]." Time Warner wasn't being terribly subtle. "They only had two price categories" on the Time Warner website, he remembered. "North Carolina and Wilson."

Time Warner also made special offers to Wilson residents for packages designed to keep them from using the city's fiber. Dathan Shows remembered: "We had significant predatory pricing. Someone would call and say 'I want to disconnect to go to Greenlight,' and they would say 'I'll give you a break on your bill.' 'Nah, you could have done that before.' 'I'll give you 10 percent off,' 'No.' 'I'll give you 20 percent off, I'll give you half off. You have $180 bill, I'll charge you $90 for a year.' It was just insane."

Wilson's residents didn't switch. They were comfortable with the city's involvement with fiber and backed their local network, with its excellent, reliable service and local people answering the phones when help was needed. "No churn. Everybody stays with Greenlight," said city manager Grant Goings. "It got to the point where our customer loyalty and word-of-mouth advertising was so strong that we quit advertising." The people signing up for RS Fiber in rural Minnesota feel the same way; they love that a local is answering the phone, they're delighted with the customer service they're getting, and they're not about to switch. This is something fiber cities have in common: people in these places trust and support the idea of community last-mile fiber.

Another thing fiber cities often have in common is a history of self-reliance and vision. Wilson has an extensive background in providing for itself. As Greenlight's general manager for its outside plant, Gene Scott, told me, "When people [incumbents] would not provide a service, we'd respond, 'Well, we'll do it ourselves.'" Wilson made sure its people had electricity, gas, water—and now fiber. It built a massive water reservoir project, city lawyer Jim Cauley told me, right before it took on the deployment of its fiber network. "This community," he said proudly, "a relatively small community to take on a project of this size, without one dollar of federal or state assistance, built Buckhorn Reservoir, which is about five to eight miles outside of the city limits and now has secured ourselves of a water supply sufficient for the next seventy-five to a hundred years." So when Time Warner Cable's representative laughed at Wilson city officials who wanted to partner with them for communications, the city was not fazed. City manager Grant Goings told me Time Warner Cable said, "'We're the second largest cable company in the United States. Why would we partner with you?" Goings responded, "Well, if you don't, we're just going to build it ourselves." The TWC representatives "sort of chuckled and left the meeting," he said. The city went ahead on its own.

The history of city planning in Chattanooga was similarly visionary and self-reliant. As David Steele told me, "As we identify problems, we are going to fix them. We just are. So even if somebody doesn't like fish, the aquarium makes this a better place. Even if you don't really care about the gig, the gig makes this a better place. But how we got that stuff, to me, is just about magical."

Fiber cities also know the difference between publicly overseen networks, aimed at providing a utility service, and wholly private "demand-driven" communications networks. There is no single meaning of the word *utility*, but the concept is familiar to many people. The basic idea is that a utility is a service that (1) relies on a physical network of some kind and (2) is a basic input into both domestic and economic life. A utility is not a luxury. Utility services can be sold by private or public entities, but they are always subject to public obligations to reach everyone at a reasonable price, with a service meeting public quality standards.

A utility-based approach would treat a last-mile fiber connection—likely provided on a wholesale basis—as essential physical infrastructure under a city's legal control that is required to reach everyone. The logic is that if a city controls when, how, and for whom the basic network is built, and at what cost that wholesale facility is made available to private competitors who want to directly serve customers, all premises in the city could have access to modern essential infrastructure at a reasonable cost. A demand-driven approach, by contrast, would allow a private operator to wire only those areas that made sense under its business model.

Services that start off as luxuries can become utilities as their centrality to life becomes clear—we've seen this with electricity, which was initially sold by private companies following a demand-driven model. Where investors saw the possibility of a stream of revenue that met their expectations, they would borrow or put up the initial money to wire businesses and homes with electricity. As a result, as we've seen, the electrification of America followed a consistent pattern: municipal buildings and businesses first, wealthy urban dwellers next, then poorer urban dwellers, and, last of all, rural homes and farms. This was the demand-driven model in action.

Now, after government intervention in the electricity marketplace and decades of treatment of electricity as a utility subject to public obligations, we take electricity for granted as a service that is available to every home and business at a reasonable cost. Most of the country follows the National Electrical Code, which requires every single-family dwelling to be connected to at least 100 amperes of electrical power from the local utility. This is a peak-load figure—the maximum current you can draw through your electrical system at one time—and it's the typical standard for modern usage. Houses are built for a peak electricity use so that everybody can plug in their devices and appliances and function in the modern world.

Today, fiber optic internet access is available at a reasonable cost to 100 percent of residents in South Korea, Japan, Hong Kong, and Singapore. China plans to have 100 million homes connected to fiber in short order. Sweden also has extraordinarily high fiber adoption rates. None of this happened by accident; none of these places used a demand-driven model. Cities in all of these places treat fiber access as a utility. As a result, as Owen Narita, a mid-twenties employee of a small Tokyo travel startup, told me that he never thinks about uploading large files ("It's not a drama"), works easily from home, and if he ever wants to switch providers, he has only to install a new Wi-Fi router in his home. Don Werve, an American computer programmer living in Tokyo, said the same thing: "The fiber here is amazing." He has never thought about it: "It is fast enough to the point where the speed of my internet connection just simply does not matter. It never has living here. It has never been a concern." He told me there's fiber in Tokyo because "a large group of people who were in power sat down and said, 'We know that we need connectivity. This is absolutely essential for us as the future of our country.'"

For an example of the shift from demand-driven luxury to utility, consider Singapore in 2002–3. Although about 80 percent of Singaporeans had high-speed internet access at that point, it was expensive and provided primarily by two private companies: DSL from a telephone company and cable modem service from a cable company. Though the cable company (in each location, as in the United States, there was one primary cable operator) was selling relatively fast download services (about 100 Mbps, compared with the 10 Mbps being offered by the phone company), it was charging $80 or $90 a month and its network's upload capacity was sharply limited. The government of Singapore, having received complaints from both residents and businesses about this state of affairs, decided that its citizens needed inexpensive, two-way, virtually unlimited fiber capacity.

After visiting cities around the world to investigate their fiber plans, the government of Singapore decided to ensure that many retail fiber competitors served all of their residents and businesses. The way to do that, they determined, was to have a fiber line built that would solve the island's "last-mile" fiber problem. Because that fiber connection to homes and businesses would be a natural monopoly—it wouldn't make sense to have two of them—it would be made available at a reasonable wholesale cost to retail providers. Competition would come not from having many lines running into homes and businesses, but from having at least one fiber line in place that any retail player interested in providing services could use.

The government put out a request for bidders, offering about $750 million in government support in exchange for a promise that the winning bidder would connect fiber to every home and business in Singapore.[9] The winning bidder was not permitted to sell services directly to consumers and businesses, and the maximum price it could charge for wholesale fiber was set by the government.

Today, Singapore's "last-mile" and "natural monopoly" problems have been decisively solved: gigabit symmetrical fiber subscriptions cost about $30–$40 a month, there are many competitive providers selling services at different levels of capacity and cost, and no one has been left behind. Singapore has stopped measuring residents' capacity and subscription rates for cable or copper internet access: the numbers are no longer relevant.

As we've seen, this same model has been realized in Stockholm; there as in Singapore, this approach has led to increased competition in the delivery of telecom services and has driven the adoption of high-speed internet access. A key common element of successful fiber cities and localities is the mental shift they have made. They no longer think of last-mile fiber as a luxury that should be provided only by private companies to those residents who can pay high rates.

In America, fiber cities have to be brave. That courage is essential at the state level, where the major telecom companies have been able to corral credulous state legislators into doing their collective will. Beginning in 2004, under pressure from national cable companies, telephone companies, and the American Legislative Exchange Council, many states passed laws making it difficult or impossible for most localities to have much to do with data transmission. ALEC believes that "local government entry into the provision of broadband services should be permissible only in unserved areas and only where no business case for private service exists."[10] (ALEC's members include Spectrum, AT&T, and two thousand state legislators who collaborate to draft model bills.) Today, about twenty states have such laws in place.

Both the Wilson and Chattanooga networks have faced elaborate state-law limitations on their ability to expand. The North Carolina and Tennessee statutes, which were pushed forward by the incumbents at great expense, have had the result of stopping expansion of not only the Wilson and Chattanooga networks, but also other public efforts within these states that might threaten the incumbents' monopoly positions. Areas immediately bordering both Wilson and Chattanooga have high-speed internet service that is markedly worse than the national average (which is bad enough), and no new city-overseen networks have been launched in either state since the bills were signed into law.

From the perspective of localities, life is rough in the state legislatures. "You have the cable company in charge, or AT&T, or CenturyLink, nonstop, 100 percent of the time, devoted to the legislature," Catharine Rice told me when we met in Greensboro. "They're pushing very simple arguments on people." In North Carolina, ALEC's efforts at suppressing local involvement in telecommunications are supported by advice given by the School of Government at the University of North Carolina, itself a creature of the legislature; the lawyers there, on whom under-resourced public officials across the state routinely rely, have interpreted HB 129, the state law essentially blocking localities from the "provision of communications service," to mean that cities in the state shouldn't even lease passive, dark fiber they own to private operators. You'd have to be brave to go up against that very conservative advice; it creates a presumption that cities should simply stay out of the telecom business altogether.

Holly Springs, a town of about 25,000 southwest of Raleigh, bucked this crabbed reading of the law in 2013, investing $1.9 million in a fiber network that it is now leasing to third parties interested in reaching homes and businesses there, while saving enormous amounts on the city's own bills for telecommunications services.[11] Its reasoning: leasing out city fiber to others is not the same thing as selling subscriptions directly to homes and businesses. As Jeff Wilson, Holly Springs's IT director, put it in early 2017, "Just like a town park whose primary purpose is free and open access to all people, but can be rented out for a private party for a fee, the excess fiber capacity in the town's network can be dedicated to private data providers through long-term agreements." That was brave. Today, a private provider based in Toronto, Ting, is selling fiber-based internet access in Holly Springs.[12]

Here's another story of local bravery: a Colorado law, SB 152, passed in 2008 at the urging of CenturyLink, prevents municipalities and counties from providing last-mile fiber, although it allows those localities to opt out of the ban if their citizens affirmatively vote in favor of going ahead. Referendums are expensive, and CenturyLink likely figured that cities would be unlikely to hold them. Although well-funded buzzsaws of opposition were routinely rolled out by incumbents every time a city was considering involvement in fiber, nearly a hundred Colorado localities so far have put these measures on the ballot. These referenda have uniformly passed overwhelmingly, with an average of 76 percent of voters supporting them, in both traditionally Democratic and traditionally Republican communities. Coloradans have noticed that the city of Longmont, which opted out of the state law in 2011, is offering gigabit last-mile fiber service to residents and businesses at a reasonable price, and the other cities are jealous.[13] It takes bravery to proceed with these initiatives—even to put the question to a vote, given the millions that the incumbents have been willing to invest to sow doubt—and Coloradans, regardless of party affiliation, are leading the way in reclaiming local control over their civic destinies.

As I talked to the technical, community, and public leaders across America who have participated in getting various flavors of municipal networks off the ground, I noticed a common thread. Every successful municipal effort has benefited from the presence of people on staff—or available to the locality—with the skills needed to avoid starting from scratch. Today, moreover, no city needs to feel alone. Because Chattanooga, Wilson, and about five hundred other American communities have already taken the plunge, local government officials can get ample advice as they do the painstaking work of planning a competitive fiber optic environment for their people—which, in turn, will lead to a competitive, ubiquitous 5G wireless world that depends on that fiber. Even if a local government does not have the in-house skills of Chattanooga's EPB and Wilson's Greenlight network, many more publicly oriented vendors and consultants are available than existed at the outset of this movement.

In a giant terrarium-like hotel in Nashville, Tennessee, full of artificial rivers and rainforest plantings, the Fiber to the Home Council held a large meeting during the summer of 2016. More than 1,700 people showed up to talk about fiber, and many were talking about local networks. There was Joey Durel, the former Republican mayor of Lafayette, Louisiana, talking about the five years of fighting with cable incumbents it took to launch the city's fiber utility in 2009. Now, thanks in large part to its network, Lafayette and its region—Acadiana, in southern Louisiana—is diversifying its energy-based economy by attracting manufacturing and health care businesses. "I can tell people," Mayor Durel told me, "that if you're not prepared for this, [the incumbents will] hire people who are close to you to oppose you."

Bob Whitman, a longtime Corning employee, talked to me in the vendor demonstration room next to a large mockup of a kitchen wall. He remembered starting the FTTH Council in 2001, when localities were first considering working with small independent telcos to build fiber. "None of the big guys were doing it," Whitman remembered. "So every company was coming up with their own type of products and solutions. There was a lot of disaggregation. We said, 'Look, we need to create a venue and place where we can bring things together.'" That was the start of the council: accelerating fiber-to-the-home installations by having a common educational and consultative mission across many companies. Whitman has seen the entire history of fiber: "I would have thought we would have retired the council by now, but we had that spike with Verizon, that big build, and then things slowed down for a while. Then Google lit the fire under the industry. The cable companies are thinking about it, but they're not really doing anything yet." Fifteen years later, he pointed out, "we've come full circle. We're back to communities, municipalities, townships, all starting to dive in."

Whitman is a good-natured guy with nine children, six of whom are still at home, sharing a DSL connection in Hickory, North Carolina. He can't wait for fiber: "Whenever I'm home and have to send something for work, I have to yell, 'Everybody get off the internet.' Because they all watch Netflix. And every day my fifteen-year-old says, 'Can we get new internet?'" Communities, he said, have to have community champions, and they have to have a vision about what they want. "If you are a champion in your community, you can come here, make the connections you need to make, and at least get started."

At these conferences and others like them, community leaders readily trade information and find companies to help them. Every locality needs to do a feasibility study, to figure out what its assets are (conduit, poles, money, community support), what personnel it has on hand to focus on the project, and what network design best suits its vision. Every locality needs to assess its political landscape and legal risks, given the multiplying state laws in this arena. Every community needs to think about its wireless future as part of its fiber plan; fiber is wireless's best friend, and neutral interconnection points at very frequent intervals will be essential for the 5G dreams of urban areas to happen—and to avoid control by AT&T and Verizon. Otis, Massachusetts, learned from Westfield Electric, which learned from Wilson, which learned from Chattanooga; Otis also learned from Leverett, Massachusetts, which had built its own fiber network. Otis city manager Chris Morris remembered Leverett representatives telling him: "Look, if our town can do it, your town can do it." "We were really inspired by that," he told me.

A local "champion" is crucial. For localities to believe a complicated infrastructure initiative like fiber is possible, there has to be someone with budget, staff, knowledge, and authority who pushes the project along—at least rhetorically. (As David Belitz told me in Chattanooga, "My view of mayors is that they have a great platform. They can promote, *and they can convene private and public groups to make things happen*.") Local governments and cooperatives and other publicly minded entities can be siloed and difficult to work with, and opposition from incumbents can be extraordinary—and extraordinarily well funded. Absent a decisive, empowered person dedicated to keeping things moving, it is almost impossible to carry off a fiber installation.

Chattanooga has a champion of fiber in mayor Andy Berke, who speaks fluently and at length about its importance to his city: "Chattanooga would not be a place talking about innovation without having fiber," he will say. Or, "We have overall economic vitality here in Chattanooga related to fiber. The fiber is a differentiator." Mayor C.

Bruce Rose of Wilson is an older, more homespun version of Mayor Berke: "Fiber was the best move we ever made, in our whole existence. We've got Greenlight everywhere now, all the manufacturers, the industries, and everybody's got it. It's changed our whole city around." City manager Chris Morris of Otis, Massachusetts, has a more technocratic bent. Otis has been working on a large wind turbine project for about five years. "And I think," he said, "that while it's taken forever and we've had any number of roadblocks, I think it's built the town's confidence that we can work through those things. Fiber would have seemed a lot more daunting if we hadn't already done that." Otis is run by a board of selectmen, who hired Morris, and Bill Hiller, who is on that board, is firm about the benefits of fiber: "I live in Otis, so I need to have fiber. It's all positive. It'll promote jobs. Why would you want to live down in Stamford [Connecticut] and work on your computer? Live up here, and you'll have faster internet access service, and we don't have a single stop light." Mark Farrell, who is leading the charge for San Francisco's dark fiber network, is similarly outspoken: he is vowing to deliver the twenty-first century utility—fiber internet access at home—to every San Franciscan.

This may all sound like boosterism, because it is. But one of the key reasons that both Greensboro and Grass Valley/Nevada City are making such slow progress toward any flavor of publicly oriented fiber is that there is no prominent public leader willing to stand behind it.

Skillful leadership, a determined focus on open physical infrastructure so as to avoid lock-in, access to inexpensive capital, connection to existing information sources, in-house capacity: all of these elements will remain central to cities and localities taking control of their destinies by planning for ubiquitous fiber.

The most important thread of all, however, runs invisibly through these stories. It has to do with a shared understanding of the role of government in widely shared infrastructure that encourages both economic growth and social justice. It also has to do with accepting the appropriateness of joint efforts when the market, left to its own devices, will not produce the desired results. The key element is trust. Theodore Roosevelt, laying the cornerstone of the Pilgrim

Monument in Provincetown, Massachusetts, in 1907, urged audiences to think of the Puritan as "combining in a very remarkable degree both the power of individual initiative, of individual self-help, and the power of acting in combination with his fellows." The true Puritan, he said, "could combine with others whenever it became necessary to do a job which could not be as well done by any one man individually."[14] But to combine with others, or to support *being* combined with others as beneficiaries of a shared infrastructure project, you have to trust that the aims of your local (or national) government or cooperative are worthwhile and that everyone's benefit is your benefit. "We all do better when we all do better," the late senator Paul Wellstone of Minnesota was fond of saying.

Many of the people I talked to in the brave cities where fiber projects had already been successful—or were on a straight path to success—mentioned trust and interdependence. The Chattanooga Way is shorthand for trust: local businesses, local foundations, community members, and local government all encouraging themselves to work together to reach desired ends. Wilson's elaborate Whirligig-plus-new-downtown plan is a giant leap of faith that Wilson will, someday, be the World's Greatest something. Or at least great. Its $10 per month plan for fiber access in public housing is all about giving everyone the opportunity to be successful. The people of Otis came together in town meetings to provide overwhelming support for moving ahead with a fiber network. The RS Fiber project was formed and implemented in an atmosphere of trust: the rurals need the towns, and the towns need the rurals.

San Francisco's fiber story, which is yet to be told, will be a test of trust. Will its citizens believe that government involvement in fiber is appropriate? Will they take to heart Abraham Lincoln's clarity on the subject of basic infrastructure? Government "is a combination of the people of a country to effect certain objects by joint effort," he said. These objects of collective action included "public roads and highways, public schools, charities, pauperism, orphanage, estates of the deceased, and the machinery of government itself."[15] Lincoln would have put fiber on the list. Without trust in this basic vision of government, without a shared sense of purpose, no city can hope to succeed in ensuring that its citizens have inexpensive, virtually unlimited communications capacity over fiber optic wires.

CHAPTER TEN

What Stands in the Way?

W IDELY AVAILABLE, INEXPENSIVE FIBER optic access, by itself, won't make an area thrive, but without it, thriving won't happen. Like electricity and telephones in the twentieth century, fiber is a precondition of sustained, broadly shared growth in the twenty-first. And not just local growth: American democracy requires that these localities thrive, and for this to happen, each community (and eventually the country as a whole) needs to reach the post-bandwidth era: where people don't think about how much data they have but instead think about what they want to do with it. Without that first step, we'll become an underdeveloped nation—the huge middle portion of the United States—rimmed by two modestly developed coasts.

While things look bleak today, with an endless list of political, economic, and technical challenges, it's important to remember that things weren't wholly different during the electrification era. "If you go far enough back" in the history of electrification, said David Wade, the chief executive of EPB, "we started off disjointed. There were a lot of fights and lots of 'is AC better than DC.'" Perhaps, he muses, the United States is not yet ready for a nationwide plan for fiber. "We may still be back in the fighting stage."

So how do we get there, and how do we learn from those twentieth-century electrification efforts? The first step is to decide as a country that the fiber upgrade is sufficiently valuable and necessary that it should be made available to everyone. Right now, that question is being explored by many localities, but countless others are largely ignoring it, as are many states and the federal government.

My hope is that as more Americans experience fiber connections, they will join the movement pushing to treat this technology like a utility. The World's Fair of 1893, held in Chicago, did that for electricity, its gaudy, well-lit demonstrations of municipal and domestic uses of electricity sparking the imagination of the more than 750,000 people who attended.[1] Even so, it took two generations for electricity's potential to be realized. In 2018 the South Korea Olympic experience was designed to convince the world of the country's technological leadership; we may hope it has the knock-on effect of reminding Americans of the importance of fiber.[2]

Once you have the idea that fiber is important, the other steps fall into place.

It's only money. Fiber optic last-mile networks are expensive to install, as was electrical line. But no matter what flavor of last-mile network a city or locality is interested in facilitating, there is capital available to fund it. (Also: 80 percent of the cost of fiber is labor, so we'll be putting a lot of people to work to get this done.)[3] This is basic infrastructure; it requires patient capital, meaning that loans will be paid off in ten or more years rather than five or fewer, but if planning is sensibly carried out, they will be repaid. We should beware of private and equity investors looking for 20 to 30 percent rates of return who expect to be paid back within five years. Those investors won't be interested in letting cities and localities control their own destiny to ensure that everyone is served at a low price. If the city or locality is willing to guarantee bonds, this can be a very attractive route for financing. RS Fiber, the cooperative in Minnesota, used several flavors of financing: an economic development general obligation bond guaranteed by the cities, a grant from the State of Minnesota, equity raised by members of the community, loans from a nearby electric cooperative, and bank financing. It is important that the community, the local government, have some skin in the game; the lack of such involvement in John Paul's Nevada City/Grass Valley has made it very difficult for him to privately finance the building of the Chip Carman network. Banks don't quite understand these projects as utility networks. And when it comes to bonding, taxpayers have to understand that although the town is borrowing money to launch a fiber project, if the project is successful, those taxpayers will never make a payment. The up-front payments needed to build these fixed assets are steep, but the bond will be paid off by revenues from the fiber network. They also need to understand that fiber is an investment in the community, just like water or sewer or electricity; it's part of a city's or locality's role to ensure that fiber is available. If RS Fiber and Otis, Massachusetts, can do it, any small town or rural locality can; if San Francisco can pull it off, any large city can too.

There were financial issues with a few early municipal networks in the United States, but those projects were dogged by poor initial planning. Since then, city officials have learned from one another, and fiber networks are returning value to their communities. Although many are also returning cash, most of their value does not take the form of direct payments back to the community. That's not how infrastructure works. Over time, the vast majority of these networks support everything a community wants to do. And the steady payments generated by these basic pieces of infrastructure will continue for many years, as retail operators lease dark fiber and subscribers pay reasonable but evergreen monthly rates. In all the parts of the United States and the world where open, reasonably priced fiber networks don't now exist, building them will help an area's economic growth and social cohesion.

Just as money isn't the problem—really—the architecture of fiber networks isn't the problem either: all engineers understand that the optimum connection includes fiber all the way to the home. Wireless will never trump fiber when it comes to capacity. It is true that most of our devices are mobile and detached, but we will need fiber connections as close to these devices as we can get them in order for the cascades of data those devices will generate to travel anywhere. And if we are using them for productive work, those connections will need to be symmetric, with equal upload and download speeds.

The real barrier to last-mile fiber around the world is what David Wade calls the "fight between the world of revenue and the world of making access available to everyone." That fight is going on at every level of government and at every place in the architecture of a communications network where incumbents can wield power. From getting access to public rights-of-way to finding inexpensive backhaul networks that can take data from last-mile fiber networks and deliver it to larger cross-country lines, every step can be a struggle. For example, poles and conduit are often owned or controlled by incumbents who have no interest in sharing them, or, if forced to share, will delay and delay until the younger, less-well-financed city network folds. State legislatures may be enormous obstacles to a city's effort to control its destiny. Substantial legal and policy reform will be required to lower these barriers.

The handful of companies that control residential wired access in America are very good at influencing state legislatures, devotedly pushing very simple, misleading arguments on credulous legislators, showing up in droves every time there is a hearing, supporting the legislators' pet nonprofit causes, ensuring that captive think-tanks pump out opposition literature in a steady drumbeat of free-market enthusiasm, and framing the overall story in ways that don't match reality. One of the most startling examples of this last move happened during the summer of 2017, when the national cable association put up a post on its site titled "America's competitive TV and internet markets." By including DSL connections and smartphone access in its calculations, lowering the threshold for what constitutes a high-speed connection from the FCC's current 25 Mbps down to just 3 Mbps, and assuming that all of these connections are substitutable from customers' perspectives, the cable association felt able to claim that most Americans have "choices" for high-speed internet access: "Competition is alive and well," the post said.[4] But the reality is that at the 25 Mbps level (far worse than what's common in much of Asia and northern Europe), most Americans have at most one option for residential internet access: out of 118 million U.S. households, almost 11 million can't buy wired internet access service with this capacity at any price, and about 46 million households live in places that have just one provider.[5] Wireless is a complementary service; it obviously is useful when you're mobile, but buildings, trees, weather, and distance can interfere with its signal. Americans who access the internet only on their smartphones often do so because they cannot afford both a wire at home and a smartphone plan. We are stuck on a plateau of second-rate, expensive internet access. But because this status quo provides enormous profit margins for the existing large players, they will fight fiercely to keep it in place.

Some of the most obscure—but fierce—fights happen over access to rights-of-way, or poles. In many places in America, those poles are owned by AT&T or Verizon. If a municipality doesn't have control over them, it has to negotiate with these companies to get access. And although the new network may have a *legal* right to attach to those poles, the state Public Utility Commission (often controlled by the incumbents), may be unwilling to enforce any legislated time limits—such as not permitting more than twenty days to go by before a pole attachment request will be granted. At the same time, the incumbent in charge of the pole has every incentive to delay in getting those poles ready for someone else to attach wires to it—and can claim, at every turn, that "safety" requires that the incumbent have complete dominion over timing and activities with respect to its poles. In this context, the insurgent has zero leverage to demand that the incumbent move more quickly—and has to pay whatever the incumbent claims it costs to ready the poles, often including paying to upgrade poles dramatically. As Gene Scott of Wilson's Greenlight fiber network put it, the incumbents will claim "'We want to make sure that what you do is safe. We want to make sure you don't overstress the poles so that if we have an ice storm it's going to break.' That's valid, but how could you argue against them? Then my point is, 'Yeah, but does it take you months and thousands of our dollars to figure this out?'"

If several actors already have wires in place, every one of them may demand that its trucks visit each pole, one at a time, and move its wires, slowly, to make room for the new network. No one else, they claim, can safely move those wires. Every step of this process involves lengthy, unpredictable delays. In other words: Sure, you can try to build a network. But you'll run out of money before you get anywhere.

That's why, in Otis, selectman Bill Hiller said frankly that "Verizon holds all the cards," as Otis prepared to build its fiber network with the help of Westfield Gas & Electric. Verizon owns the poles that Otis needs to use. "Getting the poles ready," he said, "might be somewhere between three hundred thousand dollars and a million"—a wide range of unpredictability that is genuinely tough on both budgets and credibility with taxpayers. Aaron Bean, the canny Westfield fiber leader who wrote his MBA paper on municipal networks, said, "They [the incumbents] could drag out the process as long as they so choose." Chris Morris, Otis's town manager, said that in his more cynical moments, he felt "'we're kinda getting shaken down to upgrade their poles.' And then, it's our money, but they're going to turn around and depreciate those assets." If they had a choice, Otis would build its network underground. But, as Bill Hiller put it, "There's rocks the size of Volkswagens. You can't go ten feet without hitting a rock that's ten feet tall." So the town is stuck with poles—and plagued by uncertainty.

In this context, time is definitely money: a young network that's financed for a set timeline of construction may find that timeline becoming completely unpredictable. And one can go broke for lack of access to poles. Even giant market entrants get tangled up over poles; Google Fiber struggled to expand its business in Nashville but couldn't get reasonable access to poles. After two years it was able to attach its fiber lines to only about forty of the city's ten thousand utility poles. When Nashville tried to adopt a city ordinance smoothing the process for pole attachments, AT&T and Comcast sued.[6]

When I visited the Minneapolis statehouse in spring 2017, I heard about so-called small cell legislation being pushed there by a platoon of AT&T lobbyists and backed, predictably, by ALEC. Ohio had already passed a similar bill with very little discussion, and least twenty states were suddenly considering legislation along the same lines.[7] These bills remove city discretion over street lights, power poles, and other public right-of-way elements by setting up a presumption that any carrier can attach wireless equipment, no matter how unsightly, without having to get additional city permits or be required to share its infrastructure with other providers. The buzzword for all this, according to ALEC, is that states are "streamlining" local permitting of small cell technology.[8] Technically, the wireless carriers want to "densify" their wireless transmitters—putting up millions more of them, attached to fiber optic lines, very close to one another in urban areas—so that future generations of wireless transmissions (5G) can carry a great deal of data over short distances. (The cells are labeled "small" because the data is traveling a shorter distance; the equipment used can actually be enormous.)

The wireless carriers (mostly AT&T, with its $240 billion market valuation, and Verizon, worth $189 billion, which together control the vast majority of the wireless market across the country) have essentially ceded the residential and business wired marketplace in urban areas to local cable monopolies. The two giants also, long ago, divided markets for the fiber they have installed under city streets that "backhauls" their data from cell towers to internet "points of presence" some distance away. Their "footprints" for backhaul fiber, in the jargon of telecommunications, never overlap. As I've discussed, 5G requires fiber very close to the wireless transmitter in order to work. No fiber, no 5G. 5G is full of potential to provide immersive wireless experiences, but if just one company controls both the fiber under the streets and has near-exclusive rights to poles—or two companies whose prices and services are essentially in lockstep offer "competing" 5G services—then all the amazing uses of data that might be possible over a neutral transmission medium will actually be impossible.

Now these two companies have joined forces at the state level in order to shore up their power over wireless. In effect, they would like to control the future of wireless services by duplicating the cable companies' playbook: get de facto exclusive rights, build a network that doesn't allow for the introduction of new content or other services without steep payments to the provider of transmission services, and, untroubled by oversight or genuine competition, charge whatever the market will bear. Poorer and rural Americans will be left behind as an unprofitable market.

It's a pernicious development, and I figured it out only after my third trip to Seoul, in August 2017, five months after I visited Minnesota. It took a translator's explanation of presentations made to me by the leading South Korean telco, Korea Telecom, for the penny to drop. (One clue: the slide reading "Achieving Overwhelming Market Dominance.") Korea Telecom is aligning its efforts with those of both Verizon and AT&T, and Verizon and AT&T are making sure they can control the wireless market throughout the United States by getting "small cell" bills passed in every state. Localities that want to be places of innovative, inexpensive fiber-plus-advanced-wireless uses should be wary, and many are fighting back.

From Verizon's and AT&T's perspective as short-term-oriented, revenue-optimizing private companies, localities are either incompetent (in need of "streamlining") or, at best, contractual partners without leverage: Verizon has already pushed several American cities, including Sacramento and Boston, to give the company free or low-cost access to small cell sites and conduit under city streets.[9] The company will then run its own fiber to those small cell connections. Significantly, Verizon recently made a deal with Corning to buy 12.5 million miles of fiber cabling each year through 2020.[10] It's important to understand what that fiber will be used for: Verizon is not interested in fiber-to-the-home installations or in leasing that fiber to anyone else, or in allowing upstarts to share the cell sites it connects to that fiber. It means to ensure that it has complete control over 5G networks in dense urban areas. Only it will be able to afford backhaul—the middle-mile transport of that 5G data back to the rest of the internet—because it will either own that backhaul or get it at reasonable prices from its peer, AT&T, which in turn needs backhaul in places where Verizon controls that market. What does the city get in exchange for giving up its future to Verizon? A few Wi-Fi hotspots and traffic cameras. Meanwhile, Boston residents who can afford Verizon's rates will be paying a great deal for wireless services. Many will be left behind. And the city itself will have lost control over its digital destiny.

Verizon and AT&T, for their part, benefit from the distraction created by this crazy nationwide push for small cell preemption laws: no one is paying attention to their lack of investment in fiber running all the way inside homes and businesses, or to the lack of competition in the wired marketplace. All, they claim, will be magically solved by 5G. But their plan is to make the 5G world even less competitive than the wired world currently dominated by cable in the United States. And they have no thought of extending 5G to rural areas.

The better plan for a city is to insist on neutral, open physical infrastructure at all levels: conduit should be open, fiber should be available to any player, wireless interfaces should be modular and open to any wireless carrier, and new homes and businesses should be required to be open to all competitive telecommunications players.

Brave cities remember that they are powerful. But state legislatures and powerful "free" public-private partnerships are quickly taking key cards out of city hands—particularly in an era when cities have trouble persuading citizens to fiscally support their operations. The costs to cities' futures may not be worth taking these "free" deals.

We are still not done. It turns out that landlords are problems too. They often seek to make exclusive deals with high-speed internet access carriers that give them useful benefits—a free subscription for the building's superintendent, for example—in exchange for control over the rates and quality of service enjoyed by the building's tenants.

I live in an apartment. Chances are good that you do, too: tens of millions of Americans live in apartment buildings, and in medium-to-large cities these structures account for between a quarter and a half of all housing units. More people are renting these days than ever before. And when you move into an apartment, you need the essentials: water, heat, and internet access.

Water and heat are regulated utilities. But when it comes to internet access, people in multiple dwelling units, or MDUs, often have the worst of both worlds: all the limitations of a utility framework—no competition, no choices—with zero consumer protection. That means unconstrained pricing. Network operators like Comcast, Time Warner Cable, and AT&T routinely use kickbacks, legal games, blunt threats, and downright illegal activities to lock up buildings in exclusive arrangements. The result is an enormous, decentralized payola scheme affecting millions of Americans. And these maneuvers will stop only when cities and national leaders require that every building have neutral fiber/wireless facilities that make it easy for residents to switch services when they choose. We've got to take landlords out of the equation—they are only looking to increase their revenue stream at their tenants' expense, and the giant telecom providers in our country are happy to pay them in return for sole access. The market is stuck, and residents have little idea these deals are happening. The current way of doing business is good for landlords and ISPs but destructive in every other way.

Today, without permission from a landlord, a competitive ISP can't enter the building to provide service. But the landlords have signed exclusivity agreements. If a consumer wants access to a service, then that provider should be able to get into the building, subject to reasonable technical limitations. Instead, developers and landlords demand revenue sharing agreements and "door fees": many real estate investment trusts (REITs) won't let service providers in the door unless they agree to share revenue. There's a whole layer of intermediaries who aggressively market "opportunities" for buildings to make additional revenue streams from de facto exclusive internet access agreements, and who manage and drive arrangements in the residential real estate market.

On the commercial side, it's the same deal: landlords, their interests aggregated and managed by third-party intermediaries, all have their hands out when it comes to internet access. This "riser management" is a huge problem for the city of New York; it's why commercial tenants in New York City pay high rates for awful internet service in the fanciest commercial buildings.

The FCC has tried in the past to encourage competition in MDU buildings. Eight years ago, the FCC clearly said landlords can't make exclusive agreements with internet access providers. It recognized the problem: "Incumbent providers commonly engage in a flurry of activity to lock up MDUs and other real estate developments in exclusive arrangements as soon as it becomes clear that a new entrant will be coming to town." Sometimes these clauses are inserted in fine print of tenants' leases.[11]

But the commission has been completely outmaneuvered. While a landlord can't enter into an exclusive agreement granting just one ISP the right to provide internet access service to an MDU, he can refuse to sign agreements with anyone else, in exchange for payments labeled in any number of ways.

Another colorful workaround is marketing exclusivity, which is apparently permitted. AT&T, Comcast, and others may sign deals with buildings requiring that only their flyers are displayed in the leasing office. No competitor is allowed to distribute material— and no events (such as wine and cheese parties for tenants) can be held on the premises by any competing provider.[12]

Here's another common, more serious move: even though exclusive agreements with buildings are illegal, the carriers will nonetheless insert clauses requiring exclusivity in their agreements with MDUs. Then they may add clauses saying, "if any part of this agreement turns out to be illegal, you can cut out that portion of the agreement and the rest of it will stand." (Lawyers call these "severability" clauses.) If you're a property manager reading that contract, you may feel compelled to enforce the exclusivity it appears to require. "Property managers don't know," Barr pointed out. "They're not experts in internet law. They're experts in how to run a property, and they will do what these agreements say. What property manager wants to be the guy to take on Comcast?"

The FCC long ago created "inside wiring" rules giving power to MDU owners, under certain circumstances, to take ownership of wires run by cable companies inside their buildings. The commission recognized that the wiring infrastructure inside an MDU gives the incumbent an advantage, and it wanted to open up that infrastructure to competition. But those rules were based on the assumption that, initially, the cable/telco company owned the wires. Time Warner Cable and others have worked around this by deeding ownership of their inside wires to the building owner, and then getting an exclusive license back from the owner to use those wires.[13] This deeding switchback apparently satisfies the law while still blocking competition.

The next barrier is often created by state law. Consider the history of North Carolina's HB 129 statute and, after it passed, what

happened to the efforts by Wilson to expand its fiber communications network to serve its electricity customers who happened to live outside the Wilson County border. The mantra repeated by the industry was that it didn't want local government competing with industry. Any town could easily counter that argument. As Jim Cauley, a lawyer for Wilson, put it, "You're not competing with business if the service doesn't exist." If there is no cheap fiber optic option in your community, you don't have adequate capacity. "And once you had the opportunity to explain that," Cauley said, "you'd get some head nodding." But then, Cauley remembered, "we had some legislators who were very supportive until their caucus instructed them, 'We're not going to approve this,' and then they would turn around on us."

For each of the three years following Wilson's hooking up of its first Greenlight customers to fiber in 2007, the town faced and defeated legislation drafted by Time Warner aimed at stopping any other city in North Carolina from trying to do what Wilson had done.[14] Gene Scott of Wilson told me he found the draft legislation enormously frustrating: "Wilson's a little city. It's 50,000 people. It's a drop in the bucket, if that, to revenues for any of these corporations. So what are they scared of? They're scared of, my opinion, that if we succeeded, other cities would go, 'Well, gosh. We can do that, too.'"

Although only public servants are permitted to draft bills in North Carolina, Dathan Shows told me, "I sat there in the committee meeting room, and watched the Time Warner lawyer-lobbyist open his big briefcase satchel, pull out twenty-five copies of the bill, and hand them to the committee chairman, who then handed them out. It was sickening, the whole thing was just sickening—to watch our government being bought, but it was bought and paid for." Wilson and its fellow cities were hopelessly outnumbered during the three years the legislation was pending. "We rolled up there for the legislative session sort of proud of ourselves," remembered Grant Goings, speaking to me in the huge Victorian house on Nash Street that serves as Wilson's town hall. The Wilson City Council had approved Goings's proposal to hire a lobbyist. He hired one, and the two walked into the committee room feeling ready to go. But, he said ruefully, "We looked around the room and counted

thirty-three lobbyists on the other side of the issue and realized that we were quite outmanned."

Committee jurisdiction over the draft bills was carefully engineered: "We could often predict," Goings said, "whether we were being sent to a committee to receive a fair hearing, or whether we were being sent to a committee to die, or whether we were being sent to a committee to delay." And once the bills were assigned to a committee, the process for considering them didn't feel fair. Goings remembers committee meetings in Raleigh that either weren't officially calendared or were canceled over and over; classic legislative gamesmanship aimed at keeping insurgents off balance. "A meeting would disappear off the calendar or pop up, and we'd get a call in the early hours of the morning: 'You've got to be here at 8:00 a.m.' A lot of our group was from other parts of the state. The city of Morganton was involved, and they're about a four- or five-hour drive, so they would have to try to make it down." Or, according to Jim Cauley, Wilson's outside lawyer: "We'd get the call the night before. Next morning, we'd head to Raleigh. I remember, one day, we got about halfway to Raleigh. We got a call, they said, 'It's canceled.'" The opportunity for genuine public input was often nullified by these games. "I had never seen this level of gamesmanship in the legislature before," said Cauley.

Nonetheless, without recruitment by anyone in Wilson, people from other towns—supporters, lawyers, local businesspeople who were fed up with expensive connectivity and had heard through the grapevine that the legislature was considering putting limitations on municipal fiber—started showing up at committee hearings in Raleigh to support the idea of independent fiber networks in North Carolina. Grant told me, "The folks that wanted to get the bills passed or were trying to ram them through a committee didn't particularly like that, and so that's when you started seeing these games going on with the scheduling."

Some committee chairs, under pressure to get a bill or resolution through their committee as quickly as possible, treated the Wilson representatives very poorly and did not give them a chance to speak. Grant noticed, though, that when TV cameras were in the room, "we were treated much more fairly." So he contacted Wilson's city hall communications department. "We sent our people up, and they had cameras that looked a lot like news channel cameras. I told them to go set up in the room, and not identify themselves as being with me, or just not identify themselves at all. We faked them out. We got treated very well, and we got a chance to speak because there were cameras in the room. They didn't know they were our cameras."

During the hearings themselves, it was frustrating to the members of the Wilson team that they were continually assaulted by false claims from the incumbents. "As a local government official, we have to be truthful," Goings said. "Any time that we're not truthful, it could end up being your job and potentially even your career." But "we were battling with folks that don't have the same ethical obligations."

For example, almost all of the public presentations made to the legislature during those three years, he remembered, were done by Time Warner lawyers. And in his view they included many howlers. Goings remembered one presentation that included four or five different untrue allegations, including a claim that the city was not letting Time Warner build in new developments but was instead reserving them for its own public service. That wasn't accurate: a private developer, on private land, putting in his own private streets, had wanted Wilson's service rather than Time Warner, but the decision had not been Wilson's. At the end of his presentation, the Time Warner lawyer said, in effect, that local government leaders were trying to enrich themselves personally by calling for municipal fiber networks to be built. Goings quoted the lawyer as saying, "This is no place for government. Just because a mayor decided he wants to drive a Ferrari, we shouldn't let local governments get into private business."

Time ran out on the committee hearing, and so Goings had an opportunity to respond the next day. He went step by step through the untrue claims made by the Time Warner side. Then he put up a slide showing the Time Warner words about the mayor wanting to drive a Ferrari, alongside a picture of Wilson's mayor, Bruce Rose, standing in front of his car. The slide read: "Mayor Bruce Rose, 1992 Buick LeSabre, 243,000 miles." "The whole place just busted out loud, and I went and sat down," Goings remembered. This was just funny, even to the lobbyists.

When they weren't actively dissembling, Time Warner lawyers mischaracterized what was going on. They said, according to Goings, "'So a city wants to get into the entertainment business. What next? Are they going to open a car dealership or a grocery store?'" The mayor was called a communist in a public hearing.

Another time, a committee chair got wind of a video presentation Wilson was using that showed, in real time, the speed of fiber versus cable versus copper when downloading a large graphic file. "You could say, 'Okay, I'm going to download an MRI file at a doctor's office.'" Grant recalled. "You hit the button, and each of those options would go across the screen, showing you how long it took." The committee chairman then made a new rule barring all audio-visual presentations at hearings—even though the room was wired for presentations and had flat screens on the walls for this purpose.

Goings told his assistant, Brian Bowman, that he was going to show the video anyway. Bowman said, "How are we going to do that?" Goings said, "I'm going to step up to the podium, and you're going to turn it on on the screen, and we're going to be live, and we're going to have cameras in the room, and the chair won't stop it." So Bowman figured out how to plug into the presentation system, and Goings showed the video. He clearly relishes this memory; it was a moment when David couldn't be silenced by Goliath.

Stamping out Wilson-like fiber efforts was not necessarily a partisan issue at the state level in North Carolina. Before 2011, when Republicans took control of both houses, "a lot of the battles in the legislature were with some powerful Democrats," Goings remembered. "When the Democrats were in power, they very heavily lobbied Democrat leadership," Goings said. The industry uses whatever approach works with the party in charge.

The legislative term of 2011 brought a new situation: North Carolina's congressional districts were redrawn to reflect population shifts in North Carolina, giving the Republicans majority control of the legislature. (This redistricting effort was later challenged as an unconstitutional racial gerrymander; in 2017, the U.S. Supreme Court ordered the state's redistricting plans to be redrawn.)[15] At this point, Wilson had been fighting industry-sponsored legislation for three years, and with the change of control, things looked bleak for Wilson: Representative Thom Tillis, one of the strongest opponents of municipal broadband, had become Speaker of the House. As a result, "by the time we got to 2010 and 2011," Jim Cauley remembered, "the legislative hearings were something of a joke."

Still, Goings remembered, early in the game "we were actually able to persuade a couple of Republicans who broke party ranks and voted with Democrats" to support Wilson's arguments. But after that vote, Goings remembered, the majority members who had voted with the minority party were invited to the Speaker's office. "They reported that they would not be breaking ranks again."

Something breathtaking happened the next day: the Republican chair of that committee called another meeting and said the legislators had been holding the wrong piece of paper in front of them when they voted, so they needed to call a revote. "It was like a do-over," Goings laughed. "They revoted the same issue after lining up their votes, and then it went down on party lines."

Wilson realized that some industry-sponsored bill was going to pass the legislature and that the city's role, at most, would be to negotiate the best outcome that it possibly could. It had already spent the money and built its system. "We were in debt," Goings said.

Because its service predated the passage of the bill, Wilson County qualified for a "grandfathering" exemption under HB 129, introduced in 2011 to prevent municipalities from offering fiber optic services. But the exemption did not permit Wilson to provide communications services to the five adjacent counties that compose the remainder of its electric service territory. Thus, although the treasurer's office had given Wilson permission to issue its debt offering, the state was now poised to pass a law that, by restricting the market Wilson could serve, would retroactively limit its ability to pay off that debt.[16]

And HB 129, pushed strenuously by Time Warner Cable, created sharp limitations on what Wilson or future Wilsons would be able to do. Not every element of the law looks like a barrier; for example, it requires municipal providers to keep separate books for their high-speed internet access services and publish an independent annual report. But taken together, the asymmetric provisions of the law—no private provider has to keep a separate set of books for its internet access services—make it almost impossible for new municipal networks to be built in North Carolina. The "clear effect" of the law, according to the FCC, is to "protect private providers from competition."[17] There's a section prohibiting a public provider from charging less for its services than a theoretical cost of service, with phantom costs imputed in this calculation that mirror those of a private provider—even though a city might not have the same costs. There are geographic limits on what a city can do—again, limits that don't exist for private providers—that make it hard for cities to achieve the economies of scale a private provider has.

If you add up all the delays required by the legislation, for hearings, multiple votes, request for proposals processes, and other steps, they fill up two years of effort—during which a public provider cannot start building its network. The town has to vote on its debt according to a particular election cycle. It has to disclose any feasibility study or business plan before it begins—something no private company would ever agree to do. (Time Warner and its North Carolina trade association made many public records requests of Wilson while it was building its network.)[18] It has to solicit public-private partnerships or proposals from outside entities to provide the service. The network has to be profitable on its first day, without the town's borrowing any money for operating expenses.

The requirement that a municipal network may exist only within city limits, and no further, creates a distinct competitive disadvantage. North Carolina law provides that any other form of public enterprise or utility may expand beyond city limits "within reasonable limitations," and the law provides that it is reasonable to look at the competition, or lack of it, beyond the utility's service area.[19]

Towns are not allowed to provide services at less than "cost," which is defined not based on the actual cost of the town's service but on the basis of a hypothetical private-sector competitor's service. The only way to escape these limitations is for a city to show that it proposes to provide services to an "unserved" area. But under the bill, "unserved" means that less than 50 percent of households have access to service at download speeds of at least 768 Kbps. Which, these days, is nothing at all.

And under HB 129, a city that does anything wrong can lose the tax exemption that gives it access to low-cost financing.[20] "If they can catch you, if they get you on any of these requirements, you lose it all," said Cauley. These elements of HB 129 heap risk, expense, uncertainty, and delay onto any North Carolina city that would like cheap fiber access for its citizens.

Although several such cities were considering building municipal networks before HB 129, their efforts ceased as soon as the bill passed. Nor have any additional fiber-to-the-home systems been built in rural North Carolina, even though Time Warner had promised that it would figure out a way to serve these areas if the bill went through.[21]

Even when public opinion was on Wilson's side and the business community was in support, it made no difference: "What we learned the hard way," Grant said, "is that when there is absolute determination for a certain outcome in the leadership and the majority party is committed to that outcome, it's what will happen. The incumbents, he said, "see every threat as a competitive threat, as that we want to take over what they perceive to be their sandbox." Goings was mystified: "We have no ambition to reach out across North Carolina. We just want to serve our electric customers. I guess it's the precedent that having a successful example brings. We're no threat to some of these largest telecommunication companies in the world. We want to be part of the solution." Goings had thought of getting involved in state government as a "lobbyist or something" once he finished his city manager career. But the fighting over HB 129 "cured me of any such desire. It is a dog-eat-dog world."

Why did Time Warner Cable have such power over North Carolina legislators? "If you look at the contribution history over those three, four years, it tells a story," said Cauley. HB 129 was sponsored by Marilyn Avila, a Republican representing Wake County. Campaign finance reports show that Avila received over $20,000 from Time Warner Cable, AT&T, and CenturyLink between 2010 and her vote in 2011. A range of co-sponsors, both Democrats and Republicans, received similar amounts from these three companies over similar periods.[22] According to the Institute for Local Self Reliance, Time Warner Cable and other incumbents in North Carolina spent more than a million dollars between 2006 and 2011 to get HB 129 passed.[23]

Even though Wilson's network was grandfathered by the 2011 law, its operations are still constrained by it. The very last day before the bill passed, Wilson's lobbyist was summoned to a meeting to determine what its permitted area of service would be. Representative Avila, representing Speaker Tillis, opened the meeting and immediately turned it over to Time Warner's lawyers, who told Wilson what the exceptions for its service would be. Although the bill limited future city fiber networks to their city limits, Wilson—already operating—would be allowed to serve everyone in its county. But nowhere else.

Again, this is breathtaking. A private party soaked in self-interest was making legislative policy. As Grant put it, "That was a fitting end to that battle."

Wilson ended up coming back to the state house a couple of years later. It felt it had to: although HB 129 limits Greenlight service to the Wilson county line, Greenlight actually serves electric customers in portions of five counties. There is much mutual benefit to be had by ensuring that its electric customers also have fiber connectivity: electricity can be measured using smart grid services, and renewables can be brought into the supply of energy on a dynamic, real-time basis. And it would help Wilson save money by deploying fiber over a broader territory—lowering the per-unit cost of selling its communications services.

For a brief period in 2015 and 2016, Pinetops, a tiny town of 1,300, mostly African Americans, in rural Edgecombe County just twenty miles from downtown Wilson, had affordable fiber connectivity as well as electricity from Wilson. Pinetops has about six hundred households and a per capita income of $16,698. About 38 percent of the population lives below the poverty line; about 65 percent are African American and about 34 percent Caucasian.[24] This affordable access to fiber was possible because in February 2015, the Federal Communications Commission blocked the effect of HB 129.[25] Its argument was that the North Carolina law was getting in the way of the FCC's mandate to remove barriers to "advanced broadband deployment" across the country.[26] Pointing to

"state-level red tape" and laws passed "due to heavy lobbying support by incumbent broadband providers," FCC chairman Tom
Wheeler said that "when local leaders have their hands tied by bu-
reaucratic state requirements, local businesses and residents are the
ones who suffer the consequences."[27]

Pinetops had long gotten its electricity from Wilson, but its
residents had been relying on copper DSL internet access from
CenturyLink that was slow and unreliable.[28] CenturyLink's customer service was equally slow. "It takes several days to get your
complaint resolved with customer service" from CenturyLink, Pinetops town commissioner Suzanne Coker Craig said. "All we want is
the choice of having better access." Following the FCC's order,
schools, public buildings, and two hundred residential and commercial customers in Pinetops connected to Greenlight's fiber service. But in August 2016, the U.S. Court of Appeals for the Sixth
Circuit ruled that Congress hadn't given the FCC clear enough
authority to allow it to preempt the North Carolina law.[29]

Pinetops's fiber services were instantly in limbo. Wilson didn't
want to disconnect the fiber running to Pinetops residences, and
felt obliged to provide services for free until its legal ability to sell
to Pinetops was clarified.[30] (Providing services for free is unobjec-
tionable to the carriers; it increases the chances that the municipal
system will fail.)

Wilson went back to the state legislature, asking for an exemption to HB 129 that would allow it to serve its existing electrical
customers, both in Pinetops and in other counties. The industry
fought the request tooth and nail. Meanwhile, CenturyLink, although it had for years been telling people in rural eastern North
Carolina that it couldn't provide high-capacity services there because its returns on investment would be too low, suddenly made a
presentation to the Pinetops town board declaring that it wanted
to sell fiber services in the tiny town: "Within a couple-week period of time, they get a project approved from corporate. They say
they've got all the engineering work done, and they're ready to
build and can be done in a few months. Wow!" said Grant Goings.

But it turns out CenturyLink doesn't have to build in Pinetops.
In late June 2017, the North Carolina legislature approved a bill,
H396, that allows Pinetops residents and businesses to be served by

Greenlight *only until another provider builds a similar fiber-to-the-home network in the area.* If CenturyLink decides to build in Pinetops, Greenlight will have thirty days to *stop* serving its customers there and migrate them to CenturyLink's network—and it will lose its entire investment in the area. The incumbents call the shots in the North Carolina state legislature.[31]

Grant Goings has no regrets about Wilson's fights over state legislation. "We had our moments," he said. "Obviously, we were successful for three or four years against an extremely powerful lobby. We had the courage to have the audacity to fight them. We were driven by the fact that we knew we were fighting for what was right." But the motivations of Time Warner Cable and its brethren are very clear. Their efforts in state legislatures have nothing to do with improving the lives of citizens, particularly in rural areas. They are motivated to squelch any threat to the status quo, and once that threat goes away, so will any promised investment on their part.

Gene Scott, the former telco engineer who designed Wilson's Greenlight network, feels bossed around. "The idea that I'm having someone else tell me that I have to accept fewer choices or even subpar services and where I can spend my money for resources that can help my children's education or to even benefit from something as simple as if my wife and I just want to stream a movie—is wrong, morally wrong. That's another reason why I did this [work with Greenlight's network] and stuck with it. It's an emotional issue." The situation in Pinetops bothers him. "Nowhere in the decision-making process in Raleigh does there seem to be a great deal of concern for the citizens that will be impacted. The concern seems to be not upsetting the big cable and telco lobby." After years of fighting for better municipal fiber in North Carolina and managing, expertly, the Greenlight network in Wilson, Will Aycock was quietly indignant: "We think our country and our state should be looking at laws that encourage expansion and service to the underserved. It's almost inexplicable that we would be more focused on writing laws to prevent somebody from providing fiber."

Even if there is no state law blocking a municipality from proceeding, and poles aren't an issue, there are still more hurdles. Once data from a city-controlled network leaves town, where does it go? You may wonder why this part of communications networks is relevant; so much of our discussion has been about the last mile, the part of the network that actually touches consumers. But for data coming to or from consumers and businesses to go farther upstream, to other cities or neighborhoods, it has to be carried over the next section of the network—variously called the "middle mile," "backhaul," "special access," or "business data services" part of the network. Think of a small local cul-de-sac connected to a medium-sized avenue.

Here's the problem: in most areas of the country, the middle mile, like the last mile, is a bottleneck monopoly. It turns out that AT&T, Verizon, Spectrum, Comcast, and CenturyLink own most of the lines running between towns.[32] That middle mile is nominally a regulable, so-called Title II service, meaning that the FCC has statutory authority to ensure that access to this leg of the network is provided at "just and reasonable" prices.[33] But over the years, through persistent, mostly invisible effort by the handful of companies that control it, it has been entirely deregulated.

It's easy to understand how overwhelming concentration in the roughly $50 billion middle-mile marketplace could cause problems for any competition in the last mile, even if the country builds last-mile fiber that is dark and open.[34] Any new player in the last-mile market will have to pay to get its data anywhere useful beyond a neighborhood or city. The result is that everyone, every business, every residence, pays indirect rent to a monopoly-controlled middle mile. The only answer is regulation, because the barriers to entry by competitors in many areas are simply too high.

In 2013, the FCC decided to dig into this "middle-mile" market and collect detailed pricing and availability data for every part of the country, including information about facilities, billing, revenue, and expenditures—so that it could regulate this crucial and broken market. If you have any doubt that detailed information about telecommunications can ever be gathered, rest assured that it can. This data now exists. It's not all available to the public, but it exists. It is the most comprehensive collection of information ever assembled for an FCC rulemaking proceeding.[35]

Based on what it learned from the telephone companies, cable companies, and other providers in this market, the FCC in May

2016 issued a proposed rule aimed at revamping the regulatory treatment of the noncompetitive portions of the middle-mile marketplace.[36] Economists noted that concentration in this market was uniformly high, with the vast majority of locations served by a monopoly provider—and over 95 percent served by either a monopoly or a duopoly. The Consumer Federation of America asserted that as a result of middle-mile providers' excessive market power, American consumers had paid over $150 billion since 2010 in overcharges and excessive pricing.[37]

Final comments were in by the end of July 2016. Chairman Wheeler's proposed regulatory revamping of the middle-mile marketplace then sat for two months. The commission had a chance to adopt appropriate regulations for uncompetitive segments of the market, based on an excellent data record, to constrain incumbent providers' market power and ensure just and reasonable rates, terms, and conditions for the middle mile, as required by law. But nothing happened. Wheeler issued a statement in October 2016 saying that he had circulated a proposed final rule to his colleagues incorporating a simplified regulatory framework.[38] He finally forced the issue, putting the proposed rules on the agenda for a public meeting in November 2017, but then pulled the item under pressure from Congress following the election of Donald Trump. Many years of effort down the drain.

This very profitable middle-mile market—the FCC estimates this business brings in between $45 billion and $75 billion a year—is almost completely uncompetitive.[39] Many towns and cities will have very few choices and enormously expensive connections. Wilson, North Carolina, was clever: Dathan Shows created alternatives for the town by trading access to the business of a large bank in Wilson to AT&T in exchange for a reasonably priced long-term lease of its backhaul from Wilson to an interconnection point in North Carolina that had more choices and competition. The town's network then had an electronic escape route. Once Shows had that deal in place, he quickly established additional, redundant ways for data to leave the area; he never wanted Wilson to be subject to AT&T bossing it around.

We are not done. Once the data leaves town and is lucky enough to have a first big link available to it at a reasonable price, it has to reach a wholesale interconnection location in a larger city. At that whole-sale service point, the data will hop onto one of several enormous fiber "backbones" running across the country to landing spots at the edge of the continent. And, presto, a town's inhabitants, using alternative, open, inexpensive fiber access, can be in touch with the world.

But those wholesale points are also places of conflict and control. There aren't enough of them in this country. And they're not sufficiently neutral: they're buildings that are often, again, owned by the incumbent carriers, who have plenty of latitude to make rules that restrict competition. They can charge what they like for entry, refuse to allow equipment from competing companies, and prohibit interconnection between two competing providers both coming into the same wholesale spot—the games are endless. The handful of enormous companies that control telecommunications in America treat only their peers fairly.

There are still more hurdles to an optimal post-bandwidth era. Several of the big carriers are transforming themselves into vertically integrated entertainment companies: Comcast owns not just wires but also content, having acquired the enormous media holdings of NBC-Universal in 2010.[40] It is a major player in the market for rights to U.S. sports as well as the Olympics. The company has said that it wants to own 80 percent of the content it offers, so it may be poised to acquire even more sources of programming—like CBS or Viacom. As of the spring of 2018, AT&T, a product of the reconsolidation of a half a dozen or more of the former Baby Bells (as well as the long-distance company also called AT&T) that were created by the 1984 breakup, hoped to swallow up Time Warner Entertainment in an $85 billion merger, giving it dominion over CNN and HBO, among other key holdings.[41] Verizon, the result of the reconsolidation of most of the other Baby Bells, has bought AOL, is heading for Yahoo, and has said it's "open to" discussions to buy Comcast, Charter (now Spectrum), Disney (which owns ESPN), or CBS.[42] Spectrum, having acquired all of Time Warner Cable's cable systems, controls rights to a huge number of regional sports networks and operates on an enormous scale.[43]

This vertical integration, consolidation, and control over sports rights and other key content, such as local news and HBO, adds up to a significant hurdle for insurgent independent fiber networks: no matter how little retail providers may be able to charge a subscriber for fiber access, a huge behemoth can charge even less for its cable internet access services—and threaten the subscriber with the loss of beloved programming should he or she contemplate signing up with the insurgent. In economic lingo, the incumbent can make the cost of switching away from its services seem impossibly high.

It is very difficult to prove predatory pricing, the idea that an incumbent deliberately underprices its services in order to drive a newer, usually undercapitalized competitor out of business. These giant companies, with their enormous margins and vanishingly low per-unit costs, have a million ways to bundle, slice, and reprice what they do in response to competition. Remember the "Wilson price," Time Warner Cable's crude response to the entrance of a Wilson network: people served by the same equipment got different prices, with those in Wilson charged less than others. The only difference was the presence of a competitor.

Prices can also be changed if a customer calls and says he or she wants to leave the incumbent. An enormous concern can always offer a new best deal—on the phone, to individual subscribers—spread those losses over millions of existing subscribers, and hold out until the insurgent gives up. This can wreak havoc on new networks. If they can't sign people up quickly, make customers loyal with their customer service and responsiveness, and keep the momentum going with advertising and demonstrations of the genuine benefits of their fiber networks, they will be destroyed.

Control over sports rights and local news is yet another weapon in the incumbents' arsenal. These are both types of programming that people want in real time and that aren't, by and large, available through substitutes. Getting access to this programming can be very expensive; Wilson, if it had to do it all over again, would stay out of the increasingly costly world of programming costs. RS Fiber managed to purchase programming through an association of smaller cable companies, but it is uncertain of its ability to keep these prices down over time.

The huge telecom incumbents—Comcast, Spectrum, AT&T, and Verizon—benefit from the lowest possible per-unit costs for programming, often paying just half or a third of what a smaller network pays. Owning must-have content like sports and news is itself a built-in advantage. A company that can provide these can bargain these rights for any other programming it needs. It's a system perfectly engineered to keep the status quo in place. All the local incumbent has to do is lower its prices temporarily and then remind people that they'll be paying extra for sports and news, and many Americans will shy away from fiber-to-the-home—even though fiber is unquestionably a better technology.

Many ploys happen at a surprisingly local level: customers' living rooms. In Wilson, Time Warner employees would say, "There's no need to switch to the Wilson network. I hear they're struggling." Or "They're just a flash in the pan." Chattanooga's utility, EPB, was extremely good at customer support, which allowed it to survive attacks in living rooms. As mayor Andy Berke put it, "Some of the [incumbent] companies don't have the best Q rating."

Finally, the major incumbents—particularly Comcast—have begun to upgrade their last-mile networks running to individual businesses to fiber. Their ability to pick off business customers and hang on to them will make it more difficult for a later upstart, however well intentioned, to make its business case work: the big whales will have been captured by a giant existing player.

If you're getting the idea that at every point in the operation of a network—access to conduit and poles, access to lines between cities large and small, access to neutral interconnection points in big cities, absence of predatory pricing—the governing principle needs to be "open" or "neutral" access for there to be any possibility of high-capacity service to everyone at a reasonable price, you're right.

Given all the game-playing, why would a local community take the risk of building a public option for connectivity—a dark-fiber, wholesale network in urban areas, allowing for lots of retail competition at reasonable prices, or a cooperatively run network in more rural areas connecting businesses and residences to world markets and opportunities? Because the fiber story has consequences not only for a city's economic development but also for the social justice experienced by its citizens—two things that are not on the minds of the distant investment companies that control the existing carriers.

Cities that take on this challenge have a tremendous opportunity to expand their thinking and planning: they will have demonstrated the capacity to see their community from a broad perspective. They will have shown that they can take a long view, that their individual elements can collaborate, and that they genuinely believe that every child deserves the opportunity to thrive. They can then begin to address the intertwined problems in public education, health care, workforce development, inequality, affordable housing, and transportation that beset every American city. That is the job of the public, in the end, and not of any private company. In turn, virtually unlimited communications capacity at a reasonable price will permit new approaches to many of those problems, lowering the cost of providing world-class services and opportunities to all citizens.

At the moment, the federal government is part of the problem when it comes to the city movement toward fiber. It doesn't see fiber as necessary, and the FCC's current chairman, Ajit Pai, has actively opposed city efforts to build fiber networks. But that's not forever.

CHAPTER ELEVEN

The Need for Federal Policy

When I began work on this book several years ago, my first instinct was to go to places outside America that had upgraded to last-mile fiber and find out how essentially unlimited communications capacity was affecting ordinary people's lives. Bringing those stories home, I thought, could change minds in my own country. So I went to Stockholm, Seoul, and Tokyo, all of which have essentially 100 percent fiber adoption in homes and businesses; I interviewed scores of millennials and government officials; I wandered around finding out all I could about new uses of fiber and how people were talking about their online lives.

Along the way I became convinced that the story hadn't happened yet.

It's true that South Korean twenty-somethings considered the flow of digital interactions with their friends merely another layer of life, inseparable from "real" life, and thought the 2018 Olympics would allow the country to demonstrate astonishing uses of high-capacity networks aimed at bringing the public closer to sports events; Swedes were stolidly convinced that inexpensive last-mile fiber connections were basic infrastructure, as essential to the life of a community as well-functioning public transport. And Tokyo residents took cheap, unlimited communications capacity for granted;

they simply never thought about it. But new industries in health care, education, and remote work based on the tremendous new capacity for two-way communications had not yet arrived in these places. There just wasn't a large enough sandbox.

The barrier to transformative uses of fiber capacity wasn't, I came to understand, just the size of the market each place could serve. Something about the culture of these three places had discouraged risk-taking. People I spoke to were aware of this limitation.

In Stockholm, city leaders were delighted that a direct flight to Silicon Valley was being launched: grit, messiness, and outrageous playfulness could perhaps inject some creativity into the tidy Swedish culture. ("Stockholm is a very efficient city," chief operating officer Staffan Ingvarsson told me in 2013, "and that's bad from a cultural perspective. The fact we're growing rapidly is good—things will get more crowded, more gritty, and that means more people meeting each other.")

Young people in Tokyo told me that the crushing effect of hierarchical corporate life is antithetical to an entrepreneurial, adventurous outlook. "If you're Japanese," said Owen Narita, a software marketer, "you want to go to a huge conglomerate and spend your entire career there. Not many people want to go into IT. Japanese companies have a very strict hierarchy of how they will function, and only people at certain levels are able to talk to people above them." When they are permitted to talk, they aren't comfortable speaking out about conflict or a need for change. "Getting people to raise issues—it's very against the Japanese culture to speak out about something that isn't working well," said Don Werve, a young software developer from America who speaks fluent Japanese and lives in Tokyo. Strong feelings of shame, fear, and guilt associated with failure are deeply cultural in both Japan and South Korea. "It's a Samurai culture," in Japan, Narita said to me. "Remember *harakiri*? Failing is not an option in Japan to many people."

And in South Korea, where they clear the airspace when high-schoolers are about to take the exam that will determine their university placement, people are impatient—they would never wait for a spinning ball online the way Americans do—but extraordinarily driven by credential-building and obedient to rules of age hierarchy. Inferiors (by age—age is the first question when you meet someone new) refrain from looking directly into the eyes of their superiors, address them differently from those younger than themselves, and even drink deferentially, taking a glass from an elder only with two hands and turning their heads away from the table when taking a sip. Education is an obsession, but much of it is sheer memorization and "incessant multiple-choice testing," as Sun Woo Lee, a Seoul native, told me. "Throughout my education in Korea," she said, "I have never been graded based on a paper, lab report, or any type of self-produced work other than a multiple-choice test."

Any innovative startup idea in South Korea, I was told, is likely to be bought up or taken by Samsung, Korea's giant conglomerate. Although Samsung is trying to make its corporate culture more innovative, it won't be easy. "Here," a *Korea Times* reporter told me, "IT is all about infrastructure. There's not much creativity." He thinks the conglomerates make innovation difficult. "If you start a business, people frown at you," he said. "'What the hell are you thinking? Just get into a company and work.'" In Korea, he reflected, "We're about groups. Startups are not groups. There is no government protection for startups."

A young man named Hyunseok Shim told me there were only two secure paths that were acceptable to middle-class Koreans: a job in a conglomerate or one in government—and those jobs were getting scarcer. Shim had had trouble joining the civil service, even though he had passed a multiple-choice test and a five-day written test of five subjects. After failing an interview—he didn't know the reason for his failure—he had tried again. He told me he would be assigned to a ministry within the government only after he was graded on six months of training with three hundred other people. His dreams, he said, were getting smaller and smaller. In the past, he wanted to change the world, but now all he wanted was a happy retirement; he told me he was worried that his health would deteriorate at about age fifty-five, because that happens to most people who work at the pace required in government ministries. Shim felt he had no freedom to be innovative.

Stockholm wants the world to know that people are moving there from southern Europe, that the city has the highest percentage of technology workers of all European cities, the highest smartphone penetration, and a very large number of programmers. It has a history of quietly promoting itself: "We've come from a careful culture," Michael Joseph of Invest Stockholm told me in 2016, "where we don't want to stand out too much, and we don't like to brag, and we don't want to pat ourselves on the back." He thinks that's changing. As of 2015, Sweden had the second largest concentration of billion-dollar companies ("unicorns") per capita, behind only Silicon Valley, with Spotify topping the list. At the same time, though, there are barriers to new developments: the active and vibrant innovation arena in Stockholm is suffering from a lack of affordable housing, only about nine million people speak Swedish around the world, inside the city it's hard (although not impossible) to hire anyone from outside the European Union, and, although this is changing rapidly, there is less venture capital available in Stockholm than its startups can absorb. One other barrier in Stockholm: "It's fairly cold here," Ingvarsson said to me. And dark.

I don't count either South Korea or Sweden out as a place where new things will come from. (I have less hope for insular Japan.) South Korea raised itself from rubble in a few decades and has enormous vibrancy despite its hierarchical way of doing things; Sweden is a practical, sensible place that is far more accepting of entrepreneurial behavior than either South Korea or Japan. But they are small places. Only when a critical mass of people speaking a common language is actually using last-mile fiber, and those people have gotten used to long-distance interactions with other humans that feel as real as being there, will we see transformative ways of living and thriving begin to emerge. Which large market will provide the sandbox for these dramatic developments? Who will develop the next generation of industries?

For well over a century, the United States has been the world's biggest economy, today accounting for nearly a quarter of global gross domestic product (GDP).[1] But China, with its enormous population—four times that of the United States—is swiftly catching up and moving from a reliance on manufacturing to a more modern economy.[2] Chinese homes are being wired for fiber at an astonishing rate, with 100 million already connected. Giant, shiny Shanghai will soon be a gigabit city, with fiber running to every home and business.[3]

At the same time, China is increasingly cracking down on pro-democracy activism, including by tightening its grip on free-flowing speech online. To the extent that there is a shared commitment to liberal democracy among Western nations, it would be better for the United States to lead in developing the new industries and ways of thriving that will emerge from last-mile fiber. And so I turned back to the United States, looking for stories here while continuing to keep track of what was going on in Asia and northern Europe.

If the United States can upgrade to fiber, we could be, once again, the place of opportunity and new ideas. We're primed to be that place: our national origin story is one of fearlessness and agency. How is our entrepreneurial, extroverted populace going to get connected? The visible existence of last-mile fiber networks in cities like Chattanooga and Wilson, and the benefits and changes with which those networks are associated, should help persuade other cities to get off the mark; we can believe only what we see. But even though more and more cities and localities are taking this step, the resulting patchwork of connectivity can only be fashioned into an upgraded whole with the involvement of the federal government. Mayor Andy Berke understands this well: "People talk about building a fair economy. We try really hard to do that here, to be as fair as we can in Chattanooga, but I also know that fiscal policy is set by the Federal Reserve. Tax policy is set by Congress. We operate within those constraints." Cities cannot do the work of ensuring that dark fiber is everywhere without the involvement of the federal government.

Making this upgrade will require federal involvement on at least three levels: leadership, standard-setting, and subsidization. No feds, no upgrade.

When it comes to basic physical networks that the country needs in order to stay competitive, we have always relied on federal policy to get them built and ensure they are maintained. We have also learned that federal policy doesn't emerge magically. It takes the personal vision and strength of a president to get things moving.

Franklin Delano Roosevelt's personal experiences with electricity in Warm Springs, Georgia, a place he visited dozens of times between 1924 and 1945 to treat his polio, exercise in the warm water, and relax, had a lot to do with his leadership in the electrification wars.[4] Farmers and other residents of rural Georgia weren't getting electricity in the early 1930s, which meant they didn't have electric lights, water pumps, irons, or refrigerators. Where electricity did exist, it was wildly expensive; FDR felt this personally when his first electric bill at the "Little White House" in Warm Springs in 1935 was four times greater than that of his New York home. In 1938, he publicly cited Warm Springs as the birthplace of the Rural Electrification Administration.

Abraham Lincoln played a similarly crucial role in launching America's transcontinental railroad network. Lincoln knew railroads: as a state legislator, he had supported the idea of subsidizing railroads and creating franchises for their operation, supporting the "internal improvement" of Illinois by ensuring that an extensive network of railroads would exist within the state. Six years before Lincoln was admitted to the bar of Illinois, in 1830, only thirty miles of railroad track had been laid in the state; by 1860, when he was inaugurated as president, it had over 30,626 miles of track, the state's farming and coal mining industries had been stimulated, and Illinois had seen extraordinary industrial changes, including thousands of new jobs and extensive increases in manufacturing. Lincoln had handled dozens of cases for the Illinois Central as a private lawyer beginning in the early 1850s; he had also sued railroads, gaining a reputation as a shrewd and effective advocate for whatever cause he took up. Legal scholar James Ely quoted Lincoln as celebrating "a link in a great chain of railroad communication which shall unite Boston and New York with the Mississippi," and noted that Lincoln's 1860 platform read: "That a railroad to the Pacific Ocean is imperatively demanded by the interests of the whole country; that the Federal Government ought to render immediate and efficient aid in its construction."[5] Without his personal intervention, the transcontinental railroad would have been completed much later. Lincoln had personally seen the growth and change brought by the development of rail traffic in Illinois, and he wanted the same kind of growth for the whole country.

Dwight D. Eisenhower's support for creation of the federal highway system was also spurred by personal experience. As a young lieutenant colonel in 1919, right after World War I, Eisenhower had thought it would be fun to join a military convoy of more than eighty trucks, cars, and motorcycles on a drive from Washington, D.C., to San Francisco. The trip turned out to be a grueling experience of mud, quicksand, and exhaustion: the lack of good roads, particularly in the West, often left the convoy mired for hours. "By Utah," wrote Sarah Laskow for Atlas Obscura, "the conditions of the roads were so bad, it almost stopped the convoy altogether."[6] It took more than two months to make the journey, at an average of six miles an hour. Along with the other officers who had traveled with the convoy, Eisenhower grew convinced that the "Good Roads" movement, which had been cooperatively forming associations to finance upgrades to the gravel or dirt tracks that then connected cities, needed a firm federal hand. As he put it later, "there was a great deal of sentiment for the improving of highways," and on that point, "the trip was an undoubted success."[7] Without Eisenhower, there would have been no Federal-Aid Highway Act of 1956 and no interstate highway system, 90 percent of which was funded by the federal government.

Today's analog to the unelectrified rural area or a drive across the country at an average speed of six miles per hour is, for anyone who has experienced connectivity in Asia or northern Europe, the experience of trying to get world-class, reliable, symmetric persistent internet access in the United States. We're missing a leader who has had the experience of connectivity over fiber—or at least understands that it is possible and necessary—and, like Lincoln, understands the connection between this upgrade and economic growth and social justice. That person needs to be a first-rate communicator, able to convey with color and verve why Americans should not have to settle for expensive, second-class data services, and why we cannot remain the world's leading economy without first-class connectivity.

The second key step, one only a leader backed by federal agencies and Congress can take, is to declare (enforceably) that the standard connection for a thriving life in America requires a reasonably priced, open fiber network running to homes and businesses. Such a declaration could itself drive the upgrade: ancient last-mile copper networks could be forced into retirement through tax policy and other incentives; poles and conduit could be subjected to basic openness requirements as a matter of regulation and local ordinance; new housing could be approved for habitability and federal support only with fiber-readiness or actual fiber attached. By saying that anything that wasn't fiber-ready, or actually connected to open fiber, wouldn't be supported by federal funding, the federal government could push the entire process forward. There are limits to this power: state tax rules and state constraints on local authority can get in the way, and the details are difficult. But the federal government can do a great deal in the vast portion of the marketplace that is touched, directly or indirectly, by federal funding.

The goal should be construction of open-access, dark, last-mile fiber available for lease and overseen by a public authority in every part of the country to all (or almost all) homes and businesses. It has to be open access to permit retail competition wherever possible. It has to be overseen by public authorities so that it will serve the public interests in low prices and high-quality services to everyone. The risk of allowing a private, unconstrained actor to control local dark fiber is that, quite rationally, that player will want to make as much profit for itself as possible from the facility, regardless of the public interest.

Any sensible private actor controlling dark fiber would want to charge whatever the market could bear for access and limit its competition as much as possible, even though high prices would shut some people out of the system. That same actor would inevitably want to vertically integrate upstream into the provision of services, and then privilege its own retail activities over those of others, or at least make common cause with a few retail companies so that, together, they could squeeze consumers. And a private controller of this facility would always be looking for an exit, a private equity group of some kind to buy out its investment and consolidate networks across the country. But just as we wouldn't want private actors to control highways because we want cars and freight to travel freely without being forced to pay excessive prices, so too should we ensure that our basic communications networks, now upgraded to fiber optic last miles, are held and operated in the public interest. That means regulation.

Competition in the last-mile bottleneck of communications networks happens only when wholesale basic facilities are shared. We know this from longtime experience; if you ask basic wires to compete with one another (so-called facilities-based competition), you end up with consolidation, cooperation, and divided geographic markets—just notice what happened in 2004 when we assumed that the telcos and cable companies would compete with one another by building last-mile networks for high-speed internet access, and that this feverish competition would give us low prices and great service. It didn't. Most Americans are stuck with a single provider of a not-great wire, operating without oversight, and possessed of un-constrained pricing power that necessarily leaves out huge numbers of our fellow citizens struggling to lead lives of opportunity. Today, the basic communications wire for the last mile is fiber, and once in place, it will last for decades. To ensure there is enough competition to protect consumers and businesses, that wholesale dark-fiber last mile will need to be aggressively managed in the public interest, forever.

Even where retail-level competition appears to be difficult be-cause of a low number of potential end users, as in rural areas, the country's dark fiber last miles should be separable (that is, it must be clearly physically possible to lease access to unlit fiber so as to pro-vide competing retail-level services) and separately priced according to benchmarks set in similar topographic regions in other countries that also have dark fiber facilities. (Verizon's lawyers deliberately de-signed Verizon's FiOS service to avoid any future risk that regula-tors would require "unbundling" the wholesale part of the network from retail provision of services, and cable networks are designed similarly. It will take work and money to undo this architecture, but it will be worth it for the country to have true competition in the last mile everywhere.) That way, initial retail providers in rural areas can get the advantage of reasonable pricing, and when and if a sec-ond retail player emerges, it can have access to the dark fiber on the same terms as the first. Finally, dark fiber should provide neutral in-terconnection points at the spacing needed for advanced wireless facilities—5G—to be attached to it, particularly in urban areas. We'll need competition in 5G as well as wired services, and regular interconnection points that are managed in order to ensure that any provider of a new kind of service or application will encounter only reasonable and predictable barriers to entry.

When it comes to setting standards for the country's basic communications facility, speed is secondary. The important thing is to require fiber, which is inherently a symmetric and high-capacity service, and then to get the glass in the ground and strung on poles. The electronics for fiber will continue to be improved, and competitive pressure among retail providers will make that happen.

The federal government should stop supporting installation of copper and cable wires, as it does in several programs, so as to focus investment on last-mile open-access dark fiber. Right now, the feds waste billions of dollars giving money to incumbent companies to build copper lines and beef up wireless towers: in 2015, AT&T was paid nearly $700 million, CenturyLink nearly $600 million, and Verizon $150 million, all under a program funded by fees attached to landline long-distance phone bills, to incentivize these companies to build 10 Mbps services mostly over copper wires or from spotty wireless coverage. It bears repeating: money spent on wires other than fiber is wasted. It would make sense, in fact, to give these companies tax incentives to remove copper and cable and replace it with last-mile open-access fiber.

The next step is to clear away regulatory and incumbent-created obstacles to achieving this goal. There is much to do on this front: Congress should expressly allow the FCC to preempt the nineteen state laws that obstruct sensibly planned municipal or locality networks, and the FCC, Congress, and the next administration will need to rationalize regulatory frameworks that currently get in the way of dark-fiber last-mile builds.

Preempting the state laws that constrain municipalities would not be difficult. As a technical matter, Congress would need to amend existing law only very slightly to give the FCC the express authority to do this—a bill granting this authority, called the Community Broadband Act, was introduced in the Senate in March 2017 but failed to get out of committee—and the FCC would need to rule that the state laws were interfering with federal policy supporting the deployment of advanced fiber last-mile networks.

Then the FCC will have to take on the middle mile as well. Middle-mile providers in noncompetitive areas will need to be price regulated using benchmark data from more competitive but geographically similar areas. They will need to provide facilities for competitors to install their last-mile electronics and other equipment on a neutral basis. This will not be easy, but, again, it will be worthwhile for the entire country.

There is still more work for the FCC to do. Along with taking on the last mile and the middle mile, and continuing (or, in the case of the last mile, launching) its detailed data-gathering efforts, the FCC or Congress will need to drastically streamline the myriad local barriers to deployment that have been erected by incumbent companies. If any of this sounds dull, imagine each step as an operatic libretto, full of blood and guts and battles. No romance, I'm sorry to say, but conflicts and villains are everywhere.

Anyone building last-mile fiber access needs access to utility poles and conduit—tubes beneath streets through which fiber can be pulled—as well as up-front capital. That access needs to be purchased, leased, or built, and when those poles and conduits are controlled by parties with an interest in delaying or stalling competition, competitors will not survive. Crucial pole and conduit architecture introduced in the nineteenth century turns out to be an enormous barrier to the delivery of last-mile services in the twenty-first. To begin tackling this giant issue, the FCC will need to require that information be available in a standardized, electronic form everywhere in the country about the location, accessibility, and current pricing of poles, conduits, existing fiber routes, tower locations, and other key infrastructure that is necessary to assessing gaps and efficiently targeting public policies.

While that data is being collected, the FCC needs to enact several related policies aimed at removing gatekeeper control over poles and conduits. There need to be "dig once" rules requiring anyone opening city streets to notify the public and collaborate in the installation of open, clean last-mile conduit. We need to establish "shot clocks" mandating that all steps in applications or permits to access conduit and poles be accomplished within set periods of time. Unreasonable delay in these processes can defeat any well-thought-out business plan. City control over conduit and poles needs to continue, or be established where it does not now exist, to ensure that both city aesthetic concerns and desires for neutral infrastructure fostering competition are honored; on the other hand, cities need to be constrained from seeing their poles and conduit as a source of ever increasing revenue, like traffic tickets. They are public goods, not honeypots, and only treating them like open, reasonably accessible infrastructure will truly help the public.

The federal government will need to address these issues, as well as those having to do with landlords. For new buildings, every part of America should do what Singapore, Stockholm, Paris, and Brentwood and Loma Linda, California, do: require that those buildings be fiber-ready so any competing provider can get in to a neutral connection point without the landlord's permission. For existing buildings, the feds should stop companies from being able to sign contractual provisions limiting access to inside wiring, and make it illegal for landlords to get any form of side payment for limiting tenants' choice of ISPs.

To drive a genuinely innovative online health services market into existence, Congress will need to ensure that Medicaid and Medicare reimburse telemedicine visits, but only if they are carried out over symmetric, high-capacity fiber connections. To push forward new energy uses and markets, it will need to provide incentives for investor-owned utilities to adopt smart grid functionalities. And to push forward genuinely useful online education, federal grants should support distance learning and apprenticeships carried out over fiber—as long as students actually get jobs as a result of these programs.

An essential federal step will be enforcement. Given that an enormous industry has a built-in incentive to divide markets and hide data about its operations, it will take vigilance and energy to prevent bottlenecks from stifling competition. The federal government will need to understand and fight for every part of this project, and then stay involved to ensure that wholesale services are provided at a price that promotes competition. Public support for last-mile open-access fiber is likely to be strong once the story is clearly told by an FDR-like communicator. None of this is easy, but all of it is necessary.

And then federal funding, or subsidy, in the form of loans, grants, guarantees, reverse auctions, and innumerable other vehicles, will be necessary. The existing players have no particular incentive to do anything to change our current dismal connectivity.

All of this prompts a bigger question: What can and should the federal government subsidize? The answer, it should be clear, is fiber: open, neutral, last-mile fiber networks as deep as they can go, with neutral connection points at frequent intervals to support a competitive advanced wireless ecosystem.

How much will implementation of this plan cost the country? It is difficult to say. In some areas, last-mile fiber infrastructure already exists and merely needs to be made available for lease through regulatory authority under existing law. In others, there is no dark fiber available. At the end of 2015, the Obama administration counted about 10 million existing fiber-to-the-premises connections (out of approximately 160 million residential and small- or medium-sized business locations in the country) and 56 million existing cable connections. At the beginning of 2017, officials estimated it would cost about $80 billion to bring high-capacity connections (defined as *either* cable or fiber) to homes and businesses that didn't have them, but they did not estimate how much pure fiber last-mile connectivity to those places would cost.[8]

Without question, it will cost much more than $80 billion to wire all of the country's last miles with fiber. The incumbents will fight to the death to ensure that the federal government does none of this, and it will take money to get them to reframe their businesses as competitive retail providers of internet access riding on top of public, wholesale fiber last miles.

The good news is that there is plenty of money in America looking for strong, consistent investment vehicles in the form of capital expenditures on infrastructure. Public infrastructure investment is called for as well as private money; public investment as a percentage of GDP is now at its lowest level since 1947. These investments will throw off steady, predictable returns of perhaps 4 to 5 percent for a very long time, and maintenance costs are very low for fiber—perhaps 40 percent less than for copper. Fiber last-mile networks that are integrated into energy, water, and transport systems will pay off through reduced water consumption, far more efficient energy use, and truly responsive public transport; some of these savings can be put into additional construction.

Right now, our approach to infrastructure investment is heavily reliant on tax breaks and the desires of existing incumbents. No fundamental changes will happen if we stick to this path. The federal government or Federal Reserve could establish a national infrastructure bank that would provide equity investment, risk insurance, loans, and loan guarantees to make public investment possible and dramatically lower the cost of capital for focused private investments. Like the Federal Reserve, we should have a national board setting strategy and coordinating federal investment, and the national infrastructure bank should be allied with semiautonomous regional banks that implement those policy choices while giving priority to their areas' particular needs. The national bank's powers should be modeled on those of development banks like OPIC or the European Bank for Reconstruction and Development (EBRD), which makes equity investments in addition to guaranteeing loans. The existence of these investments, in turn, will benefit pension funds, insurance companies, and others who are looking for long-term, relatively safe vehicles for their own investments. The bank should make risk insurance available, to encourage up-front investments in the current spiky regulatory landscape of permitting and access delays. Also like the Federal Reserve, it should act as a clearinghouse of accurate data and information while developing a comprehensive plan supporting long-term projects. (The Federal Reserve is beginning to think along these lines; a recent report by the Dallas branch provided a playbook for investing in high-speed internet access for local financial institutions under the Community Reinvestment Act.)[9]

This would be a novel approach, but it is needed. We have always envisioned transformational infrastructure as a federal issue: "internal improvements" paved the way for westward expansion in the early republic; federal land grants and loan guarantees in the 1860s made the transcontinental railway possible; a combination of federal "fiscal centralization with [state] administrative decentralization" characterized the spending of $4 billion by the Works Progress Administration in the 1930s to construct schools, courthouses, and highways; and federal aid through the Highway Trust Fund gave us our national highway system.[10] When we have left infrastructure to private industry, we have seen gross disparities in distribution—as with electricity in the 1930s, when 90 percent of farmers didn't have it, and today, with last-mile fiber.

In addition to a national infrastructure bank, Build America Bonds, which were introduced as part of the efforts of the American Recovery and Reinvestment Act of 2009 and provided state and local governments with a direct federal subsidy for a portion of their borrowing costs for their taxable bonds, should be revived.[11] Tax credits aimed specifically at encouraging construction of open-access last-mile fiber would also be helpful. Banks and bond issuers will need to understand fiber last-mile networks better than they do now. Builders of last-mile dark-fiber networks could be put through auctions for the right to build in particular geographic areas.

We know from the history of electrification that Roosevelt's vision included, in addition to rural electrification and the Tennessee Valley Authority, subsidizing appliance dealers to finance long-term loans to customers. Federal subsidization of new domestic uses of fiber would also drive adoption and lower prices. Eventually, the combination of these subsidies and other forms of monetary support for fiber construction would normalize high-capacity connectivity, and fiber, like electricity before it, would disappear into the background.

Innumerable political obstacles have been erected to the very idea of public involvement in communications infrastructure in America. The mainstream Washington consensus seems to be that public support for fiber is unthinkable; that view was blandly presented, without support or self-doubt, by Lawrence Summers, the former president of Harvard and economic adviser to President Obama, who wrote flatly in September 2016 that expanding high-speed internet networks was "clearly the responsibility of the private sector."[12] What is odd about this received wisdom is that, as with electricity, following an uncomfortable experiment with the purely private provision of communications services, the public sector in America has always been central to ensuring that basic communications facilities reach everyone at reasonable prices.

Ultimately, last-mile fiber is a public good. It will not pay for itself quickly—we never expected that of the highway system—and should not be expected to. It should be an industrial policy priority for America and the rest of the world. Only fiber will facilitate the exponential growth of innovation and productivity in transportation, energy, health care, manufacturing, education, job training, disability access, augmented/virtual reality, government services, and public safety that will keep our living standards rising as they have in the past. Better lives, a sense that future generations will live better than we do—this sense of hope is not just an economic good but an essential requirement for happiness, tolerance of others, and resilience in the face of difficulty. The countries that have made progress on this issue—South Korea, Japan, Hong Kong, Singapore, China, Sweden—are driving toward this future. We need fiber in the same way, and for many of the same reasons, we need liberal democracy: to ensure that all Americans have opportunities to shape their own lives. It is basic infrastructure for a good life.

Notes

Chapter One. The Fiber Future

1. Yu-Min Joo, Yooil Bae, and Eva Kassens-Noor, *Mega-Events and Mega-Ambitions: South Korea's Rise and the Strategic Use of the Big Four Events* (London: Palgrave Macmillan, 2017), 40.

2. Aaron Gordon, "With Nine Months to Go, PyeongChang Winter Olympics Faces Possible Room Shortage," Vice Sports, April 26, 2017, https://sports.vice.com/en_us/article/jp7vm4/with-nine-months-to-go-pyeongchang-winter-olympics-faces-possible-room-shortage.

3. "New Highways, Railroads Offer Better Access to PyeongChang Olympic Venues," Yonhap News Agency, August 20, 2017, http://english.yonhapnews.co.kr/culturesports/2017/08/18/0702000000AEN20170818008700320.html.

4. Erwan Lucas, "In South Korea, the Race Is on for Olympics 5G Next Year," Phys.org, February 28, 2017, https://phys.org/news/2017-02-south-korea-olympics-5g-year.html.

5. Sohn Ji-young, "KT on Track for 5G Pilot Service at 2018 Olympics," *Korea Herald*, December 13, 2016, http://www.koreaherald.com/view.php?ud=20161213000819.

6. Cho Mu-Hyun, "KT to Provide 360 Degree VR for 2018 Winter Games," ZDNet, http://www.zdnet.com/article/kt-to-provide-360-degree-vr-for-2018-winter-games.

7. Telecom Junkie, "SKT to Showcase Live Streaming 360 VR at MWC 2017," Telecom TIMES, February 19, 2017, https://thetelecomtimes.com/skt-showcase-live-streaming-260-vr-mwc-2017.html; Diamond Leung, "2018 PyeongChang Olympics Has 5G-Enabled VR, Live Holograms, Self-Driving Buses, Drones," SportTechie, March 29, 2017, https://www.sporttechie.com/2018-pyeongchang-olympics-has-5g-enabled-vr-live-holograms-self-driving-buses-drones. Because phones in common use at

the time of the 2018 Winter Olympics were not equipped with radios that could use 5G technology, these immersive experiences were limited to spectators using test phones at the arenas. Elaine Ramirez, "In the Race For 5G, South Korea Shows Off Its Tech Prowess at the Winter Olympics," *Forbes*, February 23, 2018, https://www.forbes.com/sites /elaineramirez/2018/02/23/in-the-race-for-5g-south-korea-shows-off-its-tech-prowess-at-the-winter-olympics.

8. Andrew Braun, "Why Does South Korea Have the Fastest Internet?," IDG Connect, October 20, 2014, http://www.idgconnect.com/abstract 8960/why-does-south-korea-have-fastest-internet.

9. Y. Benkler, R. Faris, U. Gasser, L. Miyakawa, and S. Schultze, *Next Generation Connectivity: A Review of Broadband Internet Transitions and Policy from Around the World* (Cambridge, MA: Berkman Center for Internet & Society, 2010); available at http://cyber.law.harvard.edu/pubrelease/ broadband.

10. Herman Wagter, "Fiber-to-the-X: The Economics of Last-Mile Fiber," *Ars Technica*, March 30, 2010, https://arstechnica.com/tech-policy/2010 /03/fiber-its-not-all-created-equal.

11. Offiber, "The Lifetime of Fiber Optic Cable," Useful Goods, May 7, 2015, https://fiberopticsof.wordpress.com/2015/05/07/the-lifetime-of-fiber-optic-cable); "Could Fiber Be the Final Frontier of High-Speed Internet?," *Government Technology*, April 18, 2017, http://www.govtech.com/ network/Could-Fiber-be-the-Final-Frontier-of-High-Speed-Internet. html.

12. Krista Tysco, "A Mid-Year Roundup of the 2017 Global FTTH Broadband Market," PPC Broadband, *PPC Blog*, August 3, 2017, http://www. ppc-online.com/blog/a-mid-year-roundup-of-the-2017-global-ftth -broadband-market.

13. Bien Perez, "China to Build World's Largest 5G Mobile Network for US$180 Billion," *South China Morning Post*, June 12, 2017, http://www. scmp.com/tech/china-tech/article/2097972/chinas-5g-network-spending -tipped-reach-us180-billion-over-seven.

14. Sung Wook Baek, "SKT T1: 'This Is Culmination of Esports Investments for Over 10 Years, Our Efforts Will Continue,'" InvenGlobal, June 1, 2017, https://www.invenglobal.com/lol/articles/2052/skt-t1-this-is-culmination-of-esports-investments-for-over-10-years-our-efforts-will-continue.

15. David E. Nye, *Electrifying America: Social Meanings of a New Technology, 1880–1940* (Cambridge: MIT Press, 1990).

16. IDATE Consulting, *FTTH/B Panorama*, Marseille, FTTH Conference 2017, http://www.ftthcouncil.eu/documents/Reports/2016/IDATE-European_ FTTH_B_panorama_2016_public.pdf.

17. Robert A. Caro, "Robert A. Caro on the Art of Biography," https://www .randomhouse.com/knopf/authors/caro/desktopnew.html.

Chapter Two. Transmitting Light

1. "Corning Innovation Timeline," Corning, 2011, http://media.corning.com/flash/corporate/2011/timeline.

2. "Research and Development," Corning, https://www.corning.com/cala/pt/about-us/news-events/resources/research-development.html.

3. Melinda Rose, "A History of the Laser: A Trip Through the Light Fantastic," Photonics Media, July 17, 2017, https://www.photonics.com/Article.aspx?AID=42279.

4. Peter Micket, "Timeline of Discoveries," *Physics of Fiber Optics*, Spring 2003, http://ffden-2.phys.uaf.edu/212_fall2003.web.dir/Peter_Micket/Timeline_of_discoveries.htm; Jeff Hecht, *City of Light: The Story of Fiber Optics* (New York: Oxford University Press, 1990), 261.

5. Rose, "A History of the Laser."

6. "How Glass Scientists Took on the Challenge of Harnessing Light," Corning, https://www.corning.com/worldwide/en/innovation/the-glass-age/science-of-glass/how-glass-scientists-took-on-the-challenge-of-harnessing-light.html.

7. Martin J. Van Der Burgt, "Coaxial Cables and Applications," Belden Electronics Division, 2003.

8. Hecht, *City of Light*.

9. Ira C. Magaziner and Mark Patinkin, *The Silent War: Inside the Global Business Battles Shaping Americas Future* (New York: Random House, 1989).

10. Sebastian Anthony, "255Tbps: World's Fastest Network Could Carry All of the Internet's Traffic on a Single Fiber," ExtremeTech, October 27, 2014, https://www.extremetech.com/extreme/192929-255tbps-worlds-fastest-network-could-carry-all-the-internet-traffic-single-fiber).

11. "Guide to Fiber Optics and Premises Cabling," Fiber Optic Association, 2005, http://www.thefoa.org/tech/fo-or-cu.htm.

12. Brigham Griffin, "Are There Any Limitations to DSL Service?," *Direct Communications Corporate Blog*, August 23, 2013, https://blog.directcom.com/2012/04/23/are-there-any-limitations-to-dsl-service.

13. "Guide to Fiber Optics and Premises Cabling."

14. Ted Dejony, "History of Fiber Optics," Timbercon.com, http://www.timbercon.com/history-of-fiber-optics; "Frequently Asked Questions on Fiber Reliability," Corning, White Paper, April 2016, http://www.corning.com/media/worldwide/coc/documents/Fiber/RC-%20White%20Papers/WP5082%203-31-2016.pdf); Pacific Light Data Communication Co., "Fiber Configuration," http://pldcglobal.com/#FiberConfiguration.

15. "OECD Broadband Statistics: Percentage of Fibre Connections in Total Broadband Among Countries Reporting Fibre Subscribers," Organisation for Economic Co-operation and Development (OECD), Excel document, June 2017, https://view.officeapps.live.com/op/view.aspx?src=https://www.oecd.org/sti/broadband/1.10-PctFibreToTotalBroadband-2017-06.xls.

16. Alan Weissberger, "Verizon to Test 5G 'Wireless Fiber' for Internet and TV in Spring 2017," IEEE Communications Society, *Technology Blog*, December 7, 2016, http://techblog.comsoc.org/2016/12/07/verizon-to -test-5g-wireless-fiber-for-internet-tv-in-spring-2017.

17. "Verizon and Corning CEOs on 5G Fiber Deal," CNBC, April 18, 2017, https://www.cnbc.com/video/2017/04/18/verizon-and-corning-ceos-on -5g-fiber-deal.html.

18. Paul Kapustka, "Texas A&M's Kyle Field: Fiber for the Future," *Mobile Sports Report*, December 2014, 32–37.

19. Kristen Chung, "Tech: What's a Google Fiber Hut?," *Cary Citizen*, June 10, 2016, http://carycitizen.com/2014/05/13/tech-whats-google-fiber-hut.

20. Neil McDonnell, "The Inside Scoop on Micro-Trenching," *Broadband Properties*, May–June 2009, 54–56.

21. McDonnell, "The Inside Scoop on Micro-Trenching."

Chapter Three. Why U.S. Internet Access Is Awful

1. "Type of Household Internet Connection," American FactFinder, October 5, 2010, https://factfinder.census.gov/faces/tableservices/jsf/pages /productview.xhtml?src=bkmk); Anne Neville, "National Broadband Map Has Helped Chart Broadband Evolution," National Broadband Map, March 23, 2015, https://www.broadbandmap.gov/blog/3328/national-broadband -map-has-helped-chart-broadband-evolution; Industry Analysis and Technology Division, Wireline Competition Bureau, Federal Communications Commission, "Internet Access Services: Status as of December 31, 2015," November 2016, https://apps.fcc.gov/edocs_public/attachmatch/DOC-342358A1.pdf.

2. Federal Communications Commission, *In the Matter of Inquiry Concerning the Deployment of Advanced Telecommunications Capability to All Americans in a Reasonable and Timely Fashion*, GN Docket No. 15-191, 2016 Broadband Progress Report, https://apps.fcc.gov/edocs_public/attachmatch/FCC-18 -10A1.pdf.

3. Jon Brodkin, "U.S. Broadband: Still No ISP Choice for Many, Especially at Higher Speeds," *Ars Technica*, August 10, 2016, https://arstechnica. com/information-technology/2016/08/us-broadband-still-no-isp-choice -for-many-especially-at-higher-speeds; Federal Communications Commission, *In the Matter of International Comparison Requirements*, GH Docket No. 15-191, Fifth International Broadband Data Report.

4. In June 2015, fiber represented 13.5 percent of high-capacity connections *for all premises;* the residential number was much lower, with cable at 85 percent. Ninety-six percent of 100 Mbps subscriptions in June 2015 were cable. Brodkin, "U.S. Broadband."

5. Darrell West and Jack Karsten, "Rural and Urban America Divided by Broadband Access," Brookings Institution, *Techtank* (blog), July 18, 2016,

https://www.brookings.edu/blog/techtank/2016/07/18/rural-and-urban
-america-divided-by-broadband-access.

6. Federal Communications Commission, *In the Matter of Inquiry Concerning the Deployment of Advanced Telecommunications Capability to All Americans in a Reasonable and Timely Fashion*, FCC 18-10, GN Docket No. 17-199, February 2, 2018, https://apps.fcc.gov/edocs_public/attachmatch/FCC-18-10A1.pdf.

7. Jon Sallet, *Broadband Competition Policy: Final Thoughts and First Principles*, U.S. Department of Justice, Remarks for the Capitol Forum Broadband Competition Conference, December 16, 2016, https://www.justice.gov/opa/speech/file/936566/download.

8. John Horrigan and Maeve Duggan, "Home Broadband 2015," Pew Research Center, December 21, 2015, http://www.pewinternet.org/2015/12/21/home-broadband-2015.

9. David Belson, "Akamai's State of the Internet: Q1 2017 Report," Akamai, February 19, 2017, https://www.akamai.com/fr/fr/multimedia/documents/state-of-the-internet/q1-2017-state-of-the-internet-connectivity-report.pdf.

10. Peter Eriksson, "A Completely Connected Sweden by 2025—a Broadband Strategy," Government Offices of Sweden, March 27, 2017, http://www.government.se/496173/contentassets/afe9f1cfeaac4e39abcdd3b82d9bee5d/sweden-completely-connected-by-2025-eng.pdf; "Swedish Access to 100 Mbps Internet Rises to 77% in 2017," Telecompaper, March 29, 2018, https://www.telecompaper.com/news/swedish-access-to-100-mbps-internet-rises-to-77-in-2017—1238255.

11. Peter Lin, "Which Internet Service Provider Has the Best 1 Gbps Fibre Broadband Plan in Singapore?," MoneySmart, April 6, 2018, https://blog.moneysmart.sg/budgeting/which-internet-service-provider-has-the-best-1-gbps-plan-in-singapore.

12. Samantha Bookman, "Verizon to Introduce 500 Mbps FiOS for $310 per Month," FierceTelecom, July 22, 2013, http://www.fiercetelecom.com/telecom/verizon-to-introduce-500-mbps-fios-for-310-per-month; Edward Baig, "Verizon Launches Near-Gigabit Speed Fios, Rivaling Google Fiber," *USA Today*, April 24, 2017, https://www.usatoday.com/story/tech/columnist/baig/2017/04/24/verizon-pushing-fios-speeds-near-gigabit/100843224.

13. "FTTH/B Deployments in Asia Pacific—Keys to Enhancing Service Availability, Proposition and Uptake," GlobalData, November 2014, https://www.globaldata.com/store/report/tc0270mr—ftthb-deployments-in-asia-pacific-keys-to-enhancing-service-availability-proposition-and-uptake.

14. "Breaking News from the FTTH Conference 2016: Croatia, Germany and Poland Join the FTTH Ranking," Fibre to the Home Council Europe, February 17, 2016, http://www.ftthcouncil.eu/documents/Press Releases/2016/PR20160217_FTTHranking_panorama_award.pdf.

15. "Breaking News from the FTTH Conference 2016"; "Optical Upgrades in China Will Resonate Worldwide," Fibre Systems, July 21, 2016, https://www.fibre-systems.com/news/optical-upgrades-china-will -resonate-worldwide.

16. OECD Broadband Portal, "Percentage of fibre connections in total broadband among countries reporting fibre subscribers," June 2017, http://www.oecd.org/sti/broadband/broadband-statistics.

17. Katie Dowd, "140 Years Ago, the Lights Were Turned on in San Francisco for the First Time," SFGate, July 4, 2016, http://www.sfgate.com /bayarea/article/public-lights-electricity-san-francisco-neri-8328034. php; "Timeline of San Francisco 1893–1929," Timelines of History, http://www.timelines.ws/cities/SF_B_1893_1929.HTML.

18. James Baller, "The Essential Role of Consumer-Owned Electric Utilities in Developing the National Information Infrastructure: A Historical Perspective," November 1, 1994, https://www.baller.com/1994/11/the-essential -role-of-consumer-owned-electric-utilities-in-developing-the-national -information-infrastructure.

19. Robert Beall, *Rural Electrification* (Washington, DC: U.S. Department of Agriculture, 1940).

20. Richard Rudolph and Scott Ridley, *Power Struggle: The Hundred Year War Over Electricity* (New York: Harper & Row, 1986), 32–38.

21. William Emmons, "Franklin D. Roosevelt, Electric Utilities, and the Power of Competition," *Journal of Economic History* 53, no. 4 (1993): 880–907.

22. Sharon O'Malley, "*Private Utility Propaganda and the Creation of Wisconsin REA News* (Washington, DC: National Rural Electric Cooperative Association, 1991); available at http://sea.coop/wp-content/uploads/2015/03 /privateutilitypropaganda.pdf.

23. Franklin D. Roosevelt, "Campaign Address in Portland, Oregon on Public Utilities and Development of Hydro-Electric Power," September 21, 1932, http://www.presidency.ucsb.edu/ws/?pid=88390.

24. Paul Webbink, "Publicly-Owned Power Plants," *Editorial Research Reports 1930* (Washington, DC: CQ Press, 1930), 3:531–46, http://library.cqpress .com/cqresearcher/cqresrre1930080400.

25. Deward Clayton Brown, "Rural Electrification in the South, 1920–1955," PhD dissertation, University of California at Los Angeles, 1970.

26. *Stock Exchange Practices: Hearings Before the Committee on Banking and Currency, United States Senate*, 72nd Cong. (1931–1933), and 73rd Cong. (1933–1935), 2nd sess. (1934), https://fraser.stlouisfed.org/title/87.

27. Richard Munson, *From Edison to Enron: The Business of Power and What It Means for the Future of Electricity* (Washington, DC: Northeast-Midwest Institute, 2005), 67.

28. James Burns, *The Story of American Money* (self-pub., Lulu.com, 2016), 310.

29. Burns, *The Story of American Money*, 310.

30. Franklin D. Roosevelt, "Campaign Address in Portland, Oregon on Public Utilities and Development of Hydro-Electric Power," September 21, 1932, http://www.presidency.ucsb.edu/ws/?pid=88390.

31. Public Utility Holding Company Act of 1935, 15 U.S.C. § 79 (1935); Federal Power Act of 1935, 16 U.S.C. § 791 (1935).

32. Exec. Order No. 7037, Establishing the Rural Electric Administration (April 8, 1935).

33. "The Electric Cooperative Story," National Rural Electric Cooperative Association, https://www.electric.coop/our-organization/history; Harry S. Truman, "Statement by the President Upon Signing Bill Providing for Improved Rural Telephone Facilities," October 28, 1949, http://www.presidency.ucsb.edu/ws/index.php?pid=13342.

34. "The Father of Public Power," Tennessee Valley Authority, https://www.tva.com/About-TVA/Our-History/The-Father-of-Public-Power.

35. U.S. Bureau of the Census, *U.S. Census of Agriculture: 1954*, Vol. III, Special Reports Part 4, Agriculture, 1954, A Graphic Summary (Washington, DC: U.S. Government Printing Office, 1956), 85.

36. Federal Communications Commission, *Fixed Broadband Deployment Data: December, 2016 Status V1*, November 14, 2017, distributed by FCC Wireless Competition Bureau, https://www.fcc.gov/general/broadband-deployment-data-fcc-form-477.

37. Federal Communications Commission, "Explanation of Broadband Deployment Data," November 20, 2017, https://www.fcc.gov/general/explanation-broadband-deployment-data.

38. Federal Communications Commission, "More About Census Blocks," March 26, 2015, https://transition.fcc.gov/form477/Geo/more_about_census_blocks.pdf.

39. Industry Analysis and Technology Division, Wireline Competition Bureau, Federal Communications Commission, "High-Speed Services for Internet Access: Status as of December 31, 2008," February 2010, https://apps.fcc.gov/edocs_public/attachmatch/DOC-296239A1.pdf.

40. United States Census Bureau, "Geographic Terms and Concepts—Census Tract," (https://www.census.gov/geo/reference/gtc/gtc_ct.html.

41. Federal Communications Commission, *Fixed Broadband Deployment Data*.

42. "FCC Acts to Ensure Continuity of the national Broadband Map," Connected Nation, June 12, 2014, https://connectednation.org/wp-content/uploads/2018/01/20140612_cn_policy_brief_-_fcc_ensures_continuity_of_national_broadband_map_final.pdf.

43. Industry Analysis and Technology Division, Wireline Competition Bureau, Federal Communications Commission, "FCC Urban Rates Survey Data Collection: Filing Instructions," https://transition.fcc.gov/Bureaus/Common_Carrier/Reports/FCC-State_Link/IAD/urs_filing_instructions.pdf.

44. "Dial-Up Modem Standards," TelecomWorld 101, http://www.telecom-world101.com/DialUpModemStandards.html.

45. "Competing for That Last Mile: A Comparison of High-Speed Data Technologies: Cable vs. xDSL," University of Washington, Computer Science and Engineering Courses, Spring 1997, https://courses.cs.washington.edu/courses/csep561/97sp/paper1/paper10.html.

46. Tom Simonite, "First Detailed Public Map of U.S. Internet Backbone Could Make It Stronger," *MIT Technology Review*, September 15, 2015, https://www.technologyreview.com/s/540721/first-detailed-public-map-of-us-internet-backbone-could-make-it-stronger.

47. "Frequently Asked Questions on Fiber Reliability," Corning, April 2016, http://www.corning.com/media/worldwide/coc/documents/Fiber/RC-%20White%20Papers/WP5082%203-31-2016.pdf.

48. "Frequently Asked Questions on Fiber Reliability."

49. Michael Powell, "Preserving Internet Freedom: Guiding Principles for the Industry," Federal Communications Commission, February 8, 2004, https://apps.fcc.gov/edocs_public/attachmatch/DOC-243556A1.pdf; "FCC Adopts Policy Statement: New Principles Preserve and Promote the Open and Interconnected Nature of Public Internet," Federal Communications Commission, August 5, 2005, https://apps.fcc.gov/edocs_public/attachmatch/DOC-260435A1.pdf.

50. Susan Crawford, *Captive Audience* (New Haven: Yale University Press, 2013).

51. James Granelli, "SBC Plans a Huge Outlay," *Los Angeles Times*, June 23, 2004, http://articles.latimes.com/2004/jun/23/business/fi-sbc23.

52. Federal Communications Commission, *In the Matters of Appropriate Framework for Broadband Access to the Internet Over Wireline Facilities et al.*, CC Docket Nos. 02-33, 01-337, 95-20, 98-10, WC Docket Nos. 04-242, 05-271, Report and Order and Notice of Proposed Rulemaking, 20 FCC Rcd 14853 (2005) (Wireline Broadband Classification Order), https://apps.fcc.gov/edocs_public/attachmatch/FCC-05-151A1.pdf.

53. "CenturyLink Reports Fourth Quarter and Full-Year 2016 Results," Century Link, February 8, 2017, http://ir.centurylink.com/File/Index?KeyFile=37959961.

54. Ben Rubin, "Verizon CEO McAdam Named Board Chairman; Seidenberg Retires," *Wall Street Journal*, December 1, 2011, https://www.wsj.com/articles/BT-CO-20111201-713380; Jon Brodkin, "Verizon Sells Three-State Territory, Including 1.6 Million FiOS Users," *Ars Technica*, February 5, 2015, https://arstechnica.com/business/2015/02/verizon-sells-three-state-territory-including-1-6-million-fios-users.

55. "2.7 Million Added Broadband from Top Providers in 2016," Leichtman Research Group, March 17, 2017, http://www.leichtmanresearch.com/press/031717release.html.

56. "2.7 Million Added Broadband from Top Providers in 2016."

57. "U.S. Cable: Will the Broadband Burden Be Too Heavy to Bear? Downgrading Sector and Comcast to Neutral," MoffettNathanson Research, June 20, 2017, 20. Craig Moffett's reports are available to subscribers at https://www.moffettnathanson.com/research.aspx.

58. Jon Brodkin, "50 Million U.S. Homes Have Only One 25 Mbps Internet Provider or None at All," *Ars Technica*, June 30, 2016, https://arstechnica.com/information-technology/2017/06/50-million-us-homes-have-only-one-25mbps-internet-provider-or-none-at-all.

59. Bruce Kushnick, "Time Warner Cable's 97 Percent Profit Margin on High-Speed Internet Service Exposed," *Huffington Post*, December 6, 2017, http://www.huffingtonpost.com/bruce-kushnick/time-warner-cables-97-pro_b_6591916.html.

60. "Satellite Internet in the United States," Broadband Now, https://broadbandnow.com/Satellite.

61. Paul de Sa, "U.S. Telecom: Cable v. Telco, Who Competes with Who in Two Charts," June 15, 2015, Bernstein Research.

62. Sean Buckley, "CenturyLink: FTTP Deployment Costs Range from $500–800 Per Home," FierceTelecom, August 17, 2016, https://www.fiercetelecom.com/telecom/centurylink-fttp-deployment-costs-range-from-500-800-per-home.

63. Sean Buckley, "CenturyLink Says FTTH Is Helping It Beat Cable, Raise Overall Broadband Speed Awareness," FierceTelecom, January 8, 2016, http://www.fiercetelecom.com/telecom/centurylink-says-ftth-helping-it-beat-cable-raise-overall-broadband-speed-awareness.

64. "AT&T's Digital Redlining of Cleveland," Connect Your Community, http://connectyourcommunity.org/atts-digital-redlining-of-cleveland-report.

65. Bruce Kushnick, "AT&T's 1000 Foot Violation of AT&T-DirecTV Merger Conditions?," *Huffington Post*, December 7, 2015, http://www.huffingtonpost.com/bruce-kushnick/atts-1000-foot-violation_b_10449612.html.

66. Jeff Baumgartner, "AT&T Expands Fiber to 17 More Metros," *Multichannel News*, March 24, 2017, http://www.multichannel.com/news/technology/att-expands-fiber-17-more-metros/411714. AT&T ended this program in September 2016. See Jon Brodkin, "AT&T to End Targeted Ads Program; Give All Users Lowest Available Price," *ArsTechnica*, September 30, 2016, https://arstechnica.com/information-technology/2016/09/att-to-end-targeted-ads-program-give-all-users-lowest-available-price.

67. "2.7 Million Added Broadband from Top Providers in 2016."

68. Leena Rao, "The Final Tally: More Than 1100 Cities Apply for Google's Fiber Network," TechCrunch, March 27, 2010, https://techcrunch.com/2010/03/27/the-final-tally-more-than-1100-cities-apply-for-googles-fiber-network.

69. John Sutter, "Topeka 'Renames' Itself 'Google, Kansas,'" CNN, March 2, 2010, http://www.cnn.com/2010/TECH/03/02/google.kansas.topeka/index .html.

70. Jacob Davidson, "Google Fiber Has Internet Providers Scrambling to Improve Their Service," *Money*, April 13, 2015, http://time.com/money /3820109/google-fiber-has-internet-providers-scrambling-to-improve-their-service; Klint Finley, "White House Backs Cities That Want to Build Their Own Super-Speed Internet," *Wired*, January 14, 2015, https://www. wired.com/2015/01/white-house-community-broadband.

71. Associated Press, "Google Fiber to Cut Jobs and Halt Expansion of U.S. Internet Service," *The Guardian*, October 26, 2016, https://www .theguardian.com/technology/2016/oct/26/google-fiber-internet-stops -alphabet-layoffs.

72. Bill Callahan, "AT&T's Digital Redlining of Cleveland," National Digital Inclusion Alliance, March 10, 2017, https://www.digitalinclusion.org /blog/2017/03/10/atts-digital-redlining-of-cleveland.

73. Bruce Kushnick, "Have You Received a Disconnect Notice from Verizon or AT&T Yet?," *Huffington Post*, February 4, 2016, http://www .huffingtonpost.com/bruce-kushnick/have-you-received-a-disco_b _9164866.html.

74. *In the Matter of Protecting and Promoting the Open Internet*, Federal Communications Commission, GN Docket No. 14-28 (Report and Order on Remand, Declaratory Ruling, and Order).

75. Cecilia Kang, "F.C.C. Chairman Pushes Sweeping Changes to Net Neutrality Rules," *New York Times*, April 26, 2017, https://www.nytimes.com /2017/04/26/technology/net-neutrality.html.

76. Office of Science and Technology Policy and the National Economic Council, *Four Years of Broadband Growth*, June 2013, https://obamawhite house.archives.gov/sites/default/files/broadband_report_final.pdf.

77. "Deployment to Rural Areas and Underserved Populations," AT&T, February 7, 2018, http://about.att.com/content/csr/home/issue-brief -builder/people/deployment-to-rural-and-underserved-areas.html.

78. "Millimeter Waves," Engineering and Technology History Wiki, http:// ethw.org/Millimeter_Waves.

79. Andy Walton, "The Causes of Wireless Interference," It Still Works, http://itstillworks.com/causes-wireless-interference-4354.html.

80. Harold Furchtgott-Roth, "Open Spectrum: A Major Step for U.S. Innovation and Economic Growth," Hudson Institute Initiative on Future Innovation, July 2013, https://www.hudson.org/content/researchattachments /attachment/1134/open_spectrum_final.pdf.

81. New America Open Technology Institute, "Citizen's Guide to the Airwaves," July 2, 2013, https://www.newamerica.org/oti/policy-papers /citizens-guide-to-the-airwaves.

82. National Telecommunications and Information Administration, Office of Spectrum Management, "United States Frequency Allocations," U.S. Department of Commerce, October 2003, https://www.ntia.doc.gov /files/ntia/publications/2003-allochrt.pdf.

83. "Frequencies by Provider," Wilson Amplifiers, October 12, 2014, https:// www.wilsonamplifiers.com/frequencies-by-provider.

84. Steven Berry, "The Fight for Spectrum and Why You Should Care," *The Hill*, December 4, 2013, http://thehill.com/blogs/congress-blog /technology/191945-the-fight-for-spectrum-and-why-you-should-care.

85. John Leibovitz, "Breaking Down Barriers to Innovation in the 3.5 GHz Band," Federal Communications Commission, April 21, 2015, https:// www.fcc.gov/news-events/blog/2015/04/21/breaking-down-barriers -innovation-35-ghz-band.

86. Guy Daniels, "Nokia Bell Labs Close in on Shannon Limit with Munich Optical Trial," TelecomTV, http://www.telecomtv.com/articles/network- innovation/nokia-bell-labs-close-in-on-shannon-limit-with-munich- optical-trial-13958.

87. Monica Alleven, "Editor's Corner—Spectrum Bands Above 24 Ghz: Lots of Love for Licenses," Fierce Wireless, November 1, 2017, https://www. fiercewireless.com/wireless/editor-s-corner-spectrum-bands-above-24- ghz-lots-love-for-licenses.

88. Ywh-Ren Tsai and Jin-Fu Chang, "Using Spread Spectrum Techniques to Combat Multipath Interference in Mobile Random Accessed Net- works," IEEE, April 1995, http://ieeexplore.ieee.org/document/380051.

89. Amy Nordrum, "Verizon and AT&T Prepare to Bring 5G to Market," *IEEE Spectrum*, December 30, 2016, http://spectrum.ieee.org/telecom/ wireless/verizon-and-att-prepare-to-bring-5g-to-market.

90. *In the Matter of Use of Spectrum Bands Above 24 GHz For Mobile Radio Ser- vices et al.*, Federal Communications Commission, GN Docket No. 14- 177, IB Docket Nos. 15-256, 97-95, RM-11664, WT Docket No. 10-112, Report and Order and Further Notice of Proposed Rulemaking.

91. Susan Crawford, "Why Can't We Be Like South Korea?," *Wired*, July 23, 2015, https://www.wired.com/2015/07/why-cant-we-be-like-south-korea); Nadia Babaali, "Sweden: A Showcase for Rural FTTH," Fibre to the Home Council Europe, June 26, 2013, http://www.ftthcouncil.eu/documents /Opinions/2013/Rural_FTTH_Nordics_Final.pdf.

92. Jacob Kastrenakes, "Japanese Internet Provider Offers Twice the Speed of Google Fiber for Less Money," *The Verge*, April 15, 2013, https://www. theverge.com/2013/4/15/4226428/sony-so-net-2gbps-download- internet-tokyo-japan.

93. Aaron Pressman, "Verizon Is Not Interested in a Big Cable Merger Right Now," *Fortune*, April 18, 2017, http://fortune.com/2017/04/18/verizon- ceo-charter.

94. Pressman, "Verizon Is Not Interested."

95. Community Networks, "Community Network Map," Institute for Local Self-Reliance, https://muninetworks.org/communitymap.
96. Community Networks, "Community Network Map."

Chapter Four. Community Stories

1. Susan Crawford, "Ajit Pai's Shell Game," *Wired*, November 29, 2017, https://www.wired.com/story/net-neutrality-fiber-optic-internet.
2. Ann Treacy, "RS Fiber Broadband Initiative Moving Forward to Bring Service to Rural Minnesota," Blandin Foundation, November 24, 2014, https://blandinonbroadband.org/2014/11/24/rs-fiber-broadband-initiative-moving-forward-to-bring-service-to-rural-minnesota.
3. Keri Brenner, "Spiral Internet Gearing Up for Fiber Optic Network in Nevada County," *The Union*, October 3, 2014, http://www.theunion.com/news/local-news/spiral-internet-gearing-up-for-fiberoptic-network-in-nevada-county.
4. Dan Raile, "Having Been Burned Before, Google Won't Bring Fiber to San Francisco," *Pando*, February 25,2014, https://pando.com/2014/02/25/having-being-burned-once-before-google-wont-bring-fiber-to-san-francisco.
5. Lisa Gonzalez, "Santa Monica City Net: An Incremental Approach to Building a Fiber Optic Network," Institute for Local Self-Reliance, March 5, 2014, https://ilsr.org/santa-monica-city-net.
6. Benoît Felten, "Stockholm's Stokab: A Blueprint for Ubiquitous Fiber Connectivity?," *Diffraction Analysis*, July 2012, https://www.stokab.se/Documents/Stockholms%20Stokab%20-%20A%20Blueprint%20for%20Ubiquitous%20Fiber%20Connectivity%20FINAL%20VERSION.pdf.
7. Marco Forzati and Crister Mattsson, "Stokab: A Socio-Economic Study," Acreo Swedish ICT, July 1, 2013, https://www.acreo.se/sites/default/files/pub/www.acreo.se/upload/publications/acro55698en_-_stokab_-_a_socio-economic_analysis.pdf.
8. Madhumita Venkataramanan, "Europe's Hottest Startups 2015: Stockholm," *Wired*, July 30, 2015, http://www.wired.co.uk/article/100-hottest-european-startups-2015-stockholm.
9. Jeff Barr, "Coming in 2018—New AWS Region in Sweden," *Amazon Web Services* (blog), April 4, 2017, https://aws.amazon.com/blogs/aws/coming-in-2018-new-aws-region-in-sweden.
10. "Cities100: Stockholm—Becoming Fossil Fuel-Free by 2040," C40 Cities, October 30, 2015, http://www.c40.org/case_studies/cities100-stockholm-becoming-fossil-fuel-free-by-2040.
11. Gonzalez, "Santa Monica City Net."
12. "Santa Monica City Net 100 Gigabit Community Broadband," Santa Monica CityNet, http://www.smcitynet.com.

13. Sheila Marikar, "Network? Let's Party!," *New York Times*, March 14, 2014, https://www.nytimes.com/2014/03/16/fashion/Santa-Monica-Venice-Technology-Start-ups.html; "Santa Monica City Net: 10 Gigabit Broadband for Business Attraction and Retention," League of California Cities, 2012, https://www.cacities.org/Top/Partners/California-City-Solutions/2012/Santa-Monica-City-Net-10-Gigabit-Broadband-for-Bu.

14. Chuck Flynn, "Walnut Street Bridge," *Atlas Obscura*, http://www.atlasobscura.com/places/walnut-street-bridge.

15. Dave Flessner, "Chattanooga's EPB Rated Top Utility by J.D. Power," *Times Free Press* (Chattanooga), July 22, 2017, http://www.timesfreepress.com/news/business/aroundregion/story/2017/jul/22/epb-rated-top-utility-jd-power/439589.

16. U.S. Department of Energy, "A Smarter Electric Circuit: Electric Power Board of Chattanooga Makes the Switch," https://energy.gov/sites/prod/files/2016/12/f34/EPB_Profile_casestudy_0.pdf.

17. Kevin McCarthy, "Chattanooga High Speed Broadband Initiative," Office of Legislative Research (OLR) Research Report 2012-R-0515, December 14, 2012, https://www.cga.ct.gov/2012/rpt/2012-R-0515.htm.

18. "Our History," Electric Power Board of Chattanooga, https://epb.com/about-epb/our-history.

19. "Speed Up with the Nation's Fastest Internet," Electric Power Board of Chattanooga, https://epb.com/home-store/internet.

20. "2016 Financial Report," Electric Power Board of Chattanooga, August 31, 2016, https://static.epb.com/annual-reports/2016/media/EPB_2016_Financial_Report.pdf.

21. Tribune Newsroom, "RS Fiber Coop Moving Forward with Rural Broadband Network," *West Central Tribune*, November 24, 2014, http://www.wctrib.com/content/rs-fiber-coop-moving-forward-rural-broadband-network).

22. Jennifer Vogel, "Sibley County Opts Out of Fiber Project, May Give Rise to Farmer Cooperative," Minnesota Public Radio, October 29, 2012, http://blogs.mprnews.org/ground-level/2012/10/sibley-county-opts-out-of-fiber-project-gives-rise-to-farmer-cooperative.

23. Lisa Gonzalez, "Local Communities Still Committed to RS Fiber Cooperative," Institute for Local Self-Reliance, February 9, 2015, https://ilsr.org/local-communities-still-committed-to-rs-fiber-cooperative-2.

24. Fritz Busch, "RS Fiber Co-op Seeks to Bring High-Speed Internet to Rural Areas," *The Journal*, February 27, 2015, http://www.nujournal.com/news/local-news/2015/02/27/rs-fiber-co-op-seeks-to-bring-high-speed-internet-to-rural-areas.

25. Busch, "RS Fiber Co-op."

26. "New Markets Tax Credit Program," U.S. Department of the Treasury, Community Development Financial Institutions Fund, https://www.cdfifund.gov/programs-training/Programs/new-markets-tax-credit/Pages/default.aspx.

27. Joe Kukura, "Engineering Internet for All of San Francisco," *SF Weekly*, June 21, 2017, http://www.sfweekly.com/news/news-news/engineering-internet-for-all-of-san-francisco.

28. Mike Parker, "Best and Worst Cities for Mobile Network Performance: The Full RootMetrics Rankings," *RootMetrics*, August 2, 2016, http://rootmetrics.com/en-US/content/2016-1h-metro-ranking.

29. Budget and Legislative Analyst's Office, "Financial Analysis of Options for a Municipal Fiber Optic Network for Citywide Internet Access," *City and County of San Francisco Board of Supervisors*, March 15, 2016, http://sfbos.org/sites/default/files/FileCenter/Documents/55324-BLA.Muni GigabitFiberFinance031516.pdf.

30. Verne Kopytoff, "S.F. Stalling Wi-Fi plans, Google Executive Charges," *SF-Gate*, September 16, 2006, http://www.sfgate.com/news/article/S-F-stalling -Wi-Fi-plans-Google-executive-2551901.php.

31. Joaquin Palomino, "Expect 'Major' Disruption as S.F. Races to Fix Old Water Pipes," *San Francisco Chronicle*, October 5, 2015, http://www .sfchronicle.com/bayarea/article/Expect-lots-of-construction-as-S-F-races-to-fix-6549030.php.

32. "Financial Analysis of Options for a Municipal Fiber Optic Network for Citywide Internet Access," Budget and Legislative Analyst's Office, San Francisco, California.

33. Janie Har, "U.S. Soda-Tax Battle Bubbles Up in San Francisco Bay Area," *U.S. News*, September 28, 2016, https://www.usnews.com/news/business/articles/2016-09-28/soda-tax-battle-bubbles-up-in-san-francisco-bay-area.

34. Mark Farrell and Eric Mar, "San Francisco Needs Internet Access for All," *San Francisco Chronicle*, February 14, 2014, http://www.sfchronicle.com/opinion/openforum/article/San-Francisco-needs-Internet-access-for-all-10932836.php.

Chapter Five. Sustaining Economic Growth

1. "The City of Chattanooga, Tennessee: Entrepreneurial Livable Community Award," Partners for Livable Communities, 2010, http://livable.org/livability-resources/best-practices/447-the-city-of-chattanooga-tennessee.

2. David Eichenthal and Tracy Windeknecht, "Chattanooga, Tennessee," A Restoring Prosperity Case Study, Metropolitan Policy Program at Brookings, September 2008, https://www.brookings.edu/wp-content/uploads/2016/06/200809_Chattanooga.pdf.

3. Eleanor Cooper, "Citizens Changing Ideas into Action: A Phenomenological Study of Community Learning of the Graduate School Education, and Professional Studies," 2013, https://www.academia.edu/7643062/CITIZENS_ CHANGING_IDEAS_INTO_ACTION_A_PHENOMENOLOGICAL_STUDY_OF_COMMU- NITY_LEARNING_of_the_Graduate_School_Education_and_Professional

_Studies, quoting extensively from Longo's 1980 report "Perceptions of Chattanooga."

4. Eichenthal and Windeknecht, "Chattanooga, Tennessee."

5. "Tennessee Aquarium History," Tennessee Aquarium, http://www.tnaqua.org/about-us/tennessee-aquarium-history.

6. "Best Practice: Chattanooga Venture/Community Vision," Best Manufacturing Practices, January 18, 2007, http://www.bmpcoe.org/bestpractices/internal/chatt/chatt_8.html.

7. Eichenthal and Windeknecht, "Chattanooga, Tennessee."

8. Ellis Smith, "CreateHere Mission Almost Accomplished," *Times Free Press* (Chattanooga), January 8, 2012, http://www.timesfreepress.com/news/business/aroundregion/story/2012/jan/08/createhere-mission-almost-accomplished/67746.

9. Studio C. Rushing et al., "City Center Plan," River City Company, December 2013, http://www.rivercitycompany.com/new/pdf/FinalCity-CenterPlan_RS.pdf.

10. Keith Schneider, "Chattanooga's Innovation District Beckons to Young Entrepreneurs," *New York Times*, August 16, 2016, https://www.nytimes.com/2016/08/17/realestate/commercial/chattanoogas-innovation-district-beckons-to-young-entrepreneurs.html.

11. Dave Flessner, "Jobless Rate in Hamilton County Falls to 15-Year Low," *Times Free Press*, June 23, 2016, http://www.timesfreepress.com/news/business/aroundregion/story/2016/jun/23/jobless-rate-hamilton-county-falls-15-year-low/372615.

12. Bento J. Lobo, "The Realized Value of Fiber Infrastructure in Hamilton County, Tennessee," Department of Finance, University of Tennessee at Chattanooga, June 18, 2015, http://media-cdn.timesfreepress.com/news/documents/2015/09/15/realizedvalueoffiberlobofinaljune18201515650443634.pdf.

13. "Data Standards," Wilson Economic Development Council, Wilson, North Carolina website, http://www.wilsonedc.com/why-choose-wilson/data-standards.

14. Lauren K. Ohnesorge, "From Google Fiber to AT&T to Frontier: Competition Is Making Raleigh-Durham Area's Internet Speeds Faster," *Triangle Business Journal*, February 2, 2017, https://www.bizjournals.com/triangle/news/2017/02/02/from-google-fiber-to-at-t-to-frontier-competition.html.

15. Mike Schoch, "Jane Nickles—City of Greensboro, North Carolina," *ToggleMAG* (blog), January 3, 2017, https://www.togglemag.com/case-studies/jane-nickles-city-of-greensboro-north-carolina.

16. An Act to Protect Jobs and Investment by Regulating Local Government Competition with Private Business, Gen. Assemb., H.B. 129 (N.C. 2011), http://www.ncga.state.nc.us/Sessions/2011/Bills/House/PDF/H129v7.pdf.

17. Greensboro Connected, "Beyond Traffic: The Smart City Challenge" (Greensboro, NC, 2016), http://www.greensboro-nc.gov/modules/show document.aspx?documentid=30070.

18. "Greensboro: History," City-Data.com, http://www.city-data.com/us-cities/The-South/Greensboro-History.html.

19. North Carolina Department of Commerce, "Employment & Wages," Labor & Economic Analysis, https://www.nccommerce.com/lead/data-tools /occupations/employment-wages.

20. City of Greensboro Planning Department, "Demographic and Income Comparison Profile," February 2, 2015, http://www.greensboro-nc.gov/modules/ showdocument.aspx?documentid=26515; City of Greensboro Planning Department, "Growth & Development Trends," January 2017, https://www. greensboro-nc.gov/Modules/ShowDocument.aspx?documentID=33021; "Greensboro residents work to break cycle of poverty," WUNC, August 15, 2017, http://wunc.org/post/greensboro-residents-work-break-cycle-poverty# stream/0.

21. Nancy Nelson Hodges and Elena Karpova, "Employment in the U.S. Textile and Apparel Industries: A Comparative Analysis of Regional vs. National Trends," *Journal of Fashion Marketing and Management* 10, no. 2 (2006): 209–26.

22. "Chattanooga, Tennessee (TN) Profile," City-Data.com, http://www. city-data.com/city/Chattanooga-Tennessee.html.

23. "Major Employers," Wilson Economic Development Council, Wilson, North Carolina, http://www.wilsonedc.com/wp-content/uploads/2017/03 /Table-3-2017_btg04iw27-1.pdf.

24. Richie Bernardo, "2017's Best & Worst Small Cities to Start a Business," *WalletHub* (blog), April 17, 2017, https://wallethub.com/edu/best-small-cities-to-start-a-business/20180.

Chapter Six. Education and Fiber

1. "STEM School Links to 4K Microscope at USC Using the Gig," *The Chattanoogan,* May 11, 2015, http://www.chattanoogan. com/2015/5/11/300159/STEM-School-Links-To-4K-Microscope-At. aspx.

2. David Morton, "Biology Seen Through a Microscope 1,800 Miles Away," *Nooga.Com* (blog), May 15, 2015, http://nooga.com/169977/biology-seen-through-a-microscope-1800-miles-away.

3. "About the School," STEM School Chattanooga, http://www.stemschool chattanooga.net/?PageName=%27AboutTheSchool%27.

4. "STEM FAQs," STEM School Chattanooga, http://www.stemschool chattanooga.net/?PageName=bc&n=161741.

5. Barry Courter, "Chattanooga Public Library's New System Creates Instantaneous Collaborations," *Times Free Press,* June 27, 2016, http://www.

timesfreepress.com/news/life/entertainment/story/2016/jun/27/lo-lo-lo-lo-lola-librarys-new-system-creates/372848.

6. Bento J. Lobo, "The Realized Value of Fiber Infrastructure in Hamilton County, Tennessee," Department of Finance, University of Tennessee at Chattanooga, June 18, 2015, http://media-cdn.timesfreepress.com/news/documents/2015/09/15/realizedvalueoffiberlobofinaljune18201515650 443634.pdf.

7. Kendi A. Rainwater, "State Threatens to Take Over Hamilton County's 5 Lowest Performing Schools if They Don't Improve," *Times Free Press*, November 11, 2016, http://www.timesfreepress.com/news/local/story/2016/nov/11/state-educatileaders-demand-progress-lowest-p/397202; Kendi A. Rainwater, "School Board Approves Balanced Budget, List of $24 Million in 'Critical Needs' [Photos]," *Times Free Press*, April 28, 2017, http://www.timesfreepress.com/news/local/story/2017/apr/28/school-board-approves-balanced-budget-list-24/425268.

8. Kendi A. Rainwater, "Tiffanie Robinson Unseats George Ricks from School Board in District 4," *Times Free Press*, August 5, 2016, http://www.timesfreepress.com/news/local/story/2016/aug/05/robinsunseats-ricks-board-seat/379667.

9. Dave Flessner, "Lamp Post Properties President Working on a Second Story for Downtown," *Times Free Press*, August 1, 2017, http://www.timesfreepress.com/news/edge/story/2017/aug/01/young-guns-tiffanie-robinson/439922.

10. U.S. Census Bureau, "Grass Valley City, California," American FactFinder, https://factfinder.census.gov/faces/tableservices/jsf/pages/product view.xhtml?src=bkmk.

11. U.S. Census Bureau, "Nevada City, California," American FactFinder, https://factfinder.census.gov/faces/tableservices/jsf/pages/productview. xhtml?src=bkmk.

12. "About Us," Spiral, http://www.spiralinternet.com/aboutspiral.php. (Their office is in Nevada City.)

13. Sharon McLoone, "Stimulus Billions Fund Rural Broadband Internet Expansion—Aug. 11, 2009," *CNN Money* (blog), August 11, 2009, http://money.cnn.com/2009/08/11/smallbusiness/stimulus_billions_for_rural_broadband.smb.

14. "Nevada City's Bid for Google Fiber for Communities," 95959google, http://www.95959google.com.

15. Keri Brenner, "Spiral Internet Gearing up for Fiberoptic Network in Nevada County," *The Union* (blog), October 3, 2014, https://www.theunion.com/news/local-news/spiral-internet-gearing-up-for-fiberoptic-network-in-nevada-county.

16. Sierra College, "Background Information," https://www.sierracollege.edu/_files/resources/about-us/public-relations/documents/SC-background-2011-v3.pdf; "Sierra College: Choose from Four Beautiful

Campuses," Sierra College, https://www.sierracollege.edu/about-us/visit/index.php.

17. "Key Facts," California Community Colleges Chancellor's Office, http://californiacommunitycolleges.cccco.edu/PolicyInAction/KeyFacts.aspx.

18. "Internet Providers in 95986 (Washington, CA) & Cable/TV," Decision-Data.org, https://decisiondata.org/tv-internet-by-zip/95986-internet.

19. Wireline Competition Bureau and Office of Strategic Planning and Policy Analysis, "E-Rate Data Update," November 17, 2014, https://apps.fcc.gov/edocs_public/attachmatch/DOC-330505A1.pdf.

20. Evan Marwell, "Using Fiber Optics to Bring Schools up to Internet Speed," *Washington Post*, November 13, 2013, https://www.washingtonpost.com/opinions/using-fiber-optics-to-bring-schools-up-to-internet-speed/2013/11/12/210bc1b8-48c7-11e3-b6f8-3782ff6cb769_story.html.

21. "Global Experience," Minerva Schools at KGI, http://www.minerva.kgi.edu/global-experience.

22. "Small Seminars," Minerva Schools at KGI, http://www.minerva.kgi.edu/academics/small-seminars; Tricia Bisoux, "Global & Campus Free," *BizEd*, November 3, 2016, http://bized.aacsb.edu/articles/2016/11/global-and-campus-free.

23. Fergus I. M. Craik and Robert S. Lockhart, "Levels of Processing: A Framework for Memory Research," *Journal of Verbal Learning and Verbal Behavior* 11, no. 6 (1972): 671–84, https://doi.org/10.1016/S0022-5371(72)80001-X.

24. Jeffrey Young, "Three Years In, Minerva's Founder on For-Profits, Selectivity, and His Critics," EdSurge, May 10, 2017, https://www.edsurge.com/news/2017-05-10-three-years-in-minerva-s-founder-on-for-profits-selectivity-and-his-critics.

25. Bisoux, "Global & Campus Free."

26. Andrew Edgecliffe-Johnson, "San Francisco Start-Up Minerva 'More Selective Than Ivy League,'" *Financial Times*, April 4, 2016, https://www.ft.com/content/7216d448-f9fb-11e5-8f41-df5bda8beb40.

27. "Tuition & Fees," Minerva Schools at KGI, http://www.minerva.kgi.edu/tuition-aid/tuition-fees.

28. "The Most Popular Courses of 2016," Coursera, January 3, 2017, https://blog.coursera.org/popular-courses-2016.

29. "Partners Directory," Coursera, https://www.coursera.org/directory/partners.

30. "Chattanooga State Community College," College Scorecard, https://collegescorecard.ed.gov/school/?219824; Tennessee Higher Education Commission, "2015–2016 Tennessee Higher Education Fact Book," https://www.tn.gov/content/dam/tn/thec/bureau/research/other-research/factbook/2015–2016_Fact_Book.pdf.

31. "Volkswagen Mechatronics Apprentice Programs Graduate 3 Classes," *The Chattanoogan*, August 11, 2016, http://www.chattanoogan.com/2016/8/11/329767/Volkswagen-Mechatronics-Apprentice.aspx.

32. "Arizona Vet School Installs Haptic Cow, Horse," *Veterinary Practice News*, September 29, 2015, https://www.veterinarypracticenews.com/arizona-vet-school-installs-haptic-cow-horse.

33. "Electrical Goods and Appliances in the 1920s Prices Examples From," The People History Site, http://www.thepeoplehistory.com/20selectrical.html.

34. Daniel Webster and Edward Everett, *The Works of Daniel Webster . . .: Biographical Memoir [by Edward Everett] and Speeches on Various Occasions* (C.C. Little and J. Brown, 1851).

Chapter Seven. Health and Fiber

1. OECD, "Health at a Glance 2015: How Does the United States Compare?," 2015, http://www.oecd.org/unitedstates/Health-at-a-Glance-2015-Key-Findings-UNITED-STATES.pdf; OECD, "Infant Mortality Rates," http://data.oecd.org/healthstat/infant-mortality-rates.htm; "The Cost of Diabetes," American Diabetes Association, March 6, 2013, http://www.diabetes.org/advocacy/news-events/cost-of-diabetes.html.

2. Fiber Broadband Association, "Fiber Growth Remains Strong: Now Passing 30 Million Homes in the U.S.," *Medium* (blog), October 27, 2016, https://medium.com/@fiberbroadband/fiber-growth-remains-strong-now-passing-30-million-homes-in-the-u-s-5461eb03216b.

3. "How It Works," KRY, https://kry.se.

4. Jens Krey, "Värmlänningar verkar nöjda med digital vård," Dagens Medicin, March 13, 2017, https://www.dagensmedicin.se/artiklar/2017/03/13/varmlanningar-verkar-nojda-med-digital-vard.

5. "The Future Population of Sweden, 2015-2060," Statistiska Centralbyrån, http://www.scb.se/en_/finding-statistics/statistics-by-subject-area/population/population-projections/population-projections/aktuell-pong/14505/behallare-for-press/389899.

6. Sandra L. Colby and Jennifer M. Ortman, "Projections of the Size and Composition of the U.S. Population: 2014 to 2060," Current Populations Reports, Population Estimates and Projections, United States Census Bureau, March 2015, https://www.census.gov/content/dam/Census/library/publications/2015/demo/p25-1143.pdf; "Survey, What Makes a Community Livable?," AARP, 2014, http://www.aarp.org/livable-communities/info-2014/aarp-ppi-survey-what-makes-a-community-livable.html.

7. "Health Care in Sweden," sweden.se, June 12, 2015, https://sweden.se/society/health-care-in-sweden.

8. Joan Garrett McClane, "The Poverty Puzzle," *Times Free Press*, 2016, http://cluster.timesfreepress.com/poverty-puzzle/index.html.

9. "'State of the Air' 2017 Report Finds Chattanooga Air Quality Improved," readMedia, April 19, 2017, http://readme.readmedia.com/State-of-the-Air-2017-Report-Finds-Chattanooga-Air-Quality-Improved/14690892.

10. Jan Johnson, "Transformation Funded Teledentistry Pilot Kicks off in Rural Polk County," *The Lund Report*, October 12, 2015, https://www. thelundreport.org/content/transformation-funded-teledentistry-pilot-kicks-rural-polk-county.

11. Tony Pugh, "CDC Says 20 Percent of U.S. Children Have Mental Health Disorders," *Washington Post*, May 19, 2013, https://www.washingtonpost. com/politics/cdc-says-20-percent-of-us-children-have-mental-health-disorders/2013/05/19/8c316b42-c0b3-11e2-8bd8-2788030e6b44_story. html.

12. American Academy of Child and Adolescent Psychiatry, "Practice Parameters for the Assessment and Treatment of Children and Adolescents with Posttraumatic Stress Disorder," 1998, https://www.aacap.org/App_ Themes/AACAP/docs/practice_parameters/PTSDT.pdf.

13. "Mental Health by the Numbers," NAMI: National Alliance on Mental Illness, https://www.nami.org/Learn-More/Mental-Health-By-the-Numbers.

14. Amy Novotney, "A Growing Wave of Online Therapy," American Psychological Association, 2017, http://www.apa.org/monitor/2017/02/online -therapy.aspx.

15. "Massachusetts Telemedicine Reimbursement Guide," Northeast Telehealth Resource Center, January 2015, http://netrc.org/wp-content/up-loads/2015/06/NETRC-Telemedicine-Reimbursement-Guide-MA.pdf.

16. Joshua Kendall, "Telepsychiatry and Mental Health," Undark.org, April 20, 2016, https://undark.org/2016/04/20/telepsychiatry-mental-health-services.

17. Kendall, "Telepsychiatry and Mental Health."

18. John Lundy, "Arrowhead Region Connects Mental Health Patients with Help Via . . .," *Bemidji Pioneer*, May 8, 2017, http://www.bemidjipioneer. com/news/4263629-arrowhead-region-connects-mental-health-patients-help-video-links.

19. Kate Murphy, "Psst. Look Over Here," *New York Times*, May 16, 2014, https://www.nytimes.com/2014/05/17/sunday-review/the-eyes-have-it. html.

20. Heather Mack, "Montana Telemedicine Bill Would Require In-Person or Video for First-Time Visits, and More State Telemedicine Updates," MobiHealthNews, April 13, 2017, http://www.mobihealthnews.com/content /montana-telemedicine-bill-would-require-person-or-video-first-time-visits-and-more-state.

Chapter Eight. Inequality and Fiber

1. "Looking for Progress in America's Smaller Legacy Cities: A Report for Place-Based Funders," 2017, https://www.chicagofed.org/region/community -development/community-economic-development/looking-for-progress-report.

2. Federal Communication Commission, "2015 Broadband Progress Report and Notice of Inquiry on Immediate Action to Accelerate Deployment," January 29, 2015, https://apps.fcc.gov/edocs_public/attachmatch/FCC-15-10A1.pdf.

3. Jonathan Sallet, "Better Together: Broadband Deployment and Broadband Competition," Brookings Institution, *Techtank* (blog), March 15, 2017, https://www.brookings.edu/blog/techtank/2017/03/15/better-together-broadband-deployment-and-broadband-competition.

4. Federal Communication Commission, "2015 Broadband Progress."

5. Dave Flessner, "Chattanooga Job Growth Expected to Jump Four-Fold in Next Five Years," *Times Free Press*, December 13, 2015, http://www.timesfreepress.com/news/business/aroundregion/story/2015/dec/13/chattanooga-job-growth-expected-jump-four-fold-next-five-years/340269.

6. Kendi A. Rainwater, "New Definition Means Fewer Tennessee Students Are Considered Economically Disadvantaged," *Times Free Press*, February 6, 2017, http://www.timesfreepress.com/news/local/story/2017/feb/06/state-redefines-student-poverty/411354.

7. "Chattanooga 2.0: Building the Smartest Community in the South," 2015, Executive Summary, http://media-cdn.timesfreepress.com//news/documents/2015/12/12/1449976255_Chattanooga-2.0-12-11-15.pdf.

8. Mike Pare, "Workforce Training Goes High-Tech in Chattanooga's High-Revving Economy," *Times Free Press*, July 1, 2017, http://www.timesfreepress.com/news/edge/story/2017/jul/01/learning-earn/435784.

9. Laura Faith Kebede and Grace Tatter, "Here's Where Tennessee's Lowest-Performing Schools Stand a Year Before the State's Next Priority List," *Chalkbeat* (blog), https://www.chalkbeat.org/posts/tn/2016/04/20/heres-where-tennessees-lowest-performing-schools-stand-a-year-before-the-states-next-priority-list.

10. "Chattanooga 2.0: Building the Smartest Community in the South," 22

11. "Chattanooga 2.0: Building the Smartest Community in the South," 24; Kendi A. Rainwater, "As Chattanooga Grows, Businesses Struggle to Find Qualified Local Applicants," *Times Free Press*, December 13, 2015, http://www.timesfreepress.com/news/local/story/2015/dec/13/chattanooga-business-growth-local-applicants/340250.

12. "The Poverty Puzzle," *Times Free Press*, March 6, 2016, http://projects.timesfreepress.com/2016/03/povertypuzzle/povertypuzzle-ebook.pdf.

13. Raj Chetty and Nathaniel Hendren, "The Impacts of Neighborhoods on Intergenerational Mobility I: Childhood Exposure Effects," Working Paper, National Bureau of Economic Research, December 2016, https://doi.org/10.3386/w23001; Elizabeth Kneebone and Natalie Holmes, "The Growing Distance between People and Jobs in Metropolitan America," Brookings, March 24, 2015, https://www.brookings.edu/research/the-growing-distance-between-people-and-jobs-in-metropolitan-america.

14. "Vote for America's Best Town," *Outside Online* (blog), May 4, 2015, https://www.outsideonline.com/1972941/best-towns-2015.

15. "TN State Report Card," Tennessee Department of Education, https://www.tn.gov/education/data/report-card.html.

16. In the report, this reads "Do we have the collective will and courage as a community to do whatever it takes to ensure that all residents are able to benefit from the growing economic opportunity?" Rainwater, "As Chattanooga Grows, Businesses Struggle to Find Qualified Local Applicants."

17. Chattanooga 2.0, "Ten Urgent Strategies to Transform Our Future," September 2016, https://chatt2.org/wp-content/uploads/2017/05/Chattanooga-2.0-Sep.-2016-Report.pdf.

18. Polina Marinova, "One of America's Most Startup-Friendly Cities Is in Tennessee," *Fortune*, May 8, 2017, http://fortune.com/2017/05/08/tech-startup-innovation-chattanooga-tennessee.

19. Kendi A. Rainwater, "Local Couple Hopes to Open All-Boys Charter School to Serve Chattanooga's Poorest," *Times Free Press*, November 6, 2016, http://www.timesfreepress.com/news/local/story/2016/nov/06/chattanoogprep-local-couple-hopes-open-all-bo/396328.

20. Estelle Sommeiller, Mark Price, and Ellis Wazeter, "Income Inequality in the U.S. by State, Metropolitan Area, and County," Economic Policy Institute, June 16, 2016, https://www.epi.org/publication/income-inequality-in-the-us; "Income Inequally," *Times Free Press*, 2016, http://projects.timesfreepress.com/2016/03/povertypuzzle/Popup1.jpg.

21. U.S. Census Bureau, "Quintiles of Gini Index by County: 2006–2010," 2012, https://www2.census.gov/library/visualizations/2012/acs/acsbr10-18-fig01.pdf.

22. Sommeiller, Price, and Wazeter, "Income Inequality in the U.S."

23. "Greensboro–High Point, North Carolina Job Growth," Department of Numbers, http://www.deptofnumbers.com/employment/north-carolina/greensboro.

24. "Greensboro (Zip 27406), North Carolina," Best Places to Live, https://www.bestplaces.net/crime/zip-code/north_carolina/greensboro/27406.

25. "Locked Out: Education, Jobs and Justice," National Urban League, 2016, http://nul.iamempowered.com/sites/nul.iamempowered.com/files/black-white-index-051316.pdf.

26. Thom Patterson, "After 50 Years of Racial Strife: Why Is Greensboro Still So Tense?," CNN, June 7, 2011, http://www.cnn.com/2011/US/06/07/greensboro.race/index.html.

27. Dave Flessner, "EPB to Offer Discounted Internet for Low-Income Households," *Times Free Press*, April 28, 2015, http://www.timesfreepress.com/news/business/aroundregion/story/2015/apr/28/epb-offer-discounted-internet-low-income-hous/301146.

28. "One-to-One Technology Integration," STEM School Chattanooga, http://www.stemschoolchattanooga.net/?PageName=bc&n=163127.

29. Aaron Smith, "Detailed Demographic Tables," Pew Research Center, *Internet, Science & Tech* (blog), January 6, 2014, http://www.pewinternet.org/2014/01/06/detailed-demographic-tables.

30. John B. Horrigan and Maeve Duggan, "Home Broadband 2015," Pew Research Center, *Internet, Science & Tech* (blog), December 21, 2015, http://www.pewinternet.org/2015/12/21/home-broadband-2015.

31. U.S. Department of the Interior, "National Register of Historic Places: Multiple Property Documentation Form," https://npgallery.nps.gov/pdf-host/docs/NRHP/Text/64500361.pdf.

32. "Report of the Real Property Survey, Greensboro, North Carolina," University of North Carolina Greensboro, Digital Collections, http://libcdm1.uncg.edu/cdm/ref/collection/UrbanDevGSO/id/7668.

33. Interview with Jim Ingraham, August 7, 2017

34. David Eichenthal and Tracy Windeknecht, "Chattanooga, Tennessee," Brookings Institution, Metropolitan Policy Program, September 2008, https://www.brookings.edu/wp-content/uploads/2016/06/200809_Chattanooga.pdf.

35. "Internet in Greensboro, NC," Broadband Now, https://broadbandnow.com/North-Carolina/Greensboro.

36. Josh Bergeron, "Fibrant in Focus: Story of Wilson's, Salisbury's Fiber Optic Networks a 'Tale of Two Cities,'" July 27, 2017, https://www.salisburypost.com/2017/07/27/fibrant-in-focus-story-of-wilsons-salisburys-fiber-optic-networks-a-tale-of-two-cities.

37. "Wilson City, North Carolina," U.S. Census Bureau QuickFacts, https://www.census.gov/quickfacts/fact/table/wilsoncitynorthcarolina/POP060210.

38. "Industry Facts," Wilson EDC, http://www.wilsonedc.com/why-choose-wilson/industry-facts.

39. Anthony King, "Technology: The Future of Agriculture," *Nature* 544 (2017): S21–S23, https://doi.org/10.1038/544S21a.

40. "World Population Projected to Reach 9.8 Billion in 2050, and 11.2 Billion in 2100—Says UN," United Nations, *Sustainable Dvelopment* (blog), June 21, 2017, http://www.un.org/sustainabledevelopment/blog/2017/06/world-population-projected-to-reach-9-8-billion-in-2050-and-11-2-billion-in-2100-says-un.

41. "Financial Management Review," Division of Local Services, Town of Otis, Massachusetts, March 12, 2013, http://www.mass.gov/dor/docs/dls/mdmstuf/technical-assistance/finmgtrev/otis.pdf.

42. "Technology Committee," Town of Otis, Massachusetts, May 31, 2017, http://townofotisma.com/commissions-councils/technology-committee.

43. Jim Kinney, "Welcome to the 'Fiberhood': Westfield's Whip City Fiber Aims for Connected City," *Mass Live* (blog), March 31, 2017, http://www.masslive.com/business-news/index.ssf/2017/03/welcome_to_the_fiberhood_westfields_whip.html.

44. Kinney, "Welcome."

Chapter Nine. Lessons from American Communities

1. Dave Flessner, "EPB Fiber Surpasses 90,000 Customers," *Times Free Press*, May 2, 2017, http://www.timesfreepress.com/news/business/aroundregion/story/2017/may/02/epb-fiber-tops-over-90000-customerstelecom-se/425825.

2. Dave Flessner, "EPB Holds Line on Rates, but Monthly Fuel Rates Edge Higher," *Times Free Press*, June 1, 2017, http://www.timesfreepress.com/news/business/aroundregion/story/2017/jun/01/epb-holds-line-ratesmonthly-fuel-rates-edge-h/431132.

3. Dave Flessner, "Conservative Think Tank Seeks to Minimize Benefits of Chattanooga, Tenn.'s Ultra-High-Speed Broadband," *Government Technology* (blog), May 8, 2016, http://www.govtech.com/network/Conservative-Think-Tank-Seeks-to-Minimize-Benefits-of-Chattanooga-Tenns-Ultra-High-Speed-Broadband.html.

4. "Annual Report 2014," EPB, April 2014, https://static.epb.com/annual-reports/2014/EPB-Annual-Report-2014.pdf.

5. Dave Flessner, "Chattanooga's EPB Rated Best Internet Provider in America," *Times Free Press*, December 9, 2016, http://www.timesfreepress.com/news/business/aroundregion/story/2016/dec/09/chattanoogas-epb-rated-best-internet-provider-america/402271.

6. Dave Flessner, "EPB Readies $250 Million Bond Issue with Upgraded Rating," *Times Free Press*, July 9, 2015, http://www.timesfreepress.com/news/business/aroundregion/story/2015/jul/09/epb-readies-250-millibond-issue-upgraded-rati/313639.

7. Dave Flessner, "Tennessee Lawmakers Gearing up for Broadband Battle," *Times Free Press*, January 20, 2016, http://www.timesfreepress.com/news/business/aroundregion/story/2016/jan/20/legislature-gears-broadband-battle/345557.

8. Lisa Gonzalez, "Transcript: Community Broadband Bits Episode 230," Community Networks, December 2, 2016, https://muninetworks.org/content/transcript-community-broadband-bits-episode-230.

9. "About the Next Gen NBN NetCo," Infocomm Media Development Authority, November 3, 2017, http://www.imda.gov.sg/industry-development/infrastructure/next-gen-national-infocomm-infrastructure/wired/next-gen-nbn/what-is-next-gen-nbn/industry-structure/about-the-next-gen-nbn-netco.

10. "Six Principles for Communications and Technology," American Legislative Exchange Council, https://www.alec.org/model-policy/six-principles-for-communications-and-technology.

11. Paul A. Specht, "Holly Springs Completes Fiber Network," *News & Observer*, June 27, 2014, http://www.newsobserver.com/news/local/community/southwest-wake-news/article10336514.html.

12. "Interview with Jeff Wilson, IT Director of Holly Springs," *Ting.Com* (blog), January 26, 2017, https://ting.com/blog/internet/hollysprings/ interview-jeff-wilson-director-holly-springs.

13. Trevor Hughes, "Town Creates High-Speed Revolution, One Home at a Time," *USA Today*, November 19, 2014, https://www.usatoday.com/ story/news/nation/2014/11/19/longmont-internet-service/19294335.

14. Theodore Roosevelt, *Presidential Addresses and State Papers of Theodore Roosevelt . . . with Portrait Frontispiece . . .* (New York: P. F. Collier & Son, 1905), 1345, http://archive.org/details/presidentialaddooroosgoog.

15. Abraham Lincoln, *Collected Works of Abraham Lincoln*, vol. 2 (Ann Arbor: University of Michigan Digital Library Production Services, 2001), 221, http://name.umdl.umich.edu/lincoln2.

Chapter Ten. What Stands in the Way?

1. "1893 Chicago World Fair," Hay Genealogy, http://haygenealogy.com/ hay/1893fair/1893fair.html.

2. Erwan Lucas, "In South Korea, the Race Is On for Olympics 5G Next Year," Phys.Org, February 28, 2017, https://phys.org/news/2017-02- south-korea-olympics-5g-year.html.

3. Susan Crawford, "Google Fiber Was Doomed from the Start," *Wired*, March 14, 2017, https://www.wired.com/2017/03/google-fiber-was- doomed-from-the-start.

4. Jon Brodkin, "Cable Lobby Claims U.S. Is Totally Overflowing in Broad-band Competition," *Ars Technica*, July 27, 2017, https://arstechnica.com/ information-technology/2017/07/cable-lobby-claims-us-is-totally- overflowing-in-broadband-competition.

5. "Internet Access Services," Industry Analysis and Technology Division, Wireline Competition Bureau, Federal Communications Commission, April 2017, https://apps.fcc.gov/edocs_public/attachmatch/DOC-344499A1.pdf.

6. Jamie McGee and Joey Garrison, "Comcast Sues Nashville over Google Fiber-Backed Pole Ordinance," *The Tennessean*, October 25, 2016, https://www.tennessean.com/story/news/local/2016/10/25/comcast-sues- metro-over-google-fiber-backed-pole-otmr-ordinance/92748490.

7. Austin Jenkins, "Wireless Industry Lobbies Statehouses for Access to 'Street Furniture,'" NPR, April 11, 2017, https://www.npr.org/2017/04 /11/522246173/wireless-industry-lobbies-statehouses-for-access-to-street- furniture.

8. "Resolution Encouraging the Support of Infrastructure Buildout to Pave the Pathway for Next Generation Networks—American Legislative Exchange Council," American Legislative Exchange Council, https:// www.alec.org/model-policy/resolution-encouraging-the-support-of- infrastructure-buildout-to-pave-the-pathway-for-next-generation- networks.

9. Anita Chabria, "Verizon and Sacramento Want to Make a Deal. What's in It for You?," *Sacramento Bee*, June 1, 2017, http://www.sacbee.com/news/local/article153716914.html; Mari Silbey, "Verizon Hails Boston Fios Launch but Eyes 5G," *Light Reading*, December 7, 2016, https://www.lightreading.com/gigabit/ultra-broadband/verizon-hails-boston-fios-launch-but-eyes-5g/d/d-id/728821.

10. Anjali Athavaley, "Verizon, Corning Agree to $1.05 Billion Fiber Deal," Reuters, April 18, 2017, https://www.reuters.com/article/us-corning-verizon/verizon-corning-agree-to-1-05-billion-fiber-deal-idUSKBN17K201.

11. FCC Record 10-35A1, "Exclusive Service Contracts for Provision of Video Services in Multiple Dwelling Units and Other Real Estate Developments," March 20, 2010.

12. Susan Crawford, "The New Payola: Deals Landlords Cut with Internet Providers," *Wired*, June 27, 2016, https://www.wired.com/2016/06/the-new-payola-deals-landlords-cut-with-internet-providers.

13. "Are the FCC's Inside Wiring Rules Still Relevant? Part I: Home Run Wiring Rules," Carl Kandutsch Law Office, January 2011, http://www.kandutsch.com/articles/are-the-fccs-inside-wiring-rules-still-relevant-part-i-home-run-wiring-rules.

14. "About," *Save NC Broadband* (blog), April 9, 2009, https://savencbb.wordpress.com/about.

15. Madison Park and Keith Allen, "North Carolina Given September Deadline to Draw New Legislative Maps," CNN, August 1, 2017, https://www.cnn.com/2017/08/01/politics/north-carolina-gerrymander-case/index.html.

16. Joe Schwartz, "Cities, Consumers Lose Municipal Broadband Fight," *Indy Week*, May 4, 2011, https://www.indyweek.com/indyweek/cities-consumers-lose-municipal-broadband-fight/Content?oid=2440390.

17. "Memorandum Opinion and Order," Federal Communications Commission, February 26, 2015, https://apps.fcc.gov/edocs_public/attachmatch/FCC-15-25A1.pdf.

18. "Memorandum Opinion and Order."

19. Quality Water Supply, Inc. v. Wilmington, No. 895SC413 (Court of Appeals of North Carolina February 20, 1990).

20. "Memorandum Opinion and Order."

21. Jon Brodkin, "Muni ISP Forced to Shut Off Fiber-to-the-Home Internet After Court Ruling," *Ars Technica*, September 16, 2016, https://arstechnica.com/information-technology/2016/09/muni-isp-forced-to-shut-off-fiber-to-the-home-internet-after-court-ruling.

22. David Hudnall, "What's Standing Between Rural North Carolina and Reliable Internet Service?," *Indy Week*, November 9, 2016, https://www.indyweek.com/indyweek/whats-standing-between-rural-north-carolina-and-reliable-internet-service/Content?oid=5084640.

23. Todd O'Boyle and Christopher Mitchell, "The Empire Lobbies Back: How National Cable and DSL Companies Banned the Competition in

North Carolina," Institute for Local Self-Reliance, January 2013, http://ilsr.org/wp-content/uploads/2013/01/nc-killing-competition.pdf.

24. "Pinetops, North Carolina (NC 27864)," City-Data.com, http://www.city-data.com/city/Pinetops-North-Carolina.html.

25. Leoneda Inge, "Wilson, North Carolina and Community Broadband Win with FCC Vote," February 26, 2015, http://wunc.org/post/wilson-north-carolina-and-community-broadband-win-fcc-vote.

26. "Memorandum Opinion and Order."

27. Tom Wheeler, "Broadband Communities Summit: Remarks of FCC Chairman Tom Wheeler," Austin, Texas, April 14, 2015, https://apps.fcc.gov/edocs_public/attachmatch/DOC-332988A1.pdf.

28. Cecilia Kang, "Broadband Law Could Force Rural Residents Off Information Superhighway," *New York Times*, August 28, 2016, https://www.nytimes.com/2016/08/29/technology/broadband-law-could-force-rural-residents-off-information-superhighway.html.

29. Brodkin, "Muni ISP Forced to Shut Off Fiber-to-the-Home Internet After Court Ruling."

30. Lisa Gonzalez, "Wilson to Offer Greenlight to Pinetops at No Charge," Community Networks, October 25, 2016, https://muninetworks.org/content/wilson-offer-greenlight-pinetops-no-charge.

31. "Wilson Greenlight to Continue Gigabit Fiber Service in Rural Pinetops and Vick Family Farms—with Conditions," *Coalition for Local Internet Choice* (blog), June 29, 2017, http://www.localnetchoice.org/connections/wilson-greenlight-to-continue-gigabit-fiber-service-in-rural-pinetops-and-vick-family-farms-with-conditions.

32. Ramakrishnan Durairajan et al., "InterTubes: A Study of the U.S. Long-Haul Fiber-Optic Infrastructure," *Proceedings of the 2015 ACM Conference on Special Interest Group on Data Communication*, August 17, 2015, 565–78.

33. "47 U.S. Code § 201—Service and Charges," Legal Information Institute, https://www.law.cornell.edu/uscode/text/47/201.

34. Susan Crawford, "The Internet Ripoff You're Not Protesting," *Wired*, July 12, 2017, https://www.wired.com/story/the-internet-ripoff-youre-not-protesting.

35. "Order on Reconsideration," Federal Communications Commission, September 15, 2014, https://apps.fcc.gov/edocs_public/attachmatch/DA-14-1327A1.pdf.

36. "FCC Releases Business Data Services Order and Further Notice," Federal Communications Commission, May 2, 2016, https://www.fcc.gov/document/fcc-releases-business-data-services-order-and-further-notice.

37. Mark Cooper, "The Special Problem of Special Access: Consumer Overcharges and Telephone Company Excess Profits," Consumer Federation of America, April 2016, https://consumerfed.org/wp-content/uploads/2016/04/4-16-The-Special-Problem-of-Special-Access.pdf.

38. "Chairman Wheeler's Proposal to Promote Fairness, Competition, and Investment in the Business Data Services Market," Federal Communications Commission, https://apps.fcc.gov/edocs_public/attachmatch/DOC-341659A1.pdf.

39. Brooke Fox, "The $45 Billion Market Where Businesses May Welcome Regulation," *Bloomberg*, August 22, 2016, https://www.bloomberg.com/news/articles/2016-08-22/the-45-billion-market-where-businesses-may-welcome-regulation; Federal Communications Commission, "Tariff Investigation Order and Further Notice of Proposed Rulemaking," May 2, 2016, https://apps.fcc.gov/edocs_public/attachmatch/FCC-16-54A1.pdf.

40. Reuters Staff, "Comcast Completes NBC Universal Merger," *Reuters*, January 29, 2011, https://www.reuters.com/article/us-comcast-nbc/comcast-completes-nbc-universal-merger-idUSTRE70S2WZ20110129.

41. Jacob Kastrenakes, "AT&T–Time Warner Merger Reportedly Moving Forward at Justice Department," *The Verge*, July 24, 2017, https://www.theverge.com/2017/7/24/16022978/att-time-warner-justice-department-review-exploring-conditions.

42. Jon Brodkin, "Yahoo and AOL Are Now a Verizon Subsidiary Called 'Oath,'" *Ars Technica*, June 13, 2017, https://arstechnica.com/information-technology/2017/06/oath-verizon-completes-4-5-billion-buy-of-yahoo-and-merges-it-with-aol; Scott Moritz, "Verizon's CEO Is Open to Deal Talks, from Comcast to Disney," *Bloomberg*, April 18, 2017, https://www.bloomberg.com/news/articles/2017-04-18/verizon-s-ceo-is-open-to-deal-talks-from-comcast-to-disney.

43. Brian Stelter, "Bye, Bye Time Warner Cable. Hello Charter," CNN, May 18, 2016, http://money.cnn.com/2016/05/18/media/time-warner-cable-charter/index.html.

Chapter Eleven. The Need for Federal Policy

1. Mike Patton, "U.S. Role in Global Economy Declines Nearly 50%," *Forbes*, February 29, 2016, Advisor Network, https://www.forbes.com/sites/mikepatton/2016/02/29/u-s-role-in-global-economy-declines-nearly-50/#7be6b3e45e9e.

2. Tim Worstall, "China's Only 15% of the Global Economy but Contributes 25–30% of Global Growth," *Forbes*, October 30, 2016, https://www.forbes.com/sites/timworstall/2016/10/30/chinas-only-15-of-the-global-economy-but-contributes-25-30-of-global-growth/#4857c68c7b76; Sarah Hsu, "China Takes Another Step Towards a Service Economy," *Forbes*, February 21, 2017, https://www.forbes.com/sites/sarahsu/2017/02/21/china-takes-another-step-towards-a-service-economy/#1898496c28c1.

3. China Telecom Americas, "China Telecom Aims to Make Shanghai a Gigabit City," June 13, 2016, http://www.ctamericas.com/china-telecom-aims-to-make-shanghai-gigabit-city.

4. "Roosevelt's Little White House State Historic Site and Roosevelt Warm Springs Institute for Rehabilitation," Warm Springs Historic District, National Park Services, https://www.nps.gov/nr/travel/presidents/roosevelts_little_white_house.html.

5. James W. Ely, Jr., "Abraham Lincoln as a Railroad Attorney," 1–2, https://mafiadoc.com/abraham-lincoln-as-a-railroad-attorney-indiana-historical-society_5a3183201723ddoed6cebcob.html.

6. Sarah Laskow, "In 1919, Eisenhower Suffered Through History's Worst Cross-Country Road Trip," *Atlas Obscura*, August 13, 2015, Stories, http://www.atlasobscura.com/articles/in-1919-dwight-d-eisenhower-suffered-through-historys-worst-cross-country-road-trip.

7. Laskow, "Eisenhower Suffered."

8. "Internet Access Services: Status as of December 31, 2015," Figure 11: Connections over 200 kbps in at Least One Direction by Technology 2011–2015, Federal Communications Commission, Industry Analysis and Competition Division, https://apps.fcc.gov/edocs_public/attachmatch/DOC-342358A1.pdf.

9. Federal Reserve Bank of Dallas, *Closing the Digital Divide: A Framework for Meeting CRA Obligations*, December 2016, https://www.dallasfed.org/assets/documents/cd/pubs/digitaldivide.pdf.

10. Quote from Robert D. Leighninger, *Long-Range Public Investment: The Forgotten Legacy of the New Deal* (Columbia: University of South Carolina Press, 2007), 201.

11. "What Are Build America Bonds?," Municipal Bonds.com, June 24, 2015, http://www.municipalbonds.com/education/what-are-build-america-bonds.

12. Lawrence Summers, "The Next President Should Make Infrastructure Spending a Priority," *Washington Post*, September 11, 2016, https://www.washingtonpost.com/opinions/whoever-wins-the-presidential-election-must-make-infrastructure-spending-a-priority/2016/09/11/406efoee-76c2-11e6-b786-19docb1edo6c_story.html?utm_term=.8c5b6cf3f485.

Index

245